The Economics of Input-Output Analysis

Input-output analysis is the main tool of applied equilibrium analysis. This textbook provides a systematic survey of the most recent developments in input-output analysis and their applications, helping us to examine questions such as: Which industries are competitive? What are the multiplier effects of an investment program? How do environmental restrictions impact on prices? Linear programming and national accounting are introduced and used to resolve issues such as the choice of technique, the comparative advantage of a national economy, its efficiency and dynamic performance. Technological and environmental spillovers are analyzed, at both the national level (between industries) and the international level (the measurement of globalization effects). The book is self-contained, but assumes some familiarity with calculus, matrix algebra, and the microeconomic principle of optimizing behavior. Exercises are included at the end of each chapter, and solutions at the end of the book.

THIJS TEN RAA is Associate Professor of Economics at Tilburg University.

The Economics of
Input-Output Analysis

THIJS TEN RAA

CAMBRIDGE
UNIVERSITY PRESS

CAMBRIDGE UNIVERSITY PRESS
Cambridge, New York, Melbourne, Madrid, Cape Town, Singapore,
São Paulo, Delhi, Dubai, Tokyo, Mexico City

Cambridge University Press
The Edinburgh Building, Cambridge CB2 8RU, UK

Published in the United States of America by Cambridge University Press, New York

www.cambridge.org
Information on this title: www.cambridge.org/9780521602679

First published 2005

A catalogue record for this publication is available from the British Library

ISBN 978-0-521-84179-5 Hardback
ISBN 978-0-521-60267-9 Paperback

Contents

Figures

Tables

Preface

Input-output analysis is the main tool to help us answer three key questions that pertain to the economy as a whole. What is the performance of an economy, in terms of efficiency and productivity growth? What is the comparative advantage of an economy *vis-à-vis* the rest of the world? How are these measures affected when environmental constraints are taken into account? Of course, many other interesting questions can be posed.

The focus on the economy as a whole gives input-output analysis a macroeconomic flavor, but its foundation and techniques are more microeconomic, including a rigorous grounding in production and consumption. Some people argue that it is at the interface of the two and define it as the study of industries or sectors of the economy. The name mesoeconomics has been coined for this.

Input-output analysis may be considered a rather mechanical tool, not be easily applicable to free market economies with competitive valuations. Specialized as well as general textbooks reinforce this perception, but it is my goal to undermine it.

This book presents input-output analysis from a mainstream economic perspective. It offers a unified, simultaneous treatment of the so-called "quantity and value systems." The main framework is the United Nations' System of National Accounts (SNA), an ingenious device to provide a coherent snapshot of all the sectors of an economy; the main tool is that of linear programming. The book is self-contained – the elements of input-output analysis, linear programming, and national accounting are introduced starting from scratch and all the derived constructs (such as efficiency and applied equilibrium analyzes) follow naturally. The book provides a complete synthesis of linear economic models and neoclassical theory and offers a thorough basis in linear programming as well as input-output analysis.

The reduction of the economic structure to fundamental primitives is undertaken rigorously and the results are significant and deep. Let me mention a few. The conditions for the existence of the so-called "Leontief inverse" are simple, yet necessary and sufficient. An intuitive result on inequalities facilitates quick proofs of the main results of linear programming. This, in turn, is used to establish the most general form of the so-called "substitution theorem". The main neoclassical tool of macroeconomics, the Cobb–Douglas production function, is derived from a microeconomic analysis of production units with different input-output coefficients. These theoretical elements are entered into the System of

National Accounts and thus produce concrete results: the questions on national economies posed above are answered.

To put the book in perspective, a short historical note is in order. Originally I was invited to write a modern version of Gale's out-of-print but still-demanded monograph *The Theory of Linear Economic Models*. In 1995, my *Linear Analysis of Competitive Economies* came out in the *LSE Handbooks in Economics* series published by Harvester Wheatsheaf. After a quick reprint, the title sold out and the publishing house was swallowed by ever-larger ones: Prentice-Hall, Pearson, Paramount, and Time Warner. To cut a long story short, the entertainment industry threw me back to square one, but Cambridge University Press stepped in and convinced me of the need to rewrite the book entirely. *The Economics of Input-Output Analysis* is the resulting textbook, with detailed treatment of new applications, including globalization and spillovers.

Strictly speaking, there are no prerequisites. In other words, if you are a bright Liberian who completely missed out on education for reasons of prolonged civil war rather than lack of capabilities you will be able to comprehend the contents after an in-depth study. This having been said, it is only fair to admit that a few preliminaries do help. Familiarity with the analysis of maximizing behavior subject to constraints, as treated in any course on microeconomics, is one. Calculus is another. And although I define them, some familiarity with vectors and matrices would be very useful. The final chapter 14 also presumes basic knowledge of random variables (the concepts of mean and variance), but it can be skipped if the reader wishes. In short, I target advanced undergraduate or new graduate students of economics who do not panic when a function is differentiated or integrated.

Input-output analysis is probably the most practical tool of economic analysis. Yet my background as a theorist is apparent in the text: The results are quite general, and this feature facilitates the use of the book as a reference source, particularly by applied equilibrium economists and national accountants using input-output measures.

I have been teaching the material in this book at Tilburg, New York, Jadavpur (Calcutta), and Utrecht Universities and also in specialist courses – one organized by the Vienna-based International Input-Output Association for the PhD students of three Montreal schools and another by Statistics Finland for PhD students from six Finnish schools. I am grateful for the feedback received; more is welcome at tenRaa@UvT.nl.

Borrowing the words of my teacher and friend Will Baumol, I dedicate this volume to my "three ladies": Anna, Rosa, and Miryam.

Glossary

c.i.f	cost, insurance, freight
EC	Efficiency change
f.o.b	free-on-board
FP	Frontier productivity
GDI	Gross domestic income
GNP	Gross national product
IODB	Input-Output Data Base
ISDB	Industrial Structure Data Base
NAMEA	National Accounting Matrix including Environment Accounts
PPF	production possibility frontier
R&D	Research and development
SAM	Social Accounting Matrix
SNA	System of National Accounts
SR	Solow residual
TFP	Total factor productivity
VAT	Value-added tax

1   Introduction

1.1   The definition of economics

In *An Essay on the Nature and Significance of Economic Science* (1984) Lionel Robbins (1898–1984) defines economics as "the science which studies human behavior as a relationship between given ends and scarce means which have alternative uses." This famous "all-encompassing" definition of economics is still used to define the subject today, according to *The Concise Encyclopedia of Economics* (http://www.econlib.org/library/CEE. html). The underlying idea is that absent scarcity, all needs could be satisfied, no choices would have to be made, and, therefore, no economic problem would be present. But which resources are scarce? Is air scarce? If not, maybe clean air is scarce? If we stick to the traditional definition of economics, these questions must be answered prior to any economic analysis: in some mysterious way, all the scarce resources are known. In my opinion, however, the enumeration of scarce resources should be included in the definition of economics. I therefore modify Robbins' definition by omitting the adjective "scarce." In short, I define economics as the study of the allocation of resources among alternative ends – or, more precisely, the study of the allocation of resources to production units for commodities and the distribution of the latter to the population. Some resources may be scarce, others may not be. Scarcity will be signaled by a price. If resources are not scarce, they will have a zero price.

It is not necessary to be very specific at this stage as regards the concepts of "production units," "commodities," "distribution," and "households." The essence of economics is merely that something is maximized. Production units, or firms, maximize profits and households maximize their levels of income or well-being. The objectives can be fulfilled only to limited extents because of resource constraints. Maybe air is not scarce, but there is certainly only a limited stock of it, however large. The limited availability of some resources will act as a bottleneck in the furthering of the objectives. The economic problem can thus be summarized as the maximization of some objective subject to constraints. It is crucial to understand the principles of *constrained maximization*, and to relate them to the basic economic concept of a price, but first we must quickly review some elementary principles of mathematics.

1.2   Mathematical preliminaries

The two main streams of elementary mathematics are calculus and matrix algebra. *Calculus* is about functions, particularly of real numbers, and the manipulations that can be done with them, such as taking derivatives or integrals. *Matrix algebra* extends operations such as addition and multiplication to higher dimensions. It is handy for the extension of calculus to functions of several variables.

By definition, a *function*, f, maps *every* element, x, of one set (the domain) to *precisely one* element of a second set (the range), $f(x)$. The standard case is where both the domain and the range are the set of real numbers. Examples are given by (1)–(3) and counterexamples by (4) and (5):

(1) $f(x) = x$ the identity function
(2) $f(x) = cx + d$ a linear function
(3) $f(x) = x^n$ a power function
(4) $f(x) = \sqrt{x}$ the square root
(5) $f(x) = \pm\sqrt{x}$ the solution to $y^2 = x$

Counterexample (4) is not a function from the real numbers to the real numbers, because it does not take every element to another one. However, by restricting the domain to the non-negative numbers, it becomes a function. Counterexample (5) is not a function from the real numbers to the real numbers, because it does not take elements to precisely one other. By restricting the value to either the non-negative or the non-positive one, counterexample (5) becomes a function. The *inverse* of function f is the function f^{-1} defined by $f^{-1}(y) = x$ with $f(x) = y$. The inverse of function 1 is $f^{-1}(y) = y$. The inverse of function 2 is $f^{-1}(y) = (y - d)/c$. The inverse of function 3 is $f^{-1}(y) = x^{1/n}$ for n odd. For n even, say 2, case (4) would be the candidate solution, but it is not a function.

Let x be input and $f(x)$ output. Then *average* product is $f(x)/x$. The *marginal* product is the rate at which output increases:

$$\frac{f(x + \Delta x) - f(x)}{\Delta x}, \Delta x \to 0 \tag{1.1}$$

Expression (1.1) is called the *derivative* of f in x and is denoted $f'(x)$. The symbol $\to$ means "tends to." The derivative of x^n is nx^{n-1}:

$$(x^n)' = nx^{n-1} \tag{1.2}$$

Let me illustrate the rule for $n = 2$: By definition (1.1) the derivative of x^2 is

$$\frac{(x + \Delta x)^2 - x^2}{\Delta x} = 2x + \Delta x$$

with $\Delta x \to 0$, hence $2x$. If Δx does not tend to zero but is small, the quotient

$$\frac{(x + \Delta x)^2 - x^2}{\Delta x}$$

is approximately equal to the derivative, as we overlook the residual term, Δx. In general:

$$\frac{f(x + \Delta x) - f(x)}{\Delta x} \approx f'(x), \quad \Delta x \quad \text{small} \tag{1.3}$$

The approximate equality (1.3) is called the first-order approximation. Other handy rules of differentiation are the *sum*, *product* and *chain rules*:

$$(f + g)' = f' + g' \tag{1.4}$$

$$(fg)' = f'g + fg' \tag{1.5}$$

$$f[g(x)] \text{ has the derivative } f'[g(x)]g'(x) \tag{1.6}$$

The proof of the sum rule (1.4) is trivial. The proof of the product rule needs a little work. By definition,

$$(fg)'(x) = \frac{f(x + \Delta x)g(x + \Delta x) - f(x)g(x)}{\Delta x}$$

$$= g(x + \Delta x)\frac{f(x + \Delta x) - f(x)}{\Delta x} + f(x)\frac{g(x + \Delta x) - g(x)}{\Delta x} \tag{1.7}$$

with $\Delta x \to 0$, so that (1.7) proves the rule (1.5). Finally, the proof of the chain rule (1.6) is straightforward. The derivative of $f[g(x)]$ is

$$\frac{f[g(x + \Delta x)] - f[g(x)]}{\Delta x} = \frac{f[g(x + \Delta x)] - f[g(x)]}{g(x + \Delta x) - g(x)} \cdot \frac{g(x + \Delta x) - g(x)}{\Delta x} \tag{1.8}$$

with $\Delta x \to 0$. Substituting $y = g(x)$ and $\Delta y = g(x + \Delta x) - g(x)$, the first factor on the right-hand side of (1.8) reads

$$\frac{f(y + \Delta y) - f(y)}{\Delta y}$$

Since Δy tends to zero as $\Delta x \to 0$, the proof of the chain rule is complete.

Taking the derivative of a product function, one obtains the marginal product function. Now the reverse operation from differentiation is taking the *integral* – or, briefly, integration. Hence by integrating the marginal products one retrieves the underlying production function. The symbol for an integral is $\int$. For example, by (1.2), $\int nx^{n-1}dx = x^n$. Since the derivative of a constant is zero, one may add this to the integral. So, strictly speaking, $\int nx^{n-1}dx = x^n + c$, where c is any constant number.

Integrating the marginal products between a and b, one obtains the total output that comes with an increase of input from a to b: $\int_a^b f'(x)dx = f(b) - f(a)$. For example, $\int_0^1 nx^{n-1}dx = (1^n + c) - (0^n + c) = 1$. Hence $\int_0^1 x^{n-1}dx = 1/n$.

Let us model the production of a single output from *two* inputs. Then x in $f(x)$ is a list of two numbers or a *vector*, with components x_1 and x_2. The marginal product of the first input is the partial derivative of $f(x_1, x_2)$ with respect to x_1. By definition, this is the ordinary derivative of the function of x_1 keeping x_2 fixed. It is denoted f_1'. The row vector of partial derivatives is denoted $f' = (f_1'\quad f_2')$. For example, if the production function is $f(x_1, x_2) = x_1^{\alpha} x_2^{1-\alpha}$, then the marginal products are given by $(\alpha x_1^{\alpha-1} x_2^{1-\alpha}\ (1-\alpha)x_1^{\alpha} x_2^{-\alpha})$. If both inputs are rewarded according to their marginal products, the total cost is

$$\alpha x_1^{\alpha-1} x_2^{1-\alpha} x_1 + (1-\alpha)x_1^{\alpha} x_2^{-\alpha} x_2.^1$$

It is also possible to model *multiple outputs*. The two inputs may produce two outputs, each with its own production function. The vector of outputs is denoted

$$\begin{pmatrix} f_1(x_1, x_2) \\ f_2(x_1, x_2) \end{pmatrix}$$

We may now list for each output the row vector of marginal products:

$$\begin{pmatrix} \dfrac{\partial f_1(x_1, x_2)}{\partial x_1} & \dfrac{\partial f_1(x_1, x_2)}{\partial x_2} \\[2ex] \dfrac{\partial f_2(x_1, x_2)}{\partial x_1} & \dfrac{\partial f_2(x_1, x_2)}{\partial x_2} \end{pmatrix}$$

This table is a $2{\times}2$-dimensional *matrix*. The first index indicates the row (output, in this case), the second index the column (input, in this case). The (i, j)th element of the matrix represents the marginal i-product of input j.

The numbers of inputs and outputs need not match. In fact, we have dealt with the case of one output and two inputs, where we had a row vector of marginal products $f' = (f_1'\quad f_2')$. This is a $1{\times}2$ matrix. In general an $m{\times}k$-dimensional matrix B has m rows and k columns. The element in row i and column j is denoted b_{ij}. $b_{i\bullet}$ denotes row i and $b_{\bullet j}$ denotes column j. Notice that the dimension of any row of matrix B is k, which is the number of columns. Similarly, the dimension of any column is m, the number of rows.

1.3   Constrained maximization

An objective function ascribes values to the various magnitudes of all the variables of an economy. If the variables are $x_1, \ldots, x_n$ (representing the activity levels of the production units, for example), then the outcome (national income, for example), will be some real number $f(x_1, \ldots, x_n)$, or $f(x)$ for short, where f is the objective function. Formally, an objective function f maps the n-dimensional variable space to the one-dimensional space of the real numbers, that is $f : \mathbb{R}^n \to \mathbb{R}$. It is important to distinguish the objective function, f, and the values it may take, $f(x)$. The latter merely measure the performance of the economy for given magnitudes of all the underlying variables, while the former denotes the relationship between performance and the underlying variables. In other words, function f summarizes the structure of the economy. There may be many constraints. With each level of the variables of an economy $x = (x_1, \ldots, x_n)$, we may associate labor requirements – say, $g_1(x)$ – and other resource requirements – say, $g_i(x)$ – where resource i is any input

---

[1] This expression happens to be equal to $f(x_1, x_2)$, a finding that reflects the constant returns to scale property of f.

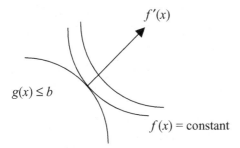

$f'(x)$

$g(x) \leq b$

$f(x) = \text{constant}$

Figure 1.1 The feasible region of constraint function g and two isoquants and the derivative of objective function f

that must be present before production takes place, such as mineral resources, equipment, etc. Let the number of resources be m. Then the requirements are $g_1(x), \ldots, g_m(x)$ and the resource constraints can be written by $g_1(x) \leq b_1, \ldots, g_m(x) \leq b_m$, where the right-hand sides are the available quantities of the resources. The inequalities may be summarized by:

$$g(x) = \begin{pmatrix} g_1(x) \\ \vdots \\ g_m(x) \end{pmatrix} \leq \begin{pmatrix} b_1 \\ \vdots \\ b_m \end{pmatrix} = b \qquad (1.9)$$

In constraint (1.9) g is the constraint function and b is the bound. Function g associates with every n-dimensional list of variables, x, m requirements, that is a point in m-dimensional space. Formally, we write $g : \mathbb{R}^n \to \mathbb{R}^m$. Constrained maximization is the problem:

$$\max_{x} f(x) : g(x) \leq b \qquad (1.10)$$

The colon in program (1.10) stands for the phrase "*subject to.*" The program can be depicted graphically in the variable space, particularly when there are two variables ($n = 2$) and only one constraint ($m = 1$). The set of points that fulfills the constraint, (1.9), is the *feasible region*. The objective function can be represented by so-called *isoquants*, which connect points x of equal value, $f(x)$. Perpendicular to these isoquants are the vectors of steepest ascent which are given by the partial derivatives:

$$f'(x) = \left(\frac{\partial f}{\partial x_1}(x) \cdots \frac{\partial f}{\partial x_n}(x) \right) \qquad (1.11)$$

For example, if the isoquant is given by $3x_1 + x_2 = 6$, which is a steep line with horizontal intercept $x_1 = 2$ and vertical intercept $x_2 = 6$, then the vector perpendicular to the isoquant is $(3\ 1)$. For a non-linear example see figure 1.1.

The objective function f takes a maximum value on the feasible region where the isoquant is tangent to the boundary. Since the boundary is an isoquant of the constraint function, g, an equivalent condition is that the vectors of steepest ascent point in the same direction:

$$f'(x) = \lambda g'(x), \lambda \geq 0 \qquad (1.12)$$

In (1.12) proportionality constant λ cannot be negative, for then a movement in the direction $f'(x)$ would go into the feasible region and constitute an improvement, contradicting the assumed maximization. Note also that the above condition covers the case where the constraint is *not* binding. Then maximization merely requires that the objective function is flat: $f'(x) = 0$. This is covered by a *zero* λ in (1.12).

First-order condition (1.12) of constrained maximization holds in the general case where $g : \mathbb{R}^n \to \mathbb{R}^m$. In short, the derivatives of the objective function are proportional to those of the constraint function and the proportions are non-negative. The following matrix defines the derivative of g:[2]

$$g' = \begin{pmatrix} \dfrac{\partial g_1}{\partial x_1} & \cdots & \dfrac{\partial g_1}{\partial x_n} \\ \vdots & \ddots & \vdots \\ \dfrac{\partial g_m}{\partial x_1} & \cdots & \dfrac{\partial g_m}{\partial x_n} \end{pmatrix} \tag{1.13}$$

The proportionality constants, one for each constraint, are listed in row vector $\lambda = (\lambda_1 \ldots \lambda_m)$ and the product of λ and matrix g' is defined in the usual way by a row vector (of the same dimension as f'):[3]

$$\lambda g' = (\lambda_1 \cdots \lambda_m) \begin{pmatrix} \dfrac{\partial g_1}{\partial x_1} & \cdots & \dfrac{\partial g_1}{\partial x_n} \\ \vdots & \ddots & \vdots \\ \dfrac{\partial g_m}{\partial x_1} & \cdots & \dfrac{\partial g_m}{\partial x_n} \end{pmatrix}$$

$$= \left(\lambda_1 \dfrac{\partial g_1}{\partial x_1} + \cdots + \lambda_m \dfrac{\partial g_m}{\partial x_1} \quad \cdots \quad \lambda_1 \dfrac{\partial g_1}{\partial x_n} + \cdots + \lambda_m \dfrac{\partial g_m}{\partial x_n} \right) \tag{1.14}$$

Mathematicians call the proportionality constants λ in (1.12) *Lagrange multipliers*. Again, when a constraint is *not* binding, the Lagrange multiplier is *zero*:

$$g_i(x) < b_i \Rightarrow \lambda_i = 0 \tag{1.15}$$

Because of inequality (1.9), implication (1.15) may be written as:

$$\lambda_i[b_i - g_i(x)] = 0 \tag{1.16}$$

Using the fact that a sum of non-negative terms is zero if and only if every term is zero, the system of all equations (1.16) is equivalent to the single equation:

$$\sum_{i=1}^m \lambda_i[b_i - g_i(x)] = 0 \tag{1.17}$$

Invoking the notation of the product of row vector λ and a matrix, (1.14), (1.17) simply

---

[2] This notation is consistent with that of the partial derivatives of a real-valued function (such as f), as the case $m = 1$ shows.

[3] In (1.14), the first component is the product of λ and the first column of matrix g', etc. A precise treatment of matrix multipication is postpond to chapter 2.

reads:

$$\lambda[b - g(x)] = 0 \qquad (1.18)$$

Equation (1.18) is a brief reflection of the condition that a constraint is binding or has a zero Lagrange multiplier.

The first-order conditions (1.12) and the so-called *complementary slackness* conditions (1.18), are a concise mathematical statement of the solution to the constrained maximization problem, (1.10). The proportionality constants between the objective function derivatives and the constraint function derivatives (the Lagrange multipliers) have an economic interpretation, which we shall establish below. As a matter of fact, we shall show that the Lagrange multipliers measure the marginal productivities of the constraining entities. By definition, a marginal productivity is the amount by which the objective value goes up when an additional unit is available. So consider the situation in which one unit is added to the bound of the ith constraint. The new bound is $b + e_i$, where e_i is the ith unit vector:

$$e_i = \begin{pmatrix} 0 \\ \vdots \\ 0 \\ 1 \\ 0 \\ \vdots \\ 0 \end{pmatrix} \leftarrow \text{place } i \qquad (1.19)$$

In (1.19), the ith entry is one and all others are zero. Let x^* be the new optimum, reserving unstarred x for the old optimum (bounded by b). Making first-order approximations (1.3) to the increase of both the objective and the constraint function values and substituting (1.12) and the new bound we get:

$$f(x^*) - f(x) \approx f'(x)(x^* - x) = \lambda g'(x)(x^* - x)$$
$$\approx \lambda[g(x^*) - g(x)] = \lambda[g(x^*) - b] \leq \lambda e_i = \lambda_i \qquad (1.20)$$

Inequality (1.20) indicates that the marginal productivity of the ith constraining entity does not exceed λ. If $\lambda = 0$, this "increase" in the value is attained trivially by $x^* = x$. If $\lambda > 0$, the increase in the value is actually attained by the solution x^* to the equation defined by (1.20) with a *binding* inequality. In either case, the value of the objective function goes up by an amount of λ when one unit is added to the ith bound. The derivation will be presented rigorously in the context of linear objective and constraint functions in chapter 4.

1.4   Linear analysis

This section is a quick introduction to material that will be explained in detail in subsequent chapters. Readers who do not know matrices should proceed directly to chapter 2.

If an economy features constant returns to scale and the objective is to maximize the value of the net product, then the constraints and the objective function are linear. Problem (1.10) turns out as:

$$\max_{x} ax : Cx \leq b \tag{1.21}$$

The constrained maximization problem (1.21) is called a *linear program*. The first-order conditions (1.12) turn out as:

$$a = \lambda C, \lambda \geq 0 \tag{1.22}$$

Finally, the complementary slackness conditions (1.18) turn out as:

$$\lambda(b - Cx) = 0 \tag{1.23}$$

Multiplying (1.22) by solution x and substituting (1.23), we derive the important result:

$$ax = \lambda b \tag{1.24}$$

Equation (1.24) imputes the optimal value to the bounds. Each binding unit gets a value of λ_i. The result confirms that the marginal productivities of the bounds (given by vector b) are the components of row vector λ. There is a neat way to characterize these Lagrange multipliers. Consider *any* row vector μ fulfilling condition (1.22):

$$a = \mu C, \mu \geq 0 \tag{1.25}$$

Then we have, using the inequality in (1.21), the equality in (1.25), and (1.24):

$$\mu b \geq \mu Cx = ax = \lambda b \tag{1.26}$$

According to (1.24) the inequality is binding for λ. In other words, λ minimizes the left-hand side of (1.26). In other words, the Lagrange multipliers solve:

$$\min_{\lambda \geq 0} \lambda b : \lambda C = a \tag{1.27}$$

Minimization problem (1.27) is the dual program associated with the original maximization problem or primal program (1.21). Notice that the values of the primal and dual programs are equal according to (1.24). If a so-called *shadow price* of λ_i is assigned to the entity of constraint i, then the value of the ith bound is $\lambda_i b_i$ and the total value of bound b exhausts the value of the objective function. Since the shadow prices are equal to the marginal productivities, a competitive mechanism can bring them about. This approach is borne out in the following example.

In traditional input-output analysis, variable x lists the gross outputs of the sectors of an economy. Assuming constant returns to scale and fixed input proportions, sector 1 requires $a_{11}x_1, \ldots, a_{n1}x_1$ units of the various sectors as inputs in its production of x_1 units of output. Demand for the product of sector 1 amounts to $a_{11}x_1$ by sector 1 itself, $a_{12}x_2$ by sector 2, $\ldots$, $a_{1n}x_n$ by sector n, and y_1 final demand by the non-producing sectors of the economy, such as the households. Organize these demand coefficients in a row vector:

$$a_{1\bullet} = (a_{11} \cdots a_{1n}) \tag{1.28}$$

The condition that total demand for the product of sector 1 is bounded by supply can be written succinctly as follows:

$$a_{1\bullet}x + y_1 \leq x_1 \tag{1.29}$$

Organize the different row vectors in a matrix A:

$$A = \begin{pmatrix} a_{1\bullet} \\ \vdots \\ a_{n\bullet} \end{pmatrix} = \begin{pmatrix} a_{11} & \cdots & a_{1n} \\ \vdots & \ddots & \vdots \\ a_{n1} & \cdots & a_{nn} \end{pmatrix} \tag{1.30}$$

Then constraint (1.29) is the first component of the following inequality:

$$Ax + y \leq x \tag{1.31}$$

Let the economy maximize the value of the net output, py, on world markets. Here p is a given row vector of *world prices*. If the net output y does not agree with household demand, it is traded for other commodities. The maximization of the value of net output yields the greatest purchasing power in world markets, which is clearly in the interest of the domestic households. Since the value of net output is constrained by commodity balance (1.31), the factor balances, and a non-negativity constraint, we face the program:

$$\max_{x,y} \underline{py} : Ax + y \leq x, kx \leq M, lx \leq N, x \geq 0 \tag{1.32}$$

In program (1.32) row vector k lists the amount of capital required per unit of output in each sector, M is the available stock of capital, and l and N are the corresponding labor statistics. Introduce matrix notation for the objective function and constraint coefficients, respectively:

$$a = (0 \quad \underline{p}), C = \begin{pmatrix} A - I & I \\ k & 0 \\ l & 0 \\ -I & 0 \end{pmatrix} \tag{1.33}$$

Then program (1.32) reads

$$\max a \begin{pmatrix} x \\ y \end{pmatrix} : C \begin{pmatrix} x \\ y \end{pmatrix} \leq \begin{pmatrix} 0 \\ M \\ N \\ 0 \end{pmatrix} \tag{1.34}$$

In program (1.34) multiplication of the first row of coefficients matrix C of (1.33) with the stacked vector $\begin{pmatrix} x \\ y \end{pmatrix}$ reproduces the first inequality, (1.31). Multiplication of the other rows of matrix C with the vector of variables reproduces the further inequalities in program (1.32).

Denote the shadow prices associated with the material constraints, the capital and labor constraints, and the non-negativity conditions by:

$$\lambda = (p \quad r \quad w \quad \sigma) \tag{1.35}$$

The notation (1.35) suggests commodity price, rental rate of capital, wage rate, and slack, as will be explained shortly. The shadow prices are determined by the first-order condition (1.22) – or, substituting specifications (1.33) and (1.35),

$$(p \quad r \quad w \quad \sigma) \begin{pmatrix} A-I & I \\ k & 0 \\ l & 0 \\ -I & 0 \end{pmatrix} = (0 \quad \underline{p}) \tag{1.36}$$

The first component of (1.36) is the product of the row vector and the first column of the matrix – or, after a slight rearrangement of terms:

$$p = pA + rk + wl - \sigma \tag{1.37}$$

The second component of (1.36) reads:

$$p = \underline{p} \tag{1.38}$$

By (1.38) the shadow prices of the materials are simply *equal* to the world prices. And by (1.37) the prices are equal to the sum of the material costs of the inputs, the capital costs, the labor costs, and the slack. If the slack is positive, costs exceed price. However, since the slack is a Lagrange multiplier, the underlying constraint is binding by the complementary slackness conditions (1.23). But since this is a non-negativity constraint, it means that the output of such a sector is zero. Thus, unprofitable sectors are inactive. Conversely, if sectors are active, the non-negativity constraint is not binding, the associated slack variable is zero, and, therefore, price equals cost by (1.37). Thus, the shadow prices, particularly of capital and labor, make the active sectors break even while rendering the inactive sectors unprofitable. Profit maximizing entrepreneurs would target the right sectors. Moreover, since the shadow prices are minimal, yielding negative or zero profits, a process of free entry can bring them about. The competitive market mechanism is a device for the *optimal allocation of resources*.

The value of final demand, $\underline{p}y$, accrues to the resources in proportion to their marginal productivities, rM for capital and wN for labor. Thus, if resources are rewarded according their shadow prices, the value of the net output of the economy is exhausted. This equality of costs and revenues reflects the constant returns to scale. A precise derivation is by the application of the equality of the primal and dual solution values, (1.24):

$$(0 \quad \underline{p}) \begin{pmatrix} x \\ y \end{pmatrix} = (p \quad r \quad w \quad \sigma) \begin{pmatrix} 0 \\ M \\ N \\ 0 \end{pmatrix} \tag{1.39}$$

Equation (1.39) is the well-known macroeconomic identity of the national product and the national income:

$$\underline{p}y = rM + wN \tag{1.40}$$

In (1.40), national income comprises no profit under constant returns to scale and competition. If resources are paid according to their marginal productivities, income matches the value of the national product. Moreover, since non-binding constraints carry zero shadow prices by complementary slackness conditions (1.23), only scarce resources have a price.

1.5   Input-output analysis

In the first input-output study Leontief (1936) presented the so-called *closed model*: All outputs are also used as inputs. Industries produce commodities using commodities as well as factor inputs. Households produce these factor inputs using commodities. This, of course, is very much in the spirit of the contemporaneous work of von Neumann (1945).[4] Leontief's *tour de force* was his breakthrough in relating general equilibrium theory to the data for an economy. The input-output matrix encompasses the data for all branches of the economy, including consumption coefficients.

The weak element in the closed model is the treatment of *investment*. It is represented in a manner similar to household consumption – which can indeed be treated appropriately as an instantaneous activity, as people consume a flow of goods and services to maintain their standard of living. Investment, however, is a function of *future output*. Von Neumann circumvented the problem by assuming balanced growth – in which current levels of output also represent their future values – but Leontief was not content in proceeding this way. His solution was to assume fixed and given capital coefficients. Changes in output, in this approach, imply rigidly predetermined changes in the quantities of capital required – and, hence, determinate quantities of investment. The model of the economy thus becomes a system of differential equations. Another more pragmatic solution was to separate out the factors that engendered problems. Leontief felt at ease modeling production sectors by means of equations using intermediate input coefficients. The difficult final demand sector could then be left exogenous. This defines the open model, which was launched and studied by Leontief (1941, 1977).

The theory of input-output analysis is a major leap forward from the work of those who led up to Leontief's analysis (1966, particularly chapter 7). The advance here was formulation of the structure of the *interdependencies of an economy* in a way that was less abstract and far more operational than anything that had appeared before. Models are quantified with the aid of empirical data for an economy, enabling their use as a guide for concrete policy decisions as well as for pure understanding. In dealing with a substantial set of such simultaneous economic interrelationships, nothing like that had ever been done before. While some of the areas of application of the quantified input-output models are obvious – as, for example, their use as a guide to central planning – the applications go far beyond that, sometimes in totally unexpected directions. Thus, Leontief's (1970) application to environmental issues was, surely, far from obvious, though once it had been carried out, it does seem an evident and natural way to go about the analysis of its subject. Perhaps an even more striking and unexpected application was that to international trade. Leontief (1953) showed that US imports are more capital-intensive than its exports. This "Leontief

---

[4] Von Neumann (1945) alludes to Marx, without mentioning him explicitly.

paradox" has, for evident reasons, generated a stream of literature seeking to shed light on the puzzling finding and to draw out its implications for the field.

The approach to input-output analysis in this book is both "closed" and "open." In conformity with the closed model, household consumption will be modeled using consumption coefficients; in fact, the level of household consumption will define the objective of the economy. At the same time, the approach is "open" in the sense that production techniques are not predetermined but chosen from a menu. The profit motive and the market mechanism are analyzed concretely.

The theory developed in this book is quite powerful and enables us to address a wide range of themes and policy issues. How does taxation affect the different industries? How inefficient are national economies, and what is the diagnosis? What are the gains to free trade? Does it harm the environment? What arc the sources of growth? Does technological change spill over to other industries and countries? Input-output analysis not only presents a framework for discussion of these issues, but also actually puts numbers on them.

Exercises

In exercises of this type throughout the book, tick in the circle against your answer.

1. Consider the linear program (1.21).

What is the number of variables?	O m	O n
What is the number of constraints?	O m	O n
What is the number of Lagrange multipliers?	O m	O n
Are the variables non-negative?	O Yes	O No
Are the Lagrange multipliers non-negative?	O Yes	O No

2. Consider the linear program (1.32) where p is positive, A has n rows and n columns, and A, k, l, M, and N are non-negative.

What is the number of variables?	O n	O $2n$	
What is the number of constraints?	O 4	O $2n+2$	
Are the material balances binding?	O Yes	O No	O Some
Are the factor constraints binding?	O Yes	O No	O Some
Are the non-negativity constraints binding?	O Yes	O No	O Some

3. Consider the capital and labor constraints, $kx \leq M$ and $lx \leq N$. Show that if the macroeconomic capital/labor intensity, M/N, falls short of all the sectoral ratios, k_i/l_i, then labor will not be scarce and the wage rate will be zero.

References

Baumol, W. J. (1977). *Economic Theory and Operations Analysis*, Englewood Cliffs, N J, Prentice Hall

Baumol, W. J. and Thijs ten Raa (2005). "Wassily Leontief: In Appreciation," *Journal of Economic and Social Measurement* 27, 1–10

Leontief, W. (1936). "Quantitative Input and Output Relations in the Economic System of the United States," *Review of Economics and Statistics* 18 (3), 105–25

(1941).*The Structure of the American Economy, 1919–1929*, Cambridge, MA, Harvard University Press

(1953). "Domestic Production and Foreign Trade: The American Capital Position Re-Examined," *Proceedings of the American Philosophical Society* 97 (4), 332–49

(1966). *Input-Output Economics*, New York, Oxford University Press

(1970). "Environmental Repercussions and the Economic Structure – An Input-Output Approach," *Review of Economics and Statistics* 52 (3), 262–70

(1977). *Studies in the Structure of the American Economy*, White Plains, NY, International Arts and Sciences Press (now M. E. Sharpe))

von Neumann, J. (1945). "A Model of General Economic Equilibrium," *Review of Economic Studies* 13 (1), 1–9

Robbins, L. (1984). *An Essay on the Nature and Significance of Economic Science*, New York, New York University Press

2   Input-output basics

2.1   Introduction

The core of input-output analysis is a matrix of technical coefficients that summarizes the interdependencies between the sectors of production. To produce output, sectors require each other's inputs. What matters, of course, is the *net output of an economy*, which is the difference between output and the inputs used. Conversely, to fulfill a wanted bill of final deliveries, how much must be produced, taking into account the intermediate input requirements? The answer will be given by the so-called "Leontief inverse" of a matrix. In this chapter we derive conditions for the existence and the non-negativity of the Leontief inverse of a matrix. In itself, this is not new. However, the conditions presented here are economically intuitive and, at the same time, mathematically rigorous.

Traditional input-output analysis (Leontief 1966) is characterized by two simplifying assumptions. First, a common classification is used for commodities and production units: The economy is classified by "sector." Second, although sectors may have a variety of commodities as inputs, their outputs are not mixed. Each sector is identified with "the" commodity that it produces. By definition, a technical coefficient measures the requirement of some input per unit of some output – for example, the amount of sugar needed to bake a cake. In production, sector 1, for example, the technical coefficients are denoted a_{11} through a_{n1} and measure the input requirements (amounts of commodities 1 through n) per unit of output (commodity 1). Here n is the number of commodities. These coefficients are organized in a column vector, denoted $a_{\bullet 1}$:

$$a_{\bullet 1} = \begin{pmatrix} a_{11} \\ \vdots \\ a_{n1} \end{pmatrix} \tag{2.1}$$

The vector (2.1) summarizes the recipe for the production of commodity 1. We find it on p. 1 of a cookbook. The cookbook has n such pages, one for each product, and is denoted A:

$$A = (a_{\bullet 1} \ldots a_{\bullet n}) = \begin{pmatrix} a_{11} & \cdots & a_{1n} \\ \vdots & \ddots & \vdots \\ a_{n1} & \cdots & a_{nn} \end{pmatrix} \tag{2.2}$$

14

Matrix (2.2) is a *square* matrix, with the same number of rows as of columns; we say it is $n \times n$-dimensional, where the first n refers to the number of rows (i.e. the length of the columns) and the second n refers to the number of columns. The first row of matrix A collects all the first entries of the columns and is denoted $a_{1\bullet}$. Reproducing (1.28):

$$a_{1\bullet} = (a_{11} \cdots a_{1n}) \tag{2.3}$$

If two matrices – say, B and C – have the same dimension – say, $m \times n$ (m rows and n columns) – they can be summed to $B + C$. This is a third $m \times n$-dimensional matrix of which the entry in row i and column j is obtained by adding the respective entries of B and C.

Multiplication is trickier. The idea is to take a row of a first matrix (say, B) and a column of a second matrix (say, C), and to take the sum of the products of their components. This procedure works only if a row of B has precisely as many entries as a column of C – or, in other words, if the number of columns of B matches the number of rows of C. In short, if B is $m \times k$-dimensional, C must be $k \times n$-dimensional, where n is any number. Then BC is an $m \times n$-dimensional matrix of which the entry in row i and column j, $(BC)_{ij}$, is obtained by taking the product of row i of B and column j of C:

$$(BC)_{ij} = b_{i\bullet}c_{\bullet j} = \sum_{l=1}^{k} b_{il}c_{lj} \tag{2.4}$$

The last equality in (2.4) defines the product of a row and a column vector. Indexing matrices by their dimensions we see that $B_{m \times k}C_{k \times n} = D_{m \times n}$. Clearly D inherits the number of rows of B and the number of columns of C. The numbers of columns of B and of rows of C do not matter, but must be equal.

An immediate consequence of definition (2.4) is that the product is *associative*, in the sense that:

$$(AB)C = A(BC) \tag{2.5}$$

Formula (2.5) is meaningful if the products are defined. The dimensions must be consistent: $A_{k \times l}$, $B_{l \times m}$, and $C_{m \times n}$. The proof is by repeated application of definition (2.4), working out the (i,j)th element of the products on either side of (2.5). This procedure yields the common value

$$\sum_{r=1}^{l} \sum_{s=1}^{m} a_{ir} b_{rs} c_{sj}$$

Also, for this reason, we may denote matrix (2.5) simply by ABC.

The geometry of the product of a row and column vector is as follows. If the vectors are perpendicular to each other, for example, $(1 \quad 2)$ and

$$\begin{pmatrix} -2 \\ 1 \end{pmatrix}$$

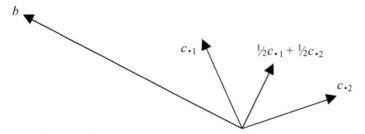

Figure 2.1 Positive and negative products of vectors

which point to the Northeast and the Northwest, respectively, then the product is zero. Otherwise they point either in similar or opposite directions, and the product is positive or negative, respectively. If two column vectors – say, $c_{\bullet 1}$ and $c_{\bullet 2}$ – are no multifold of each other, then they point in different directions. They can be separated by choosing a row vector b which is perpendicular to their mean, $\tfrac{1}{2}c_{\bullet 1} + \tfrac{1}{2}c_{\bullet 2}$. Then $b(c_{\bullet 1} + c_{\bullet 2}) = 0$, hence $bc_{\bullet 1} = -bc_{\bullet 2}$. If this expression is positive, $c_{\bullet 1}$ points in the direction of b, but not so $c_{\bullet 2}$; this situation is depicted in figure 2.1. If $bc_{\bullet 1} = -bc_{\bullet 2}$ is negative, $c_{\bullet 2}$ points in the direction of b, but not so $c_{\bullet 1}$.

Since pre-multiplication by vector b signs vectors $c_{\bullet 1}$ and $c_{\bullet 2}$ differently, vector b is said to *separate* the two vectors. Geometrically, $c_{\bullet 1}$ and $c_{\bullet 2}$ reside on opposite sides of the "subspace" perpendicular to b.

Although the product of B and C is obtained by multiplying rows of B with columns of C, the operation of multiplication amounts to combining columns of B or combining rows of C. To illustrate this observation, concentrate on a row of B, by letting $m = 1$. Then $B = (b_1 \ldots b_k) = b$ and

$$bC = (bc_{\bullet 1} \cdots bc_{\bullet n}) = (b_1 c_{11} + \cdots + b_k c_{k1} \cdots b_1 c_{1n} + \cdots + b_k c_{kn})$$
$$= b_1(c_{11} \cdots c_{1n}) + \cdots + b_k(c_{k1} \cdots c_{kn}) = b_1 c_{1\bullet} + \cdots + b_k c_{k\bullet} \qquad (2.6)$$

Equation (2.6) shows that bC is a combination of the rows of C. This procedure may be repeated for other rows of a multidimensional matrix B. Similarly (focusing on a column of C), one can show that BC comprises *combinations of the columns of B*.

A warning is in order: BC and CB may be different. The reason is that the product of row $b_{i\bullet}$ and column $c_{\bullet j}$ (constituting an element of BC) need not be equal to the product of row $c_{i\bullet}$ and column $b_{\bullet j}$ (constituting an element of CB). Worse, if BC is well defined, CB need not even exist. For example, if $B = 1$ and $C = (1 \quad 1)$, then $BC = (1 \quad 1)$, but CB is not defined, as the two-dimensional rows of C cannot be paired with the one-dimensional row of B. If the dimensions of B and C are opposites (one $m \times k$ and the other $k \times m$), this problem does not occur. In particular, for a square matrix A we may define $A^2 = AA$, $A^3 = AAA$, and so on. Notice also that in this (exceptional) case, $AA^2 = A^2 A$. It is also conventional to define $A^1 = A$ and $A^0 = I$. Here I is the *identity* matrix, with all diagonal elements 1 and all off-diagonal elements 0. (By definition, the *diagonal* elements of a matrix are the ones with the same row and column index.) Pre- or post-multiplication of any matrix with the identity matrix of the appropriate dimension preserves the matrix.

A handy column vector is given by:

$$e = \begin{pmatrix} 1 \\ \vdots \\ 1 \end{pmatrix} \tag{2.7}$$

The row vector associated with (2.7) is

$$e^{\top} = (1 \quad \cdots \quad 1) \tag{2.8}$$

Superscript $\top$ in expression (2.8) denotes *transposition*, the operation by which the roles of rows and columns are interchanged. For example, if A is given by formula (2.2), then:

$$A^{\top} = \begin{pmatrix} a_{11} & \cdots & a_{n1} \\ \vdots & \ddots & \vdots \\ a_{1n} & \cdots & a_{nn} \end{pmatrix} \tag{2.9}$$

If matrix B has b_{ij} on row i and column j, then $B^{\top}$ has b_{ji} on this place. Clearly, if B is $m \times n$-dimensional, then $B^{\top}$ is $n \times m$-dimensional. Also, the transposed matrix of a sum is easily seen to be the sum of the transposed matrices. Moreover, the string $(BC)_{ij}^{\top} = (BC)_{ji} = b_{j\bullet}c_{\bullet i} = (C^{\top})_{i\bullet}(B^{\top})_{\bullet j} = (C^{\top}B^{\top})_{ij}$ implies:

$$(BC)^{\top} = C^{\top}B^{\top} \tag{2.10}$$

Post-multiplication of A by e yields an $n \times 1$-dimensional matrix, that is a column vector, consisting of the *row totals* of A. *Pre*-multiplication of A by $e^{\top}$ yields a $1 \times n$-dimensional matrix, that is a row vector, consisting of the *column totals* of A. These properties are immediate consequences of the definition of multiplication, (2.4).

2.2   Price changes

The tack taken in this book towards input-output coefficients matrices, and their Leontief inverses is via the thought construct of a *price change*. Price changes are equivalent to changes in the physical units of measurement. If we measure the sugar requirements of a cake in dollars, the figure would increase by 100 percent if the price of sugar doubles. If the initial price were $1 per kilogram, the new price is $1 per (metric) pound. The sugar requirements of cake would also double in a single-person Robinson Crusoe economy without prices, if Robinson decides to change his unit of measurement for sugar from kilograms to (metric) pounds.[1] Now a well-known condition often imposed on input-output

---

[1] There are 2 metric pounds to the kilogram.

coefficients matrices A is that the column totals are less than one:

$$e^\top A < e^\top \tag{2.11}$$

The unit vector in (2.11) is defined in (2.8) and the idea behind the above inequality is that everything is measured in dollars. Under this assumption the first column total represents the total material cost of one unit, hence \$1, of commodity 1, and this should be less than one.[2] Condition (2.11) is unnecessarily strong, though. To understand this, let commodity 1 be sugar again and commodity 2 cake, and let the price of sugar become prohibitively high. In current dollars, the sugar requirement of cake, a_{12}, will shoot up, and condition (2.11) may no longer be valid under the new price regime, even though the technology did not change. This consideration prompts the replacement of (2.11) by the more general condition:[3]

$$\text{For some row vector } p \geq 0 : pA < p \tag{2.12}$$

If the technical coefficients are expressed in current values, then a price change from $e^\top$ to p would turn coefficient a_{ij} into $p_i a_{ij}/p_j$. The sugar requirement of cake goes up with the price of sugar, but down with the price of cake. (If cake becomes more expensive, you need less sugar per dollar of cake, simply because it represents a smaller quantity.) This stream of thought can be inverted to express a nominal matrix of technical coefficients (in *current* prices) in real a matrix of technical coefficients (in base-year or *constant* prices).

Economists separate real effects from nominal effects by expressing flows or coefficients in base-year prices. By artificially sticking to the "old" price system, all variations can be ascribed to quantity fluctuations. The nominal changes, reflecting mere price changes, are identified and removed. What are the technical coefficients expressed in base-year prices? Let the base-year price of commodity i be p_i^b and the current price be p_i^c. When there is inflation in this market, we have:

$$p_i^b < p_i^c \tag{2.13}$$

The quantities of commodity i must be deflated by p_i^b/p_i^c to express them in the base-year price unit. The transition to the base year is brought about by the price system:

$$p = \left(\frac{p_1^b}{p_1^c} \quad \cdots \quad \frac{p_n^b}{p_n^c} \right) \tag{2.14}$$

Input-output coefficients are deflated to base-year price levels by replacement of a_{ij} by $p_i a_{ij}/p_j$, or, using formula (2.14):

$$p_i a_{ij}/p_j = \left(\frac{p_i^b}{p_i^c} \middle/ \frac{p_j^b}{p_j^c} \right) a_{ij} \tag{2.15}$$

---

[2] The same argument is applied to the other commodities.
[3] Throughout the book inequality signs are presumed to hold for *all* components.

Inflation affects the change in the technical coefficient displayed in (2.15) in two ways: The increase of the price of input i ($p_i^b < p_i^c$) makes the constant value coefficient smaller than the current value coefficient, but the increase of the price of output j ($p_j^b < p_j^c$) makes the constant value coefficient larger than the current value coefficient, and the overall effect depends on the relative strengths of the commodity price inflation rates.

2.3 Value relations

A *value-added coefficient* is the difference between the revenues per unit of output (the price of the commodity) and the material costs per unit of output, hence the wedge in inequality (2.12). Organizing these figures in a row vector v we get:

$$p - pA = v \tag{2.16}$$

Now if matrix A fulfils condition (2.12) – i.e. if some price system yields positive value-added, then *any* value-added coefficients vector can be sustained by an appropriate price vector. In other words, (2.16) can be solved for any non-negative row vector v. Value-added is income, for the workers, the capitalists, and the government. An appropriate price vector can support any distribution of income between the sectors of production, provided that the technology fulfills condition (2.12). In fact, the solution to (2.16) will be shown to be:

$$p = v + vA + vA^2 + \cdots = v \sum_{k=0}^{\infty} A^k \tag{2.17}$$

Definition. The *Leontief inverse* of matrix A is:

$$\sum_{k=0}^{\infty} A^k \tag{2.18}$$

We will show that the Leontief inverse of A is the inverse of $I - A$. The latter features in the equation we want to solve, (2.16), because a simple rewrite turns it into:

$$p(I - A) = v \tag{2.19}$$

Multiplication of $I - A$ with the Leontief inverse (2.18) indeed yields the identity matrix:

$$(I - A) \sum_{k=0}^{\infty} A^k = \sum_{k=0}^{\infty} A^k - \sum_{k=1}^{\infty} A^k = A^0 = I \tag{2.20}$$

By (2.20), post-multiplication of (2.19) with the Leontief inverse actually solves it, proving (2.17).

Our analysis makes sense if the Leontief inverse exists. The question is if the infinite series (2.18) converges to something finite. A practical answer is: "Yes, if the column sums are less than one." This is condition (2.11). A more general answer is: "Yes, if for some price system the values of the columns are less than the prices." This is condition (2.12).

The latter condition will be shown to be necessary and sufficient for the existence of the Leontief inverse.

Let us first investigate the "classical" case where A fulfills condition (2.11). We will demonstrate that the column sums of A^k are geometrically declining. This will permit summation over k, hence the construction of a finite Leontief inverse. The first step is to rewrite condition (2.11) as a weak inequality:

$$e^\top A \le \alpha e^\top, 0 \le \alpha < 1 \tag{2.21}$$

In fact, α is the maximum column total. The second step is to notice that inequality (2.21) implies:

$$e^\top A^2 = e^\top AA \le \alpha e^\top A \le \alpha^2 e^\top \tag{2.22}$$

Post-multiplying inequality (2.22) by matrix A, not once, but arbitrarily many times:

$$e^\top A^k \le \alpha^k e^\top \tag{2.23}$$

Inequality (2.23) implies:

$$0 \le e^\top \sum_{k=0}^{N} A^k = \sum_{k=0}^{N} e^\top A^k \le \sum_{k=0}^{N} \alpha^k e^\top = \frac{1 - \alpha^{N+1}}{1 - \alpha} e^\top \le \frac{e^\top}{1 - \alpha} \tag{2.24}$$

Now it is an elementary fact of analysis that an increasing but bounded sequence of real numbers has a limit. Inequality (2.24) shows that the column totals of $\sum_{k=0}^{N} A^k$ are bounded as N grows. The (i, j)th elements themselves must certainly be bounded as N grows. Hence they have a limit and, therefore, expression $\sum_{k=0}^{\infty} A^k$ is finite.

Next turn to the general case, where A fulfills condition (2.12). The strategy of proof is to express the input-output coefficients in dollars and to apply the preceding case. Now, as we have seen before, transformations between units of measurement require positive prices. Hence, as a first step, we demonstrate that in condition (2.12) the price vector p may be assumed to be positive. The idea is to replace all p_i by $p_i + \varepsilon$, ε positive. We must show it fulfills condition (2.12):

$$p + (\varepsilon \cdots \varepsilon) < [p + (\varepsilon \cdots \varepsilon)]A \tag{2.25}$$

Indeed, because inequality (2.25) is true for $\varepsilon = 0$, it is still true for ε positive but small. The positivity of the price vector p permits us to define $\tilde{a}_{ij} = p_i a_{ij} / p_j$. Organize these elements in matrix $\tilde{A}$:

$$\tilde{A} = \hat{p} A \hat{p}^{-1} \tag{2.26}$$

Here, by definition, a *cap* (ˆ) creates a matrix by the placement of a vector on the diagonal (and leaving the off-diagonal elements zero). Because A fulfills condition (2.12), the column totals of the matrix in (2.26) are less than one, which is condition (2.11). By the preceding "classical" result, $\tilde{A}$ has a Leontief inverse:

$$\sum_{k=0}^{\infty} \tilde{A}^k,$$

Equation (2.26) implies:

$$\tilde{A}^k = \hat{p} A^k \hat{p}^{-1} \tag{2.27}$$

Summing the equations (2.27):

$$\sum_{k=0}^{\infty} \tilde{A}^k = \hat{p} \sum_{k=0}^{\infty} A^k \hat{p}^{-1} \tag{2.28}$$

Dividing and multiplying equation (2.28) by price:

$$\sum_{k=0}^{\infty} A^k = \hat{p}^{-1} \left(\sum_{k=0}^{\infty} \tilde{A}^k \right) \hat{p} \tag{2.29}$$

Equation (2.29) completes the proof that condition (2.12) is also a sufficient condition for the finiteness of the Leontief inverse of A.

It remains to show that condition (2.12) is a necessary condition. So let $\sum_{k=0}^{\infty} A^k$ be finite. Take a positive vector v. Then condition (2.12) can be verified for $p = v \sum_{k=0}^{\infty} A^k$:

$$pA = v \sum_{k=0}^{\infty} A^k A = v \sum_{k=1}^{\infty} A^k = v \left(\sum_{k=0}^{\infty} A^k - A^0 \right) = v \sum_{k=0}^{\infty} A^k - vI$$
$$= p - v < p \tag{2.30}$$

This completes the verification. Theorem 2.1 summarizes our findings.

Theorem 2.1. Let A be a square, non-negative matrix. The Leontief inverse $\sum_{k=0}^{\infty} A^k$ exists if and only if $pA < p$ for some row vector $p \geq 0$.

A simple example is given by:

$$A = \begin{pmatrix} 0 & 1/4 \\ 2 & 0 \end{pmatrix} \tag{2.31}$$

Not all column sums of matrix (2.31) are less than one; sector 1 uses a lot of commodity 2. However, if we value by $p = (1 \quad 1/3)$ (reducing the value of the "excessive" input), the column sums become $2/3$ and $1/4$, which are less than the respective elements of p. In short, A fails test (2.11), but passes test (2.12). The Leontief inverse exists. In practice one finds it by inversion: Call the Leontief inverse

$$\begin{pmatrix} a & b \\ c & d \end{pmatrix}.$$

Then, by (2.20) and (2.31):

$$\begin{pmatrix} 1 & -1/4 \\ -2 & 1 \end{pmatrix} \begin{pmatrix} a & b \\ c & d \end{pmatrix} = \begin{pmatrix} 1 & 0 \\ 0 & 1 \end{pmatrix} \tag{2.32}$$

Writing out the product in (2.32):

$$a - \frac{c}{4} = 1 \qquad b - \frac{d}{4} = 0$$

$$-2a + c = 0 \qquad -2b + d = 1 \qquad (2.33)$$

The system of equations (2.33) has solution $a = 2, c = 4; b = \frac{1}{2}, d = 2$.

In economic practice one tests the condition of positive value-added coefficients in theorem 2.1 by taking market prices. If a table is in current values, $p = e^\top$, the test reduces to the condition that column sums are less than one, (2.11).

A less practical but general test is the positivity of the so-called principal minors of A (Hawkins and Simon 1949). This condition is clear-cut; it demarcates the matrices that have a non-negative Leontief inverse. However, it is not as practical as the profitability conditions.

If matrix A is as in theorem 2.1, then mathematicians call $I - A$ an M-matrix (by Minc 1988). Equivalent conditions characterizing M-matrices are known in the literature, but the analysis revolves around so-called eigenvectors and eigenvalues, which are circumvented by the above economic analysis.

2.4   Quantity relations

In section 2.3, a matrix of technical coefficients, A, was pre-multiplied by a row vector, p, yielding costs. It can also be post-multiplied by a column vector, say x, of dimension n. If x_j is the output level of sector j, then $a_{ij}x_j$ is the required input of commodity i in sector j and $(Ax)_i = \sum_j a_{ij}x_j$ is the economy-wide input requirement of commodity i.

The economy is self-reliant if all required input can be provided by its own output:

$$Ax < x \qquad (2.34)$$

The wedge in the inequality, $x - Ax$, is the net output of the economy, also called *final demand*. It comprises the quantities of commodities that are not consumed by industry and may be used by the households. Theorem 2.2 shows that the economy is self-reliant if and only if the Leontief inverse exists.

Theorem 2.2. Let A be a square, non-negative matrix. $Ax < x$ for some column vector $x \geq 0$ if and only if the Leontief inverse $\sum_{k=0}^{\infty} A^k$ exists.

Proof. The proof is by means of a transposition argument and theorem 2.1. Transposition of $Ax < x$ yields $pA^\top < p$ (for $p = x^\top$). By theorem 2.1, this is equivalent to the existence of $\sum_{k=0}^{\infty} A^{\top k}$ By (2.10), this is the existence of $\sum_{k=0}^{\infty} A^{k\top} = (\sum_{k=0}^{\infty} A^k)^\top$ hence the existence of the Leontief inverse of A. □

Theorem 2.2 has a striking implication, which was first demonstrated by Gale (1960). If a technology (represented by a matrix of technical coefficients A) is capable of producing *some* net output, the Leontief inverse exists, and, therefore it is capable of producing *any* net output. If we denote the latter by vector y, we can indeed solve the material balance:

$$x = Ax + y \tag{2.35}$$

Step 1 is to rewrite (2.35):

$$(I - A)x = y \tag{2.36}$$

Step 2 is pre-multiplication of (2.36) with the Leontief inverse (2.18). This yields:

$$x = \sum_{k=0}^{\infty} A^k y \tag{2.37}$$

Equations (2.35), (2.36), and (2.37) are the quantity counterparts to the value equations, (2.16), (2.19), and (2.17), respectively.

The Leontief inverse (2.18) is by (2.20) the inverse of $I - A$. We may therefore write:

$$\sum_{k=0}^{\infty} A^k = (I - A)^{-1} \tag{2.38}$$

The existence problem of the Leontief inverse is the problem of the existence and non-negativity of the inverse matrix (2.38). In general, B is the *inverse* of a matrix A if $BA = AB = I$. That $BA = AB$ is straightforward in case of the Leontief inverse (2.18); it rests on the property that $A^k A = A A^k$. In other words, A^k and A are commutative. Unfortunately, two matrices do not commute in general with respect to the taking of the product, as we discussed after the product definition, (2.4). This complicates the inversion of a general matrix. Another way to appreciate the difficulty is as follows. Matrix B fulfilling $BA = I$ is the *left inverse* of matrix A, whereas matrix C fulfilling $AC = I$ is the *right inverse* of A. The concept of an *inverse* is unambiguous if it follows that $B = C$. This is true, but the proof is not easy and will be relegated to chapter 4.

Exercises

1. A has n rows and n columns and is non-negative. Check the nature of each the following conditions for the existence of the Leontief inverse:

$e^\top A < e^\top$	O	Necessary	O	Sufficient	O	Both
$pA < p$ for some $p \geq 0$	O	Necessary	O	Sufficient	O	Both

2. Assume the input-output coefficients matrix fulfills theorem 2.2. Show that positivity of net output implies the positivity of all sectoral outputs.

3. Determine the class of all 2×2-dimensional non-negative matrices with a non-negative Leontief inverse.

References

Gale, D. (1960).*The Theory of Linear Economic Models*, New York, Mc-Graw Hill

Hawkins, D. and H. A. Simon (1949). "Some Conditions of Macroeconomic Stability," *Econometrica* 17, 245–8

Leontief, W. (1966). *Input-Output Economics*, New York, Oxford University Press

Minc, H. (1998). *Non-Negative Matrices*, New York, Wiley

3 Multiplier effects

3.1 Introduction

In chapter 2 we analyzed the "cookbook of recipes" of an economy, given by a matrix of technical coefficients, A. The Leontief inverse (2.18) suggests a series of direct and indirect effects, culminating in a matrix of multipliers, and is a useful tool to model the multiplier effects of cost increases on prices, such as the price effects of an energy tax. The Leontief inverse can also be used to model the multiplier effects of a final demand stimulus on outputs and income, such as the income effects of a public program. Input-output analysis focuses on the multiplier effects that stem from the "roundaboutness" in production, meaning that sectors use each other's outputs as inputs. We will analyze them in sections 3.2 and 3.3 for the value and quantity systems, respectively. It is possible to incorporate the multiplier effects induced by household consumption; this will be done in sections 3.4 and 3.5.

3.2 Cost-push analysis

The difference between revenues and material costs is *value-added*. Value-added comprises factor costs and profit. Per unit of output, revenue equals price, material costs are given by the value of the column in the matrix of technical coefficients, that is an element of pA, and the difference between the two is the value-added coefficient, the corresponding element of v. In short, repeating (2.16):

$$p - pA = v \tag{3.1}$$

If factor costs go up, value-added per unit of output will be higher. This is possible only if the price goes up. However, since material costs will be increased in the process, the price must go up disproportionally. This is the multiplier effect of cost on price. An example is the analysis of an energy tax. Decompose the row vector of value-added coefficients in energy costs, u, and all other costs, w. If we tax energy at a rate t, the value-added coefficients $v = u + w$ will become:

$$(1+t)u + w = v + tu \tag{3.2}$$

What is the effect of the increase of value-added in expression (3.2) on price? If we denote the price increase by Δp, the new price, $p + \Delta p$, fulfills (3.1) with the new value-added, (3.2):

$$(p + \Delta p) - (p + \Delta p)A = v + tu \tag{3.3}$$

Subtracting (3.1) from (3.3), we obtain:

$$\Delta p - (\Delta p)A = tu \tag{3.4}$$

We solve (3.4) by taking the Leontief inverse, (2.38):

$$\Delta p = tu \sum_{k=0}^{\infty} A^k \tag{3.5}$$

The price effect equals $tu = tuA + tuA^2 + \cdots$. The first term is the direct effect of the tax. The second term is the cost increase of the direct material inputs. The further terms are the cost increases of the indirect material inputs. Even if the tax is limited to one sector – say, sector i – the effect will spread through the economy. The tax pushes up the price of commodity i directly, but this pushes up the material costs in all the other sectors and hence the prices of the other commodities as well. By definition, the cost-push multiplier effect is the price increase per unit of value-added increase. It is determined by replacing the value-added increase vector (tu) by the ith unit vector, (1.19). From (3.5) we see that the cost-push multipliers of sector i are given by the ith row of the Leontief inverse (2.18).

3.3   Demand-pull analysis

The difference between gross output and material inputs is *final demand*. Final demand comprises consumption and investment. Recall (2.36):

$$x - Ax = y \tag{3.6}$$

If final demand is increased, output must go up. However, since this will call forth higher demand for material inputs, output must go up disproportionally much. Hence final demand has a multiplier effect on output. An example is the analysis of public investment in infrastructure; denote it by commodity j. By definition, the demand-pull multiplier effect is the output increase per unit of final demand increase. It is determined by replacing the final demand vector by the jth unit vector, see (1.19). The jth column of the Leontief inverse (2.18) gives the demand-pull multipliers of commodity j.

Output increases induced by a final demand stimulus are of little interest in themselves. What matters is the income generated by the additional economic activity. To obtain this, each output increase must be multiplied by its value-added coefficient. Thus, the production income multiplier of commodity j is the product of the value-added coefficients row vector,

v, and the jth column of the (2.18). The production income multipliers are aligned in a row vector by taking the product of row vector v and the entire Leontief inverse:

Definition. A square, non-negative matrix A and a row vector v define a row vector of *production income multipliers*:

$$v \sum_{k=0}^{\infty} A^k \tag{3.7}$$

The jth production income multiplier in row vector (3.7) indicates the economy-wide increase of income per unit increase of final demand for commodity j. The first term of (3.7) is v. It shows the direct income effects of alternative commodity increases. The second term, vA, yields the income generated in the production of the direct material input requirements. The further terms, $vA^2 + vA^3 + \cdots$, yield the income generated in the production of the indirect requirements. The production effects called forth by the final demand increases multiply income. The indirect effects are quite important. If the government wants to select a public program on the basis of generated income, the commodity with the greatest value-added is not necessarily the best one. Another commodity, with a lower value-added coefficient, may have a higher production income multiplier: the further terms of the production income multiplier may overwhelm it. Such a commodity has a great demand-pull effect on the rest of the economy.

Comparing definition (3.7) to (2.17), we see that a production income multiplier equals price. Indeed, the income generated by the direct and indirect requirements of an additional unit of some final demand component adds to the price of that commodity. An additional unit generates much income if the price is high. Conversely, the production income multiplier of a dollar of final demand is always one, no matter the commodity composition. This is a reflection of the identity of the national product and national income, which we will establish in chapter 6.

3.4 Consumption effects

The production process is "roundabout" and thus creates the production income multiplier effect of government spending; the supplying sectors call forth further demands. In traditional macroeconomics, factor inputs are directly mapped into the national output and production income multiplier effects are not detected. The feedback effect of income on consumption is taken into account, however. The familiar Keynesian multiplier effect is derived from the basic final demand decomposition:

$$Y = cY + I \tag{3.8}$$

In (3.8), Y is aggregate income, c the propensity to consume, and I investment. It follows that:

$$Y = (1 - c)^{-1}I = I + cI + c^2 I + \cdots = \sum_{k=0}^{\infty} c^k I \tag{3.9}$$

For example, if the propensity to consume is 0.9, then the propensity to save is $1 - 0.9 = 0.1$ and the Keynesian multiplier of investment on income is an impressive $0.1^{-1} = 10$.

If households spend on commodities the income that comes with the production of output necessary to sustain a public investment project, the production income multiplier is reinforced by a Keynesian multiplier effect. The total income multipliers, one for each commodity, reflect the production *and* the consumption effects of increased final demand, and, therefore, are greater than the production income multipliers. The consumption effect can be modeled in a microeconomic framework by disaggregating the propensity to consume into a commodity vector. Thus, let column vector a list the quantities consumed by the households per dollar earned. Since total income is vx (value-added per unit of output times the level of output, summed over sectors) consumption is avx. Final demand, y, comprises consumption and other final demand (investment), z. The modeling of consumption thus refines (3.6) into:

$$x - Ax = avx + z \qquad (3.10)$$

Equation (3.10) features an augmented input-output coefficients matrix, as a rewrite shows more clearly:

$$x - (A + av)x = z \qquad (3.11)$$

Since a is a column vector of dimension $n \times 1$, and v a row vector of dimension $1 \times n$, in (3.11) av is a *matrix* of dimension $n \times n$. The (i, j)th element of matrix av is $a_i v_j$. In other words, the incorporation of consumption in the model augments the commodity i requirement per unit of commodity j, a_{ij}, by the consumption of commodity i called forth by the income generated per unit of commodity j, $a_i v_j$. The latter amount is necessary to feed the income earners in sector j, per unit of output. The augmentation inflates the Leontief inverse. A closed-form formula and the effects on the multipliers will be given below. The relationships are determined by the propensity to consume.

Definition. Let the input, value-added, and consumption coefficients be given by a square matrix A with Leontief inverse B, a row vector v, and a column vector a, respectively, all being non-negative. The *propensity to consume* is:

$$c = pa = vBa = v \sum_{k=0}^{\infty} A^k a \qquad (3.12)$$

Since vector a depicts the pattern of consumption per dollar earned, pa is the expenditure on consumption per dollar earned and this, indeed, is the propensity to consume. We will assume that the consumption expenditure per dollar earned is less than a dollar. The Leontief inverse of $A + av$ has been determined by Pieter Kop Jansen:

Lemma 3.1. Let A, v, and a be such that the propensity to consume c in definition (3.12) is less than one. Then the Leontief inverse of $A + av$ is:

$$C = B + BavB \sum_{k=0}^{\infty} c^k$$

Proof. We must show that the product of $I - (A + av)$ and C is the identity matrix. First rewrite C. Because $\sum_{k=0}^{\infty} c^k$ is a scalar (well defined by assumption $0 \leq c < 1$), it may be replaced between vectors a and v:

$$C = B + Ba \sum_{k=0}^{\infty} (vBa)^k vB = B \sum_{k=0}^{\infty} (avB)^l$$

The second equality is verified term by term. On the left-hand side the first, second, and mth terms are: B, $BavB$, and $Ba(vBa)^{m-2}vB$, respectively. On the right-hand side the terms are B, $B(avB)$, and $B(avB)$, respectively. This is perfectly consistent. The right-hand side involves the Leontief inverse of $D = avB$; it exists because $Da = avBa = ac < a$ admits application of theorem 2.2. Now we can take the product:

$$(I - A - av)C = (I - A - av)B \sum_{l=0}^{\infty} (avB)^l$$

$$= (I - A)B \sum_{l=0}^{\infty} (avB)^l - avB \sum_{l=0}^{\infty} (avB)^l$$

$$= \sum_{l=0}^{\infty} (avB)^l - \sum_{l=1}^{\infty} (avB)^l = (avB)^0 = I$$

$\square$

The Leontief inverse in lemma 3.1, C, consists of the standard Leontief inverse, B, and an additional term comprising two factors, namely $BavB = Bap$ and $\sum_{k=0}^{\infty} c^k$. The latter factor is the well-known Keynesian multiplier effect of an increase in non-household final demand (such as investment) generated by household consumption; see (3.9). The first factor has as typical element

$$\sum_{k,l=1}^{n} b_{ik} a_k p_j$$

A unit increase in the final demand for commodity j generates income p_j and consumption demands $a_k p_j$ for commodity j. Pre-multiplication with Leontief inverse element b_{ik} translates the additional demand for commodity j into a gross output effect of output i and summation over the various additional demand components yields the overall consumption effect on output i of a unit increase in final demand

$$\sum_{k,l=1}^{n} b_{ik} a_k p_j$$

The total income multipliers are obtained in the same way as the production income multipliers, but with matrix A replaced by $A + av$.

Definition. A square, non-negative matrix A, a row vector v, and a column vector a define a row vector of *total income multipliers*:

$$v \sum_{k=0}^{\infty} (A + av)^k \tag{3.13}$$

The jth total income multiplier in row vector (3.13) measures the economy-wide income rise per unit of final demand increase of commodity j, taking into account the consumption effects. It is bigger than the production income multiplier. The production income effects are reinforced by a Keynesian multiplier effect. In fact, all production income multipliers are inflated by a common factor, the Keynesian multiplier. This result was discovered by Sandoval (1967) and generalized by ten Raa and Chakraborty (1983).

Theorem 3.1. If the propensity to consume is less than one, $c < 1$, then the ratio of the total to the production income multipliers is the same for all commodities. In fact, the ratio is the Keynesian multiplier $\sum_{k=0}^{\infty} c^k$.

Proof. Lemma 3.1 gives the total income multipliers as:

$$v \sum_{k=0}^{\infty} (A + av)^k = vC = vB + vBavB \sum_{k=0}^{\infty} c^k = vB + cvB \sum_{k=0}^{\infty} c^k$$

$$= vB + vB \sum_{k=0}^{\infty} c^k = vB \sum_{k=0}^{\infty} c^k$$

$\square$

where vB lists the production income multipliers.

Household consumption reinforces production effects irrespective of the source of the latter. The Keynesian multiplier acts indiscriminately. Theorem 3.1 has two important implications, a practical one and a theoretical one.

The practical implication is that household behavior need not be modeled when income effects rank alternative programs. A prominent application of multiplier analysis is development economics. Here the problem is to target a sector for investment so as to boost income. The simplest approach is to determine the component of final demand with the greatest income multiplier effect by means of the Leontief inverse. It has been argued that such a policy would be misdirected as it neglects the households. Their demand-pull effects would differ from those of the production units. Theorem 3.1 invalidates this critique. The inclusion of household consumption effects would not alter the ranking of the investment projects in terms of income effects.

The theoretical implication is as follows. Theorem 3.1 provides a microeconomic foundation to a macroeconomic concept: the Keynesian multiplier. The latter applies to production shocks irrespective of the commodity composition of the sources. In other words, it is an invariant with respect to the commodities, and, therefore, a true macroeconomic concept.

3.5 Employment multipliers

When employment is the main concern, rather than income, we use employment multipliers, of which there are also two types. Production employment multipliers measure the employment requirements of unit final demand increases resulting from intermediate demand-pull effects. Analogous to the analysis of income multipliers, the inclusion of consumption effects defines total employment multipliers. In this case, however, reversals may take place. A labor-extensive sector will score low on production employment multipliers, but if value-added is high, the consequent consumption effects may have overwhelming employment implications and thus yield high total employment multipliers.

A simple example illustrates the reversal. Consider a two-sector economy without intermediate demand (matrix $A = 0$) and with a labor-extensive sector. Say the labor inputs per unit of output in the sectors are given by row vector $l = e_2^\top$, the second unit vector, (1.19) with $i = 2$. Then the production employment multiplier of sector 1 is zero. However, if value-added in this sector is high ($v_1 > v_2$), consumption effects may make it an attractive target for an employment program. For simplicity, let consumption of the two commodities be in a one-to-one proportion, say $a = e$, defined by (2.7). Now consider the two scenarios. In the first, a unit shock to the final demand of sector 1 has an immediate income effect of v_1. Employment is created only in the fulfillment of the consumption vector

$$\begin{pmatrix} v_1 \\ v_1 \end{pmatrix}$$

The direct employment effect is v_1 in sector 2. (Moreover, incomes v_1^2 and $v_2 v_1$ in the respective sectors spur further consumption and employment effects.) In the second scenario, a unit shock to the final demand of sector 2 has immediate employment and income effects, 1 and v_2, respectively. The direct consumption effect is given by vector

$$\begin{pmatrix} v_2 \\ v_2 \end{pmatrix}$$

with employment requirement v_2 in sector 2 and income effects $v_1 v_2$ and v_2^2 in the respective sectors. If we compare the immediate and direct consumption employment effects in the two scenarios, we have v_1 and $1 + v_2$, respectively. The first score may be better. Even when the indirect consumption effects are considered in terms of labor requirements, the labor-extensive sector 1 can be seen to be superior.

The example is a bit peculiar though, in the sense that commodities are measured in physical terms. We shall see below that consumption effects will no longer change the ranking of sectors in terms of employment when employment effects are measured in monetary unit of commodities.

A formal analysis is made by examination of the consumption input/gross output matrix:

$$av = ev = \begin{pmatrix} v_1 & v_2 \\ v_1 & v_2 \end{pmatrix} \tag{3.14}$$

The Leontief inverse of matrix (3.14) is (the division applying to each matrix element):

$$\begin{pmatrix} 1 - v_2 & v_2 \\ v_1 & 1 - v_1 \end{pmatrix} \Big/ [(1 - v_1)(1 - v_2) - v_1 v_2] \tag{3.15}$$

The first column of matrix (3.15) shows the gross output requirements of a unit shock to the final demand of sector 1 (the first scenario). The employment requirement is given by the second component, hence proportional to v_1. The second column shows the gross output effects with an employment requirement proportional to $1 - v_1$. If $v_1 > \frac{1}{2}$, then the total employment multiplier of sector 1 is greater, showing the reversal from the production employment multipliers. The earning capacity of sector 1 generates a lot of consumption and indirect employment effects.

Value-added is stronger in sector 1, and an investigation of the Leontief inverse confirms this. It exists and is non-negative only if the denominator in (3.11) is positive, or:

$$v_2 < 1 - v_1 \qquad (3.16)$$

Our assumption that $v_1 > \frac{1}{2}$ implies, using inequality (3.16), $v_2 < \frac{1}{2}$ and, therefore indeed, $v_1 > v_2$.

A further critical examination of the example will lead us to a positive result on the relation between total and production employment multipliers. Suppose the government has one dollar to spend. Is sector 1 a better target as regards employment effects? The total employment multiplier is greater in sector 1. But that says only that a *unit* final demand increase in sector 1 is more effective than in sector 2. So the question is: How much does the dollar buy? Well, it buys $1/p_1$ in sector 1 and $1/p_2$ in sector 2. Sector 1 is a better target if and only if v_1/p_1 exceeds $(1 - v_1)/p_2$ where the numerators represent the (relative) total employment multipliers and the denominators the prices. A low price buys you a lot. What are the prices? Because there are no material costs, prices are equal to value-added per unit: $p_1 = v_1$ and $p_2 = v_2$. Hence sector 1 is a better target if and only if $1 > (1 - v_1)/v_2$ or $v_2 > 1 - v_1$. This is not the case, in view of the condition that the Leontief inverse exists and is non-negative, (3.16).

Although the inclusion of consumption effects may reverse the ranking of sectoral employment multipliers, a sector with the greatest production employment multiplier continues to be the best target for a fixed budget. A convenient way to analyze this property is to assume that the input-output coefficients are in *values* – that is dollars per dollars. We will show that *no* reversal of employment multiplier can take place in this case.

Definition. A square, non-negative matrix A and a row vector l yield a row vector of *production employment multipliers*:

$$l \sum_{k=0}^{\infty} A^k \qquad (3.17)$$

Definition. A square, non-negative matrix A, row vectors l and v, and a column vector a constitute a row vector of *total employment multipliers*:

$$l \sum_{k=0}^{\infty} (A + av)^k \qquad (3.18)$$

Definition. A square, non-negative matrix A, a row vector l, and a column vector a constitute a row vector of *nominal total employment multipliers*:

$$l \sum_{k=0}^{\infty} \left[A + a(e^\top - e^\top A) \right]^k \qquad (3.19)$$

Definitions (3.17) and (3.18) are variations on the theme of income multipliers (3.7) and (3.13). Note, however, that consumption is still proportional to value-added. The extended input-output matrix remains $A + av$.[1] Nominal total employment multipliers are total employment multipliers with the A matrix assumed to be in current values so that the value-added coefficients equal one minus the column totals: $v = e^\top - e^\top A$.

Theorem 3.2. If the propensity to consume is less than one, $c < 1$, then the difference between the nominal total and the production employment multipliers is the same for all commodities. In fact, the difference is the product of the production employment multipliers, the column vector of consumption coefficients, and the Keynesian multiplier:

$$\left(l \sum_{k=0}^{\infty} A^k \right) a \sum_{k=0}^{\infty} c^k$$

Proof. By lemma 3.1, the nominal total employment multipliers are given by:

$$l \sum_{k=0}^{\infty} [A + a(e^\top - e^\top A)]^k = lC = lB + lBa(e^\top - e^\top A)B \sum_{k=0}^{\infty} c^k$$

$$= lB + lBae^\top \sum_{k=0}^{\infty} c^k$$

where lB lists the production employment multipliers and the jth component of the second term is:

$$lB(ae^\top)_{\bullet j} \sum_{k=0}^{\infty} c^k = lBa \sum_{k=0}^{\infty} c^k \qquad \square$$

The inclusion of consumption effects raises all nominal employment multipliers by the same amount, and the commodity with the greatest production employment multiplier continues to be the best target for fixed government expenditure.

Let us summarize the effects of household consumption. Income multipliers increase by a common relative amount (theorem 3.1) and nominal employment multipliers increase by a common absolute amount (theorem 3.2). No reversal takes place and we conclude that the Leontief inverse of the production coefficients, (2.18), determines the best target for both income and employment policies irrespective of the specifics of household consumption. The conclusion holds for closed economies, in which domestic supplies fulfill all demands.

For open economies, the situation is very transparent. The opportunity costs of the commodities are determined by the world terms of trade. The best target for income maximization is the sector where value-added per dollar output is greatest and the best target for employment maximization is the most labor-intensive sector, also per dollar output. There is no need to activate other sectors. All demands can be filled by imports as we shall see in the following chapters.

---

[1] If only workers would consume and $A + al$ were pertinent, the analysis of section 3.4, particularly theorem 3.1, would apply, with v replaced by l.

3.6 Miyazawa inverses

In the previous sections the economy was divided into many production sectors and a single consumption sector. Miyazawa (1976) addressed the case where there were different types of households. A general partition of the input-output coefficients is

$$A = \begin{pmatrix} A_{11} & A_{12} \\ A_{21} & A_{22} \end{pmatrix} \tag{3.20}$$

In the previous sections A_{11} was the ordinary input-output coefficients matrix, A_{12} the column vector with consumption coefficients, A_{21} the row vector with value-added coefficients, and A_{22} zero. The partition (3.20) is much more general; it applies not only to multiple household types, but also to different settings, such as regional economies, where A_{11} represents the internal structure of a region, A_{21} the import coefficients, A_{12} the export coefficients, and A_{22} the external structure. If we neglect the external interactions, the multiplier effects of additions to the final demand of commodities in bloc 1 on their own output levels would be given by the Leontief inverse of A_{11}. Now we have to factor in the demand on the other bloc (A_{21}), the internal multiplier effect in the other bloc, and the feedback (through A_{12}). This is determined by the Leontief inverse of A, denoted by B – or more precisely, its first (Northwestern) bloc, B_{11}:

Theorem 3.3. $B_{11} = (I - B_1 A_{12} B_2 A_{21})^{-1} B_1$, where $B_i = (I - A_{ii})^{-1}$.

Proof. Write out $B(I - A) = I$:

$$\begin{pmatrix} B_{11} & B_{12} \\ B_{21} & B_{22} \end{pmatrix} \begin{pmatrix} I - A_{11} & -A_{12} \\ -A_{21} & I - A_{22} \end{pmatrix} = \begin{pmatrix} I & 0 \\ 0 & I \end{pmatrix}$$

The top components read $B_{11}(I - A_{11}) - B_{12}A_{21} = I$ and $-B_{11}A_{12} + B_{12}(I - A_{22}) = 0$. Post-multiplication of the latter by B_2 yields $B_{12} = B_{11}A_{12}B_2$. Substitution in the former yields $B_{11}(I - A_{11} - A_{12}B_2A_{21}) = I$. Hence $B_{11} = (I - A_{11} - A_{12}B_2A_{21})^{-1} = [B_1^{-1}(I - B_1A_{12}B_2A_{21})]^{-1}$ which yields the result. □

The standard multipliers get a further boost by what Sonis and Hewings (1999) call the Miyazawa external multiplier: $(I - B_1A_{12}B_2A_{21})^{-1}$. Notice it is the Leontief inverse of $B_1A_{12}B_2A_{21}$. The latter matrix gives the requirements induced by the rest of the economy, first directly (it demands A_{21}), then expressed in its output levels (by means of its Leontief inverse B_2), and finally its feedback effect (the direct demand, A_{12}, is expressed in output levels by means of the standard Leontief inverse, B_1).

Theorem 3.3 presents the matrix of *consolidated* multipliers. Consolidated multipliers take into account not only the local indirect production requirements (B_1), but also the external requirements and their feedbacks. Leontief (1967) introduced consolidated coefficients in an indirect way (using a double inversion) as an alternative to aggregation. Ten Raa and Wolff (2001) consolidated business services in the manufacturing input-output coefficients and were able to ascribe twenty percent of the manufacturing productivity recovery in the 1980s to outsourcing.

In income analysis, the two blocs represent production and household consumption. The production input-output coefficients are in sub-matrix A_{11}. The consumption coefficients are in sub-matrix A_{12} and the value-added coefficients in sub-matrix A_{21}. Ignoring household production, $A_{22} = 0$, and this adds structure that can be exploited. In particular, B_2, see theorem 3.3, is the identity matrix, so that the matrix of consolidated multipliers reduces to $(I - B_1 A_{12} A_{21})^{-1} B_1$. As in definition (3.13), consolidated income multipliers are obtained by pre-multiplication with value-added coefficients: $A_{21}(I - B_1 A_{12} A_{21})^{-1} B_1$. Consolidated income multipliers factor in the Keynesian multipliers effects that come with household consumption. Miyazawa's fundamental equation of income formation, see Sonis and Hewings' (1999, (2.55)), rewrites the consolidated income multipliers as follows:

$$A_{21}(I - B_1 A_{12} A_{21})^{-1} B_1 = (I - A_{21} B_1 A_{12})^{-1} A_{21} B_1 \qquad (3.21)$$

The proof of (3.21) is easy. The starting point is the identity

$$(I - A_{21} B_1 A_{12}) A_{21} = A_{21}(I - B_1 A_{12} A_{21})$$

Pre- and post-multiplication with the Leontief inverses of $A_{21} B_1 A_{12}$ and $B_1 A_{12} A_{21}$, respectively, yields the result.

Notice that if there is only one income class, then the consumption coefficients, A_{12}, reduce to column vector a and the value-added coefficients, A_{21}, to row vector v. By definition (3.12) the consolidated income coefficients of (3.21) reduce to $(1 - c)^{-1} v B_1$. This confirms theorem 3.1 (where A_{11} was denoted A and $B_1 = (I - A_{11})^{-1} = (I - A)^{-1} = B$). The consolidated income multipliers are the product of the production income multipliers and the Keynesian multiplier. The latter becomes matrix $(I - A_{21} B_1 A_{12})^{-1}$ if there are multiple household classes. Here $A_{21} B_1 A_{12}$ is the matrix of propensities to consume.

Remark 3.1. We conclude this chapter with a technical mark that bridges the chapters. In the proof of theorem 3.3 we determined the components of the left-hand side inverse of the partitioned $(I - A)$-matrix. We could just as well have determined the components of the right-hand side inverse. Then we write out $(I - A)B = I$:

$$\begin{pmatrix} I - A_{11} & -A_{12} \\ -A_{21} & I - A_{22} \end{pmatrix} \begin{pmatrix} B_{11} & B_{12} \\ B_{21} & B_{22} \end{pmatrix} = \begin{pmatrix} I & 0 \\ 0 & I \end{pmatrix}$$

The left-hand components read $(I - A_{11})B_{11} - A_{12}B_{21} = I$ and $-A_{21}B_{11} + (I - A_{22})B_{21} = 0$. Pre-multiplication of the latter by B_2 yields $B_{21} = B_2 A_{21} B_{11}$. Substitution in the former yields $(I - A_{11} - A_{12} B_2 A_{21}) B_{11} = I$. Hence again $B_{11} = (I - A_{11} - A_{12} B_2 A_{21})^{-1}$ which indeed yields the same result. There is no difference because the left-hand and right-hand inverses match, as we noted and proved for Leontief inverses at the end of chapter 2 and will prove for general inverses in chapter 4.

Exercises

1. Show that the existence and non-negativity of the total income multipliers ensure the existence and non-negativity of the production income multipliers.
2. Show that for any matrix A fulfilling theorem 2.2 and propensity to consume commodity vector there are positive value-added coefficients such that the total income multipliers exist.

3. Show that an increase in one value-added/gross output ratio raises the prices.

4. Show, by example, that income and employment policies point to different targets for government expenditure.

References

Leontief, W. (1967). "An Alternative to Aggregation in Input-Output Analysis and National Accounts," *Review of Economics and Statistics* 49 (3), 412–19; reprinted in W. Leontief, *Input-Output Economics*, Oxford, Oxford University Press, 2nd edn. (1986)

Miyazawa, K. (1976). *Input-Output Analysis and the Structure of Income Distribution*, Heidelberg, Springer

ten Raa, Th. and D. Chakraborty (1983). "A Note on Induced Multiplier," *Artha Vijnana* 25 (3), 277–9

ten Raa, Th. and E. N. Wolff (2001). "Outsourcing of Services and the Productivity Recovery in US Manufacturing in the 1980s and 1990s," *Journal of Productivity Analysis* 16, 149–65

Sandoval, A. D. (1967). "Constant Relationship between Input-Output Multipliers," *Review of Economics and Statistics* 49 (4), 599–600

Sonis, M. and G. J. D. Hewings (1999). "Miyazawa's Contributions to Understanding Economic Structure: Interpretation, Evaluation and Extensions," in G. J. D. Hewings, M. Sonis, M. Madden, and Y. Kimura, *Understanding and Interpreting Economic Structure*, Heidelberg, Springer

4 Linear programming

4.1 Introduction

Linear programming is a chapter of applied mathematics concerned with the maximization (or minimization) of a linear function, subject to linear constraints. A key role is designated to the *Lagrange multipliers*. In economics, these are the marginal productivities of the constraining entities. Our development of the theory of linear programming is made through an analysis of the Lagrange multipliers. The multipliers are constructed on the basis of inequality implications (sections 4.2 and 4.3) and yield an intuitive and simple derivation of the main results (sections 4.4 and 4.5). The remaining sections characterize the multipliers (section 4.6), identify the active variables (section 4.7), and provide an economic interpretation in terms of scarcity (section 4.8).

4.2 Inequality implications

There is a close connection between linear programs and inequality implications. An inequality implication states that one set of inequalities implies another inequality. For example, the inequality pair $x_1 \geq 0$ and $x_2 \geq 0$ clearly implies the new inequality $x_1 + x_2 \geq 0$.[1] A linear program can be designed in this framework. If a point is feasible, meaning that it fulfills the inequalities of the constraints, it is implied that the value of the linear function is less than or equal to the optimal value. Lemma 4.1 will reveal the structure of inequality implications, contains the seed of the Lagrange multipliers, and enable us to quickly derive the main results of the theory of linear programming. The lemma is an observation on linear inequalities of the type:

$$c_i x \geq 0, \ i = 1, \ldots, m \tag{4.1}$$

In inequalities (4.1) c_i are row vectors of coefficients, x is a column vector of variables, and i indexes constraints. From the set of inequalities (4.1) new ones can be derived, such as non-negative combinations of the old inequalities:

$$ax \geq 0 \tag{4.2}$$

---

[1] The reverse is not true.

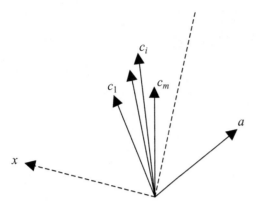

Figure 4.1 The proof of lemma 4.1

with

$$a = \lambda_1 c_1 + \cdots + \lambda_m c_m, \lambda_1, \ldots, \lambda_m \geq 0 \tag{4.3}$$

Indeed, the system of inequalities (4.1) *implies* inequality (4.2) when the coefficients are given by expression (4.3). Lemma 4.1 states that *no* other inequalities are implied. In other words, if the system of inequalities (4.1) implies an inequality of the general form (4.2), then the coefficients of the latter *must* be as in (4.3). The proof of lemma 4.1 has a nice geometry and is intuitive. It reflects a deep result of mathematics. This is the only instance in the book where such an appeal is made. Once we have established the lemma, the whole analysis flows smoothly.

Lemma 4.1. The system of linear inequalities (4.1) implies the linear inequality (4.2) if and only if the coefficients in the latter are a non-negative combination of the coefficients in the former, in the sense of (4.3).

Proof. Sufficiency (the "if" part) is trivial, as noted. To prove necessity (the "only if" part), let row vector a *not* belong to the set of vectors fulfilling (4.3). This set is a cone (see figure 4.1).

Since a is *off* the cone spanned by the vectors $c_1, \ldots, c_m$, there exists a so-called separating hyperplane.[2] More precisely, there exists a vector x (perpendicular to the separating plane), such that $c_1 x \geq 0, \ldots, c_m x \geq 0$, but $ax < 0$. Hence the former inequalities do *not* imply $ax \geq 0$.   □

If we organize the row vectors of coefficients, c_i, in a matrix:

$$C = \begin{pmatrix} c_1 \\ \vdots \\ c_m \end{pmatrix} \tag{4.4}$$

---

[2] This is Minkowski's theorem, see Rockafellar (1970) or, for a simple economic proof, Weitzman (1999).

and the weights in a row vector, $\lambda = (\lambda_1 \ldots \lambda_m)$, lemma 4.1 can be rephrased as follows:

$$(Cx \geq 0 \Rightarrow ax \geq 0) \Leftrightarrow (a = \lambda C; \lambda \geq 0) \qquad (4.5)$$

Here $\Rightarrow$ denotes 'implies' and $\Leftrightarrow$ denotes 'if and only if.' Statement (4.5) can be extended to matrices: If we consider not a single, but a number n of new inequalities, represented by row vectors a_i, then we have:

$$(Cx \geq 0 \Rightarrow a_1 x \geq 0, \ldots, a_n x \geq 0) \Leftrightarrow (a_1 = \lambda^1 C, \ldots, a_n = \lambda^n C; \lambda^1, \ldots, \lambda^n \geq 0) \quad (4.6)$$

Organizing the row vectors a_i in a matrix A and the row vectors λ^i in matrix Λ, statement (4.6) reads:

$$(Cx \geq 0 \Rightarrow Ax \geq 0) \Leftrightarrow (A = \Lambda C; \Lambda \geq 0) \qquad (4.7)$$

As before, x is a column vector of variables. A trivial variation holds for row vectors of variables. It is obtained by transposition of statement (4.7):

Corollary 4.1. $\mu C \geq 0$ implies $\mu A \geq 0$ if and only if $A = CX$ for some matrix $X \geq 0$.

Armed with lemma 4.1 and its various reformulations, we can attack the problem of linear programming. Our strategy is as follows. First we discuss the concept of independence. Then we define a linear program and derive the so-called "first-order conditions" by which the coefficients of the objective function are proportional to those of the constraints. The proportions are the Lagrange multipliers. They will be conceived as the outcome of a related linear program, the so-called "dual." The main theorem of linear programming follows and is used to establish complementary slackness between the original constraints and the Lagrange multipliers. In other words, positive Lagrange multipliers will signal the constraints without slack, the binding ones. We shall then proceed to investigate the structure of the binding constraints. By throwing out the redundant ones, we will reduce the linear program to its non-degenerate kernel. This admits an economic interpretation of the Lagrange multipliers, the so-called "marginal productivities."

4.3   Dependent and independent constraints

The first application of lemma 4.1 is the theory of *linear independence*. Constraints are either dependent or independent. Constraints are defined to be dependent if and only if at least one of them can be written as a linear combination of the others:

$$c_i = \mu_1 c_1 + \cdots + \mu_{i-1} c_{i-1} + \mu_{i+1} c_{i+1} + \cdots + \mu_m c_m \qquad (4.8)$$

A somewhat cleaner rewrite is as follows:

$$\mu_1 c_1 + \cdots + \mu_m c_m = 0 \text{ for some } \mu_i \neq 0 \qquad (4.9)$$

Equation (4.8) implies (4.9) by choice of $\mu_i = -1$. Conversely, (4.9) implies (4.8) upon division by μ_i. Hence (4.9) may be used to define dependence.

Definition. The rows of matrix C are *linearly dependent* if and only if for some non-zero row vector μ:

$$\mu C = 0 \qquad (4.10)$$

The rows of matrix C are linearly independent if they are not linearly dependent.

Definition. The rows of matrix C are *linearly independent* if and only if:

$$\mu C = 0 \Rightarrow \mu = 0 \qquad (4.11)$$

Using corollary 4.1 we can characterize independence.

Corollary 4.2. The rows of matrix C are linearly independent if and only if $CX = I$ for some matrix X.

Proof. By definition (4.11) the rows of C are linearly independent if and only if $\mu C \geq 0$ together with $\mu(-C) \geq 0$ implies $\mu I \geq 0$ and $\mu(-I) \geq 0$. In short, $\mu(C\ -C) \geq 0$ implies $\mu(I\ -I) \geq 0$. By corollary 4.1, this is equivalent to the condition that

$$(I\ -I) = (C\ -C)\begin{pmatrix} X_{11} & X_{12} \\ X_{21} & X_{22} \end{pmatrix} \qquad (4.12)$$

for some non-negative matrix, which we have partitioned for convenience. The first and second components, $I = C(X_{11} - X_{21})$ and $I = C(X_{22} - X_{12})$, are equivalent to each other as well as to the statement that $CX = I$ for some unsigned matrix. $\qquad \square$

Taken as a mapping, a matrix with linearly independent rows C reaches any vector: If you want to reach some vector – say, b, – simply apply matrix C to the vector Xb and indeed you do obtain $CXb = Ib = b$. The dimensions have to be right, though. If C is $m \times n$-dimensional, then b must be m-dimensional and X must be $n \times m$-dimensional, so that I is the $m \times m$-dimensional unit matrix. One might call X a *right inverse* of C. From the discussion of matrix multiplication following (2.6) we know that post-multiplication of C by the columns of X yields combinations of the *columns* of C. The most we obtain this way is the space of all combinations of the columns of C. This space exhausts the entire space of all m-dimensional vectors b only if there are at least m columns of C to combine. It follows that $CX = I$ for some matrix X can be valid only if C has at least m columns: $m \leq n$. Let us summarize the discussion.

Corollary 4.3. Row independence is possible only if the number of rows is less than or equal to the number of columns.

This means that constraints are independent only if their number is less than or equal to the number of variables.

Corollary 4.3 has another deep consequence: The right inverse equals the left inverse. This result is known from linear algebra, but the proofs in the literature are difficult, relying on so-called "determinants" or other mathematical animals. Luckily, I found an exceedingly simple proof.[3]

Corollary 4.4. If $n \times n$-dimensional matrices C and X fulfill $CX = I$, then also $XC = I$.

Proof. The $n + 1$ vectors comprising c_i and $e_i^\top$, see (1.19), are linearly dependent by corollary 4.3. By (4.10), we have $\mu C + v e_i^\top = 0$ for a non-zero combination μ, v. Because the rows of C are linearly independent, see (4.11), by corollary 2, it must be that $v \neq 0$. Now comes the punch line: $e_i^\top XC = -v^{-1} \mu CXC = -v^{-1} \mu IC = -v^{-1} \mu C = e_i^\top$. In other words, the ith row of XC is the ith row of I. Hence the matrices must be equal. □

Definition. Matrix X fulfilling

$$CX = XC = I \tag{4.13}$$

is called the *inverse* of C and denoted C^{-1}.

Remark 4.1. The inverse is unique: Suppose Y is also an inverse of C, then, by (4.13) and (2.5), $Y = YI = Y(CX) = (YC)X = IX = X$.

Lemma 4.2. $(CD)^{-1} = D^{-1} C^{-1}$ for $n \times n$-dimensional matrices C and D.

Proof. By corollary 4.4 it suffices to show that $(CD)(D^{-1} C^{-1}) = I$. By formula (2.5) the left-hand side of this equality is $CDD^{-1} C^{-1} = CIC^{-1} = CC^{-1} = I$, which is the indeed right-hand side. □

To close the circle, recall the Leontief inverse, (2.18). Equation (2.38) proves that the Leontief inverse of A is the inverse of $I - A$. We were able to analyze the associated multipliers in chapter 3 without the theory of inverses, particularly the equality of the right and left inverses. This was possible due to the special structure of the Leontief inverse. More precisely, it happens to be trivial that the mirror image of (2.38) is also valid:

$$\sum_{k=0}^{\infty} A^k (I - A) = I \tag{4.14}$$

Indeed, the proof of (4.14) is analogous to that of (2.38).

4.4 The main theorem

A linear program is a constrained optimization problem with linear objective and constraint functions:[4]

---

[3] My proof employs corollary 4.2, which in turn depends on lemma 4.1 and ultimately the separating hyperplane theorem. A simple, calculus-based proof of the latter has been discovered by Weitzman (1999).
[4] A linear program was introduced first in (1.21).

Definition.   A *linear program* reads

$$\max_x ax : Cx \le b \tag{4.15}$$

In expression (4.15) row vector a lists the objective function coefficients or weights, column vector x lists the variables, matrix C lists the constraint coefficients, one row for each constraint, and column vector b lists the constraint bounds. A linear program is specified by the coefficients and the bounds. Formally, a linear program is a triplet a, b, C. Throughout the book we assume that the constraints are *consistent*, meaning that they admit some vector x. We also assume throughout that the maximum is *finite*. This assumption is not essential, but keeps the analysis interesting, particularly in economics.[5] Since the objective, ax, and the constraints, Cx, are linear, the finite maximum is attained, say, by x^*. Any other *feasible x*, meaning a vector that fulfills the constraints, must be worse:

$$Cx \le b \Rightarrow ax \le ax^* \tag{4.16}$$

Since $Cx^* \le b$, implication (4.16) may be replaced by:

$$Cx \le Cx^* \Rightarrow ax \le ax^* \tag{4.17}$$

Rewrite implication (4.17):

$$C(x^* - x) \ge 0 \Rightarrow a(x^* - x) \ge 0 \tag{4.18}$$

Applying lemma 4.1 to implication (4.18), row vector a must be a non-negative combination of the constraints, the rows of C:

$$a = \lambda C, \lambda \ge 0 \tag{4.19}$$

Result (4.19) is true for any linear program that is consistent and finite. It is fairly general. Within the class of consistent linear programs, (4.19) is necessary and sufficient for finiteness.[6]

The implication for practical work is as follows. Given a linear program, check feasibility. Proceed directly to the establishment of a λ fulfilling (4.19). If this mission is impossible, stop, for the program is not finite. Otherwise you have the proportionality constants between the constraint functions and the objective function, which are the *Lagrange multipliers*.

A systematic determination of the Lagrange multipliers λ is done by associating with program (4.15), the so-called *primal program*, a *dual program*:

$$\min_{\lambda \ge 0} \lambda b : \lambda C = a \tag{4.20}$$

A warning is in order: The constraint in dual program (4.20) is *not* an inequality. The dual program is consistent by result (4.19). It is also finite: By the primal and dual constraints, respectively, we have $\lambda b \ge \lambda Cx^* = ax^*$. Consequently, if we can find a row vector $\lambda^* \ge 0$

---

[5] The finiteness excludes uninteresting cases as the maximization of x subject to $x \ge 0$.

[6] Necessity has just been derived. Sufficiency is easy. Suppose a consistent linear program fulfills (4.19). Let x be feasible. Then $Cx \le b$ or $b - Cx \ge 0$. Since λ in (4.19) is non-negative, we have $\lambda(b - Cx) \ge 0$ or $\lambda Cx \le \lambda b$. By (4.19), $ax \le \lambda b$, hence the value is finite.

which is feasible, meaning that it fulfills the constraint in dual program (4.20), but has value $\lambda^* b = a x^*$, we have solved the program. This is achieved in the proof of Theorem 4.1.

Theorem 4.1 (Main theorem of linear programming). The primal and dual programs, (4.15) and (4.20), have equal solution values: $a x^* = \lambda^* b$.

Proof. We have seen that any feasible λ of the dual program fulfills $\lambda b \geq a x^*$. Consequently, it suffices to find $\lambda^* \geq 0$ with $\lambda^* C = a$ and $\lambda^* b \leq a x^*$. This is equivalent to the existence of

$$(\lambda^* \quad \mu) \geq 0 : (\lambda^* \quad \mu) \begin{pmatrix} C & b \\ 0 & 1 \end{pmatrix} = (a \quad a x^*)$$

By lemma 4.1, this is equivalent to the statement that:

$$\begin{pmatrix} C & b \\ 0 & 1 \end{pmatrix} \begin{pmatrix} y \\ z \end{pmatrix} \geq 0 \Rightarrow (a \quad a x^*) \begin{pmatrix} y \\ z \end{pmatrix} \geq 0$$

Note that $z \geq 0$. If $z = 0$, the implication is true by inequality (4.18). Otherwise we may divide by z and must establish that

$$\begin{pmatrix} C & b \\ 0 & 1 \end{pmatrix} \begin{pmatrix} y/z \\ 1 \end{pmatrix} \geq 0 \Rightarrow (a \quad a x^*) \begin{pmatrix} y/z \\ 1 \end{pmatrix} \geq 0$$

Defining $x = -y/z$, this is true by inequality (4.16). $\qquad\square$

Theorem 4.1, the main theorem of linear programming, imputes the value of a linear program, $a x^*$, to the constraining entities. Bound b_i picks up value λ_i^* per unit. Adding one unit of the constraining entity adds value λ_i^*. In other words, the marginal value or productivity of the ith constraining entity is λ_i^*. This will be confirmed in section 4.8, but first we have to "clean" a linear program by eliminating redundancies. For example, the linear program max x subject to $x \leq b$, has solution b, and, therefore, Lagrange multiplier 1. The marginal product is indeed 1. If, however, the linear program is max x subject to $x \leq b$ and $x \leq b$, then the marginal value of each (of the identical) constraint is zero, for a relaxation of one bound by one unit is immaterial (as the other bound remains binding). In other words, we must first remove one of the two constraints. The cleansing makes use of the phenomenon of *complementary slackness*, which we present first.

4.5 Complementary slackness

The *slack* in the ith constraint of the primal program is the wedge in the inequality, $b_i - c_i x^*$, and the slack in the ith inequality of the dual program is simply λ_i itself, since the bound is zero. You cannot have slack in both: at least one of them is zero. More precisely, the main theorem has the following consequence.

Corollary 4.5 (Complementary slackness, weak form). For each constraint i in the primal and dual programs, (4.15) and (4.20), we have: $\lambda_i(b_i - c_i x^*) = 0$.

Proof. Slacks λ_i and $b_i - c_i x^*$ constitute the vectors λ^* and $b - Cx^*$, which are non-negative by the dual and primal constraints, respectively. Their product is zero by theorem 4.1 and the dual constraint. Since the product is a sum of non-negative terms, each term must be zero. $\qquad\square$

The primal program, (4.15), maximizes an objective function, ax, subject to constraints on another function, Cx. The first-order conditions stipulate that the derivatives of the objective function are proportional to the derivatives of the constraint function, $a = \lambda C$, which is the constraint of the dual program, (4.20). The proportions are the Lagrange multipliers, listed in row vector λ^*, the solution to the dual program. If a primal constraint is not binding, but features slack, then the Lagrange multiplier must be zero, yielding no slack in the inequality of the dual program. Conversely, if the dual program features slack, there is no slack in the associated primal constraint.

At least in principle, corollary 4.5 admits the possibility of no slack in both a primal constraint and the associated dual inequality. Such a coincidence, however, is artificial and will be removed by an alternative choice of the solutions, in Theorem 4.2. Consequently, we have slack in either a primal constraint or the non-negativity condition of the associated Lagrange multiplier, but not in both. This strong form of complementary slackness can be found in Schrijver (1986, p. 95), but lemma 4.1 permits a simple proof again:

Theorem 4.2 (Complementary slackness, strong form). For each constraint i in the primal and dual programs, *either* primal program, (4.15), has a solution x^* with $c_i x^* < b_i$, or the dual program, (4.20), has a solution λ^* with $\lambda_i^* > 0$.

Proof. By corollary 4.5 we cannot have both. Now suppose that we are not in the first situation. Then we have:

$$Cx \le b, ax \ge ax^* \Rightarrow c_i x \ge b_i$$

where x^* is any solution to program (4.15). Since $Cx^* \le b$ and $c_i x^* = b_i$ (as we are not in the first situation), we certainly have:

$$C(x - x^*) \le 0, a(x - x^*) \ge 0 \Rightarrow c_i(x - x^*) \ge 0$$

Consolidate the two implications:

$$\begin{pmatrix} -C & b \\ a & -ax^* \\ 0 & 1 \end{pmatrix} \begin{pmatrix} y \\ z \end{pmatrix} \ge 0 \Rightarrow (c_i \quad -b_i) \begin{pmatrix} y \\ z \end{pmatrix} \ge 0$$

(The first implication corresponds with $z > 0$ and $y = xz$, the second implication with $z = 0$ and $y = x - x^*$.) By lemma 4.1:

$$(c_i \quad -b_i) = (\lambda \quad \mu \quad v) \begin{pmatrix} -C & b \\ a & -ax^* \\ 0 & 1 \end{pmatrix} ; \quad \lambda, \mu, v \ge 0$$

If $\mu = 0$, then $(\lambda + e_i^\top)C = 0$ and $(\lambda + e_i^\top)b = -v$, so that addition of $\lambda + e_i^\top$ to a solution of program (4.20) preserves feasibility without increasing the solution value. Otherwise we may define $\lambda^* = (\lambda + e_i^\top)/\mu$ for which $\lambda^* C = (\lambda C + c_i)/\mu = \mu a/\mu = a$ and $\lambda^* b = (\lambda b + b_i)/\mu = (\mu a x^* - v)/\mu \leq a x^*$. In either case, we wind up in the second situation of the statement of the theorem. □

The constraints which fall in the first category of theorem 4.2 are redundant. Non-binding constraints may be dropped. If we drop a non-binding constraint, $c_i x^* < b_i$, x^* remains optimal.[7]

So all the essential constraints fall in the second category of theorem 4.2. We may do better and throw out some more constraints. For example, if two constraints are equal, one is redundant. More generally, a constraint implied by the others is redundant. Throwing them out, lemma 4.1 shows that the remaining constraints are not non-negative combinations of each other. We can strengthen the structure of the constraints a little further and wind up with a set of them which are neither positive nor negative combinations of each other. In other words, only a sub-set of linearly independent constraints is essential. The construction of this sub-set is the subject of section 4.6.

4.6　Non-degenerate programs

We may assume that the non-binding constraints have been eliminated, so that $Cx^* = b$, where b has now a dimension possibly less than m. Within this class of binding constraints, a further refinement can be made. Some constraints may be redundant in the sense that they are linearly dependent on the others. The Lagrange multipliers detect such constraints. In fact, condition (4.19) characterizes a solution to the dual program (4.20), for it implies $\lambda b = \lambda Cx^* = ax^*$, which is optimal. Thus, for linear programs with all constraints binding, any feasible dual variable is optimal. The signs of the Lagrange multipliers are crucial. A zero signals a redundant constraint:

Theorem 4.3. If the primal constraints are binding, then any row vector fulfilling condition (4.19) solves the dual program, (4.20). Moreover, if the primal constraints in (4.15) are linearly dependent, then some row vector fulfilling condition (4.19) has a zero component.

Proof. Any λ fulfilling (4.19) is optimal, because $\lambda b = \lambda Cx^* = ax^*$ (using $Cx^* = b$). If the primal constraints are linearly dependent, then $\mu C = 0$ for some $\mu = 0$. Let i be the non-zero component of μ which has the greatest absolute value relative to λ. Formally, i minimizes $\dfrac{\lambda_i}{|\mu_i|}$. We may assume that μ_i is positive (possibly by taking $-\mu$ instead of μ).

---

[7] The proof is by contradiction. Otherwise there would be an alternative x with $c_j x \leq b_j$ $(j \neq i)$ and $ax > ax^*$. Any weighted combination of x^* and x would also be superior to x^*. When sufficient weight is put on x^*, the combination would also fulfill constraint i and thus contradict the optimality of x^* in the full linear program, including the ith constraint.

Define $\lambda^* = \lambda - \dfrac{\lambda_i \mu_i}{\mu}$. If $\mu_j = 0$, then $\lambda_j^* = \lambda_j \geq 0$. Otherwise:

$$\frac{\lambda_j^*}{|\mu_j|} = \frac{\lambda_j}{|\mu_j|} - \frac{\lambda_i}{\mu_i} \frac{\mu_j}{|\mu_j|} \geq \frac{\lambda_j}{|\mu_j|} - \frac{\lambda_i}{\mu_i} \geq 0$$

(The last inequality is by definition of component i.) It follows that $\lambda^* \geq 0$. $\lambda^* C = \lambda C - 0 = a$. By construction, $\lambda_i^* = 0$. □

Corollary 4.6. The dual constraints admit only positive Lagrange multipliers if and only if the primal constraints are binding and linearly independent. In this case, the dual constraints admit precisely one vector of Lagrange multipliers.

Proof. Let the dual constraints admit positive Lagrange multipliers only. By the corollary to theorem 4.1, the primal constraints are binding. By theorem 4.3, they are linearly independent. Conversely, let the primal constraints be binding and linearly independent. By theorem 4.2, $\lambda^* C = a$ for some positive λ^*. If $\lambda C = a$, then $(\lambda^* - \lambda)C = 0$ and $\lambda = \lambda^*$ by linear independence. Hence λ^* is the unique vector fulfilling the dual constraints. □

The situation of the corollary is obtained by elimination of constraints. The procedure is described as follows:

Step 1.   Eliminate the non-binding constraints.
Step 2.   If the remaining constraints are linearly independent, stop. Otherwise there exists a solution to the dual program with some component zero. Eliminate the associated constraint.
Step 3.   Go to step 1.

This procedure is well defined in the light of theorem 4.3. The procedure is also justified. We have already seen that the elimination of non-binding constraints preserves the optimality of the solution, x^*. It remains to show that any constraint with zero Lagrange multiplier, $\lambda_i^* = 0$, is redundant, in the sense that the solution value cannot go up when the constraint is dropped. We have, obviously:

$$a = \sum_{j \neq i} \lambda_j^* c_j \tag{4.21}$$

Applying lemma 4.1 in reverse:

$$c_j(x^* - x) \geq 0 (j \neq i) \Rightarrow a(x^* - x) \geq 0 \tag{4.22}$$

By Step 1 above, $c_j x^* = b_j$. Hence inequality (4.22) may be replaced by

$$c_j x \leq b_j (j \neq i) \Rightarrow ax \leq ax^* \tag{4.23}$$

Inequality (4.23) completes the justification.

The three-step procedure replaces the linear program, (4.15), by

$$\max_{x} ax : \dot{C}x \leq \dot{b} \tag{4.24}$$

where $\dot{C}$ is a matrix of which the rows are a sub-set of binding and independent rows of C and $\dot{b}$ the corresponding vector of elements of b, without affecting the solution, x^*. The little dot superscript denotes the matrix (vector or row vector) of smaller dimension, which results from the omission of components. By corollary 4.6, the linear program (4.24) has Lagrange multipliers, which are positive, unique, and characterized by the equation:

$$\dot{\lambda}\dot{C} = \dot{a} \tag{4.25}$$

Augment $\dot{\lambda}$ with zeros for the constraints that have been thrown out:

$$\lambda^* = (\dot{\lambda} \quad 0) \tag{4.26}$$

Here we have rearranged the constraints, putting the binding ones up front. Augmented vector (4.26) solves the full dual program, (4.20): Feasibility extends automatically and the value, ax^*, is minimal indeed. Although $\dot{\lambda}$ is a unique solution to the dual of the reduced linear program (4.24), the augmented vector of Lagrange multipliers, (4.26), is no unique solution to the full dual program, (4.20). The reason is that alternative reductions may be possible.

Such ambiguity does not plague non-degenerate linear programs. A linear program is called *non-degenerate* if the binding constraints are linearly independent. For such programs, the elimination of constraints stops after Step 1 above and $\dot{C}$, the set of remaining linearly independent constraints, comprises all binding constraints. The Lagrange multipliers of the latter are positive and unique. The Lagrange multipliers of the non-binding constraints are zero. Note that any reduced linear program, (4.24), representing the base linear program, (4.15), is non-degenerate. The discussion is now summarized.

Theorem 4.4. For a non-degenerate linear program, λ^* is unique and $\lambda_i^* > 0$ if and only if $c_i x^* = b_i$. The positive components, $\dot{\lambda}$, are characterized by the binding constraints, $\dot{C}$, through $\dot{\lambda}\dot{C} = \dot{a}$.

Theorem 4.4 strengthens the phenomenon of complementary slackness even beyond the strong form of theorem 4.2. It shows that either a constraint is non-binding or the Lagrange multiplier is positive. Any ambiguity that is associated with multiplicity of solutions is removed when a linear program is non-degenerate.

4.7 Active variables

An important issue is the *number* of binding constraints. A binding constraint is *active* and carries a positive dual variable. Sometimes one is interested in the number of non-binding constraints (which is just the complement). For example, when constraints are simple non-negativity conditions, non-bindingness reflects that not the constraint, but the underlying variable, is active. Intuitively, one counts constraints. If the number of constraints exceeds the number of variables, the 'surplus' number of constraints must be dependent on the others by corollary 4.3. By Step 2 of the procedure outlined in section 4.6, they have zero Lagrange multipliers. By theorem 4.4 they are non-binding, at least when the linear program is non-degenerate. So the number of binding constraints is less than or equal to the number of variables. Typically, the number of binding constraints will be equal to the number of variables, as we shall see now. Bindingness is signaled by positivity of the Lagrange multipliers (theorem 4.2) and the latter are characterized by (4.25). It would be a coincidence if the vector of objective function coefficients, a, is a combination of a number of rows of C less than the number of variables.[8] In other words, generally it takes as many constraints as the number of variables to reach a through (4.25). This *equality* between the number of binding constraints and the number of variables has been derived on two assumptions: non-degeneracy and independence of the objective function coefficients vector of sub-sets of binding constraints.

Example 4.1. Let us return to the small open economy that maximizes its purchasing power in world markets: program (1.32). By (1.38), the shadow prices of the commodities equal the world prices, hence are positive. By the phenomenon of complementary slackness (corollary 4.5), the material balances are binding: (2.36). Then reintroduce the value-added coefficients (2.16). Substituting these shorthands in program (1.32), we obtain:

$$\max_{x} vx : \begin{pmatrix} k \\ l \\ -I \end{pmatrix} x \leq \begin{pmatrix} M \\ N \\ 0 \end{pmatrix} \tag{4.27}$$

Row vectors k and l list the capital and labor coefficients and scalars M and N the stocks. Program (4.27) allocates capital and labor so as to maximize earnings. Of the $n + 2$ constraints, precisely two are linearly dependent combinations of the others. By Step 2 of the reduction procedure, their Lagrange multipliers may be taken as zero and the remaining constraints are linearly independent. Since they include all the binding ones, the program is non-degenerate and the number of binding constraints is at most n. If the objective function coefficients vector, v, is independent of sub-sets of the binding constraints, then precisely n constraints are binding. At least one of the labor and capital constraints is among them (otherwise the value would go off to infinity, which we have ruled out by assumption). If both are binding, $n - 2$ of the non-negativity constraints are binding, so that all activity is concentrated in two sectors. Otherwise the pattern of specialization is even more extreme and only one sector is active. This will happen when the macroeconomic capital/labor ratio (M/N) is more extreme than required by any of the sectors (smaller than the lowest, k_i / l_i, or larger than the highest one) and, therefore, only the most capital/labor-extensive or labor-intensive sector will operate. Note that the simple counting rule applies. The number of variables is n, which is equal to the number of binding constraints, leaving two constraints non-binding for the active sectors (or for one active sector and one underemployed factor input). It should be recalled that the conclusion is weaker when the objective function coefficients vector is dependent on sub-sets of the binding constraints. Then the number of binding constraints may be less than n, meaning that fewer sectors meet the non-negativity

---

[8] Vector a would reside in a sub-space of lower dimension, an "event" with zero measure.

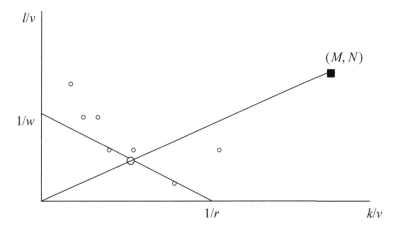

Figure 4.2 The scatter diagram of sectors in the capital/value-added and labor/value-added plane
Note: Capital-intensive sectors are in the Southeast, labor-intensive sectors in the Northwest.

constraints. In other words, more sectors may be active. This happens when two or more sectors have precisely the same unit costs, a coincidence.

The pattern of specialization is revealed by an explicit solution of the dual program,

$$\min_{r,w \geq 0} rM + wN : rk + wl \geq v \tag{4.28}$$

In program (4.28) we have eliminated the Lagrange multipliers of the non-negativity constraints by the replacement of the dual constraint by an inequality. Dividing the latter by its right-hand side, we obtain for every sector:

$$r\frac{k_i}{v_i} + w\frac{l_i}{v_i} \geq 1 \tag{4.29}$$

In inequality (4.29) ratios k_i/v_i and l_i/v_i are the capital and labor coefficients per unit of value-added. Represent each sector by the point $(k_i/v_i, l_i/v_i)$ in the capital/value-added and labor/value-added plane of all points $(k/v, l/v)$. See figure 4.2.

The value of the points (valuing their components by prices r and w) must exceed unity by constraint (4.29). Now all the points in the plane that are worth unity are on the straight line connecting the point $1/r$ on the horizontal axis and the point $1/w$ on the vertical axis. So the constraints of the dual program stipulate that the prices r and w must be selected large enough to locate the line under the cloud of points representing the sectors. The value of the dual objective, $rM + wN$, depends on how far the endowment point (M, N) is away from the unit budget line. Consequently, the value $rM + wN$ is minimized, by pushing the unit budget line towards the point (M, N). This is obtained by sliding one's hand along the straight line connecting the origin and point (M, N) and moving the unit budget line as far out as possible, until the cloud of sector points stops further movement. The intercepts of the resulting budget line are the inverse shadow prices of capital and labor. The points that are hit represent sectors for which the dual constraint (4.29) is binding:

$$r\frac{k_i}{v_i} + w\frac{l_i}{v_i} = 1 \tag{4.30}$$

By the phenomenon of complementary slackness (theorem 4.2), the sectors fulfilling (4.30) are the sectors with slack in the primal constraints, which are the non-negativity constraints. That is, these sectors are active. It would be a coincidence if three or more sectors stopped the outward movement of the unit budget line.[9] Thus, two sectors will be active in the optimal allocation. If the macroeconomic M/N ratio becomes extreme – that is, below $\min_i k_i/l_i$ or above $\max_i k_i/l_i$ – then the budget line is pushed horizontally or vertically in the approach to the allocation point (M, N). This means that $r = 0$ or $w = 0$. By the phenomenon of complementary slackness (theorem 4.2), there is unemployment of capital or labor, respectively. In these cases, only one point of the cloud is hit, hence only one sector will be active.

In all cases we have found the break-even sectors by solving the dual program graphically. By the phenomenon of complementary slackness (theorem 4.2) these are the active sectors. Their gross outputs can be determined by solving the full-employment equations for the active sectors. If sectors i and j are hit, then $k_i x_i + k_j x_j = M$ and $l_i x_i + l_j x_j = N$ determine their outputs x_i and x_j. Thus, the dual program is used to identify the active sectors and their constraints in the primal program are used to solve the problem. This completes the example.

4.8   Marginal productivity and sensitivity

We now turn to the important issue of the economics of maximization subject to scarcity constraints. The uniqueness of the Lagrange multipliers associated with a non-degenerate linear program (theorem 4.4) permits an economic interpretation. Lagrange multipliers are essentially marginal productivities, which measure the increase of the objective value per unit constraint relaxation. This is the value of the entity underlying a constraint, at the margin. The values add up by theorem 4.1 and are, therefore, also average values. The economic interpretation of Lagrange multipliers is justified by theorem 4.5.

Theorem 4.5. For a non-degenerate linear program, the rate of increase of the solution value with respect to an increase of a bound equals the Lagrange multiplier of the associated constraint.

Proof. Consider an increase of the ith bound by a positive amount ε: $Cx \leq b + \varepsilon e_i$. By the dual constraint, (4.19), and theorem 4.1,

$$ax - ax^* = \lambda^*(Cx - b) \leq \lambda^*\varepsilon e_i = \lambda_i^*\varepsilon$$

---

[9] Three sectors would reside on a straight line in the above factor intensity plane: an unlikely "event."

We must show that this increase can be attained. If constraint i was non-binding, then $\lambda_i^* = 0$ by theorem 4.4 and $x = x^*$ solves. If constraint i was binding, it is part of C, which has linearly independent constraints by assumption of degeneracy. By corollary 4.2, $\dot{C}X = I$ for some matrix X. Denote the vector obtained from e_i by deleting the components corresponding to the non-binding constraints by $\dot{e}_i$. Then $x = x^* + \varepsilon X\dot{e}_i$ fulfills the (originally) binding constraints, augmented by εe_i, and also the (originally) non-binding constraints for ε sufficiently small. In short, x is feasible. The value increase is

$$ax - ax^* = \varepsilon aX\dot{e}_i = \varepsilon \lambda^* CX\dot{e}_i = \varepsilon \dot{\lambda} \dot{C}X\dot{e}_i = \varepsilon \dot{\lambda}\dot{e}_i = \varepsilon \lambda^* e_i = \lambda_i^* \varepsilon$$

Here $\lambda^* C = \dot{\lambda}\dot{C}$ is a consequence of the definition of $\dot{\lambda}$ and (4.25) and (4.26). ☐

The proof of theorem 4.5 is constructive. The binding constraints were maintained and used to find a new point. The construction was successful thanks to the independence of the binding constraints.

The marginal productivities in degenerated programs fall short of the Lagrange multipliers. A trivial example is the inclusion of two identical constraints. Each constraint will have a zero marginal productivity, since a relaxation will render it non-binding. If the constraints are binding, however, then the Lagrange multipliers can be positive by theorem 4.2. As a matter of fact, degenerated programs have multiple Lagrange multipliers. For any constraint, the marginal productivity can be shown to be equal to the lowest value that its Lagrange multiplier may attain.

Recall that the parameters of a linear program are the objective function coefficients, the bounds, and the constraint coefficients: a, b, and C. The sensitivity of the solution with respect to the various parameters is analyzed by means of the dual variables, which are given by row vector λ^* in the solution. The latter is unique for non-degenerate programs (theorem 4.4), to which attention is confined. Equations (4.25) and (4.26) determine the Lagrange multipliers of the binding constraints. Now consider an infinitesimal perturbation of the data: da, db, and dC. Non-binding constraints ($c_i x^* < b_i$) remain non-binding. Hence (4.25) and (4.26) continue to be valid. Consequently,

$$d\lambda^* = (d\dot{\lambda} \quad 0), d\dot{\lambda}\dot{C} = da - \dot{\lambda}d\dot{C} \tag{4.31}$$

By theorem 4.1, the neglect of products of infinitesimal terms, and (4.31):

$$d(ax^*) = d(\lambda^*b) = \lambda^*db + (d\dot{\lambda} \quad 0)b = \lambda^*db + (d\dot{\lambda} \quad 0)Cx^* \tag{4.32}$$

The last equality replaces bounds by constraint values. The replacement values are no different for the binding components and the others are pre-multiplied by zero. Using (4.31), (4.32) becomes:

$$d(ax^*) = \lambda^*db + (da)x^* - \lambda^*(dC)x^* \tag{4.33}$$

Formula (4.33) is handy, at least for non-degenerate linear programs. It reveals all the sensitivities of the solution value. If we only vary the bounds, we obtain $d(ax^*) = \lambda^*db$, reconfirming theorem 4.4. If we vary only the objective function coefficients, we obtain $d(ax^*) = (da)x^*$. Only the direct effects of the coefficients changes need to be accounted for.[10] If we vary only the constraint coefficients, we obtain $d(ax^*) = -\lambda^*(dC)x^*$. The power of duality analysis asserts itself in the establishment of the rates of change formula, (4.33), without recourse to matrix inversion.

The rates of change of the Lagrange multipliers themselves are determined by (4.25) and (4.26) for non-degenerate programs. By uniqueness (theorem 4.4), (4.31) determines $d\lambda^*$ uniquely. Since db does not enter the right-hand side of the equation, the rates of change of the Lagrange multipliers with respect to bound perturbations are *zero*.

This robustness of marginal productivities with respect to bound perturbations is remarkable. If the output of an economy is constrained by labor, the marginal productivity of labor does not diminish with the stock of labor, at least when the problem of maximizing output can be represented by a linear program with a finite number of constraints, as we have seen. Neoclassical economists like diminishing marginal productivities, not only for big increases of constraint bounds, but also for perturbations. They do so by constructing models with a continuum of constraints, describing alternative techniques of producing output. The coexistence of alternative techniques will be studied in chapters, and the idealization of a continuum will be investigated in chapter 8.

Exercises

1. Consider program (4.15).   *Encircle one:*

The variables, x, must be non-negative	T	F
The bounds, b, must be non-negative	T	F
The number of constraints is the number of rows of C	T	F
The number of constraints is the number of columns of C	T	F
The shadow prices, λ, must be non-negative	T	F
The shadow prices are equal to the market prices	T	F
The shadow prices are equal to the productivities	T	F
$a = e_i^\top$ is possible	T	F
$a = I$ is possible	T	F
If x is feasible, then $ax = \lambda b$	T	F
A non-binding constraint has zero shadow price	T	F

2. Show how a minimization problem can be written as a maximization problem.
3. Show how a maximization problem for a row vector can be written as a problem for a column vector.
4. Show how an equality can be written as a system of inequalities.
5. Write the dual program in the format of a primal program.
6. Take the dual program of the latter.
7. Show that it is the primal: The dual of the dual is the primal.
8. Consider a primal program with non-negative variables. Let column vector y be the dual variable. Show that the dual is obtained by reversal of the inequality sign, transposition

---

[10] This may be seen an instance of the so-called "envelope theorem" of calculus.

of the coefficients matrix, and exchange of the objective function coefficients and the bounds.

9. The data of an economy comprise technical coefficients (for commodity and labor inputs) and a labor force. Final demand has certain desired proportions. Write out the linear program that maximizes the level of final demand. Show it is positive when the matrix of technical coefficients fulfills theorem 2.2. Show that all sectors are active. Show that the commodity prices are given by the labor coefficients, inflated by the Leontief inverse. Would all sectors remain active under free trade?

References

Schrijver, A. (1986). *Theory of Linear and Integer Programming*, Chichester, John Wiley

Tyrrell Rockafellar, R. (1970). *Convex Analysis*, Princeton, Princeton University Press

Weitzman, M. L. (1999). "An 'Economics Proof' of a Separating Hyperplane Theorem," Discussion Paper 1881, Harvard Institute of Economic Research

5 Are input-output coefficients fixed?

5.1 Introduction

Substitution is the replacement of one input vector by another in the production of a certain output. In this chapter we show that if there is only one resource, think of labor, there will be no substitution. Hence a fixed technique will be used to produce a commodity. The concept of substitution is best explained in the context of an economy with a pure make table. A *make table* lists all the commodity outputs per production unit:

$$V = \begin{pmatrix} v_{11} & \cdots & v_{1n} \\ \vdots & \ddots & \vdots \\ v_{m1} & \cdots & v_{mn} \end{pmatrix} \qquad (5.1)$$

The first row in make (5.1) lists the quantities produced by the first unit: v_{11} of commodity 1 through v_{1n} of commodity n. A make table is *pure* if every production unit produces one unit of precisely one commodity and every commodity is produced by some unit. Every row is a unit vector, with one entry equal to one and the others zero; see (1.19). Every column has at least one entry equal to one. An example of a pure make table is the following:

$$V = \begin{pmatrix} 1 & 0 \\ 1 & 0 \\ 0 & 1 \end{pmatrix} \qquad (5.2)$$

Either production unit #1 or production unit #2 can produce the first commodity. Make table (5.2) therefore features substitutability. The *use table* and the *factor employment row vector* give the input requirements:

$$U = \begin{pmatrix} u_{11} & \cdots & u_{1m} \\ \vdots & & \vdots \\ u_{n1} & \cdots & u_{nm} \end{pmatrix} \qquad (5.3)$$

$$L = (L_1 \quad \cdots \quad L_m)$$

Unlike the outputs, the inputs of the first production unit are listed in the first *column*, for reasons of national accounting that will transpire in chapter 6. Commodity quantities u_{11} to u_{n1} and factor input L_1 (think of labor) feed production unit 1. The accounts feature an asymmetry: A production unit is represented by a row in the make table, but by a column in the use table. This asymmetry will be examined in chapter 6, when considering national accounts. The example can be completed by:

$$U = \begin{pmatrix} 0 & 0 & 0 \\ 1 & 0 & 0 \end{pmatrix}$$

$$L = (0 \quad 1 \quad 1/2)$$

(5.4)

Commodity 1 can be produced by means of the second commodity (through production unit 1) or by means of the factor input (through production unit 2). The advantage of working with a pure make table is that the columns of the use table, augmented with the factor employment entries, immediately reflect the input requirements per unit of output, or the *technical coefficients*. Note that technical coefficients comprise not only material but also factor input coefficients. For the production of commodity 1 we may choose between two vectors of technical coefficients, namely

$$\begin{pmatrix} 0 \\ 1 \\ 0 \end{pmatrix}, \begin{pmatrix} 0 \\ 0 \\ 1 \end{pmatrix}$$

(5.5)

The bottom elements in techniques (5.5) represent the factor input requirements. A switch of techniques effects substitution.

5.2   Techniques and the role of demand

It is important to have a precise notion of techniques.

Definition.   A *technique* is a pair of a column vector of intermediate and factor inputs and a row vector of outputs. If the latter is a unit vector, the technique is *pure*.

For any given output, techniques are different whenever either the intermediate or the factor inputs are different. For example, if in input structure (5.4) the labor employment vector can be replaced by $L' = (1/4 \quad 2 \quad 3/4)$, the collection of techniques for the first commodity, (5.5), is expanded to four:

$$\begin{pmatrix} 0 \\ 1 \\ 0 \end{pmatrix}, \begin{pmatrix} 0 \\ 0 \\ 1 \end{pmatrix}, \begin{pmatrix} 0 \\ 1 \\ 1/4 \end{pmatrix}, \begin{pmatrix} 0 \\ 0 \\ 2 \end{pmatrix}$$

(5.6)

In addition there are now two techniques for commodity 2:

$$\begin{pmatrix} 0 \\ 0 \\ 1/2 \end{pmatrix}, \begin{pmatrix} 0 \\ 0 \\ 3/4 \end{pmatrix}$$

(5.7)

The economy comprises the six techniques given by (5.6) and (5.7); it is given formally by the following triplet of make, use, and factor input tables:

$$V = \begin{pmatrix} 1 & 0 \\ 1 & 0 \\ 1 & 0 \\ 1 & 0 \\ 0 & 1 \\ 0 & 1 \end{pmatrix}, \quad \begin{matrix} U = \begin{pmatrix} 0 & 0 & 0 & 0 & 0 & 0 \\ 1 & 0 & 1 & 0 & 0 & 0 \end{pmatrix} \\ L = \begin{pmatrix} 0 & 1 & \frac{1}{4} & 2 & \frac{1}{2} & \frac{3}{4} \end{pmatrix} \end{matrix} \qquad (5.8)$$

Comparison with the dimensions of the tables, see (5.1) and (5.3), indicates that technology (5.8) has $m = 6$ techniques and $n = 2$ commodities. However, once only two techniques are available, a whole continuum of techniques can be constructed. Any input vector

$$\begin{pmatrix} 0 \\ s_1 \\ s_2 \end{pmatrix}$$

with non-negative weights s_1 and s_2 summing to unity, is capable of generating one unit of commodity 1, at least under the assumption of constant returns to scale. The collection of all such input vectors defines an *isoquant*.

The choice between units 1 and 2 in the production of commodity 1 will depend on the relative prices of the inputs. If commodity 2 is cheaper than the factor input, then the first technique is more profitable. Substitution takes place in response to changes in relative prices, which are determined by supply and demand. Let us model demand in a simple way. Assume that households desire commodities in certain proportions, listed in commodity vector a. Assume a greater level of consumption is preferred. Then bundle ac is preferred to bundle a when the level of consumption, given by scalar c, is greater than one. As is well known (see chapter 3), the competitive equilibrium is optimal and can be analyzed by maximizing the objective function and determination of the shadow prices. Thus we consider the maximization of consumption, c, subject to a feasibility constraint.

Definition. Commodity vector (y) is *feasible* if it does not exceed the net output for a feasible activity vector; an activity vector (s) is feasible if it is non-negative and does not exceed the available stock of the factor input (N):

$$y \leq (V^\top - U)s; s \geq 0, Ls \leq N \qquad (5.9)$$

The activity vector in definition (5.9) is an m-dimensional column vector, with activity levels s_i for the production units, which are indexed by i. Since

$$(V^\top s)_j = \sum_{i=1}^{m} v_{ij} s_i \qquad (5.10)$$

is obtained by inflating the column of the make table associated with commodity j by the various activity levels and summation, expression (5.10) is the gross output of commodity j.

Similarly, $(Us)_j$ is the input requirement of commodity j exercised by the production units when their activity levels are given by vector s. This explains why $(V^\top - U)s$ is the *net output* vector of the economy. By definition (5.9) an activity vector is feasible as long as it requires no more factor input than is available.

We now maximize the level of consumption:

$$\max_{s,c} c : ac \le (V^\top - U)s,\; Ls \le N,\; s \ge 0 \tag{5.11}$$

Linear program (5.11) maps the *production possibility frontier* (PPF) of the economy. For every direction in net output space, given by consumption bundle a, it measures how much can be produced.[1] Since the *solution* of program (5.11) depends on bundle a, we denote it by $c(a)$. Final demand ac is feasible as long as $c \le c(a)$. Notice that substitution of $y = y_1$ for ac demonstrates that vector y is feasible as long as $c(y) \ge 1$. Prices are determined by the dual program, (4.20), with

$$C = \begin{pmatrix} U - V^\top & a \\ L & 0 \\ -I & 0 \end{pmatrix} :$$

$$\min_{p,w,\sigma \ge 0} wN : p(V^\top - U) = wL - \sigma,\; pa = 1 \tag{5.12}$$

In program (5.12) row vector σ is the slack variable that measures the losses in the inactive sectors. By complementary slackness (corollary 4.5), components are zero in the active sectors. Prices are thus determined by the equality of value-added, $p(V^\top - U)$, and factor costs, wL, in the active sectors. The second constraint in program (5.12) normalizes the price system. It is crucial to observe that household preferences merely serve to normalize the price system. Relative prices are determined by the cost relations embedded in the use and make tables and the employment vector. We thus have the classical economic result that in an economy with a single factor input, relative prices are determined by the *supply side*. We shall prove this claim in detail.

Substitution takes place in response to a change of relative prices, and prices are determined by supply and demand, but the pattern of final demand does not affect relative prices. A striking implication can now be drawn: Although there is a lot of scope for substitution, substitution will not take place. There is a superior set of techniques, independent of the proportions of final demand. Any point on the PPF can be produced by this same set of techniques. The formal statement of this result is the so-called "substitution theorem," which will be presented below. For obvious reasons, it is also called the non-substitution theorem.

5.3 Selection of techniques

A formal way to select techniques is by means of a non-substitution table.

---

[1] Note that a is a column vector with constraint coefficients and not a row vector of objective function coefficients. The latter are given by $(0\ 1)$.

Definition. A *non-substitution table* of a pure make table V is a pure make table V^* obtained by suppression of all but one element in each column of V. Formally, for each $j = 1, \ldots, n$ there is an

$$i(j): v^*_{i(j)j} = v_{i(j)j} = 1; v^*_{i'j} = 0, i' \neq i(j) \qquad (5.13)$$

A non-substitution table picks winners. For each commodity j it identifies a production unit $i(j)$. The input coefficients will be given by column $i(j)$ of the use table and the employment vector. For each commodity we thus obtain a unique input coefficients vector. Placement next to each other yields a fixed matrix of technical coefficients. In summary, if there is only factor input and production units make single outputs, the pattern of final demand will not influence relative prices and the choice of technique. Technical coefficients are constant, whatever final demand. This observation is due to Samuelson (1951), who considers it a justification of the use of fixed-input coefficients.

Samuelson's graphical solution to the problem is illuminating. Consider an economy with m production units but only two commodities (figure 5.1). The net output vector of the first production unit is

$$\begin{pmatrix} 1 - u_{11} \\ -u_{21} \end{pmatrix}$$

which is

$$\begin{pmatrix} (1 - u_{11})/L_1 \\ -u_{21}/L_1 \end{pmatrix}$$

per worker.

The net output vectors of the first activities, producing commodity 1, point to the Southeast. The net output vectors of the units producing commodity 2 point to the Northwest. Since all net outputs are per worker, any point on the straight segment connecting two net output vectors is also producible by one worker (by dividing her time properly). The line segment indicated gives the greatest net output she can produce. Any other combination of activities would result in a net output point relatively to the Southwest, hence with lower quantities. The two activities can be found by dropping a straight line onto the net output vectors. The pair of activities that will support it, one for each commodity, is selected. Since this analysis applies to each worker and constant returns to scale are assumed, the selected pair of activities also supports the greatest net output for the economy. The formal identification of the winning activities is a matter of specifying a non-substitution table.

A non-substitution table restricts the activities to a sub-set of production units, one for each commodity. Activity vectors take the form V^*x, where x is a non-negative commodity vector. Since matrix V^* is $m \times n$-dimensional and vector x $n \times 1$-dimensional, V^*x is m-dimensional, displaying one element for each production unit. If a production unit is a winner, $i(j)$, then it picks up output x_j. Otherwise $(V^*x)_i$ is zero. The non-substitution table that selects the first production unit as the winner (as a producer of commodity 1) in make

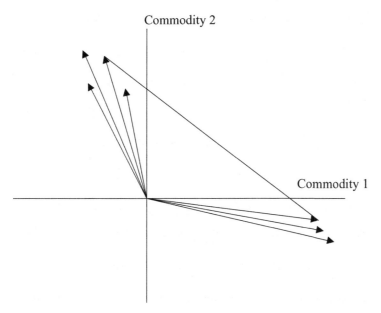

Figure 5.1 Per-worker net outputs

table (5.2) is:

$$V^* = \begin{pmatrix} 1 & 0 \\ 0 & 0 \\ 0 & 1 \end{pmatrix} \qquad (5.14)$$

Producing commodity output x with non-substitution table (5.14) yields

$$V^*x = \begin{pmatrix} x_1 \\ 0 \\ x_2 \end{pmatrix}$$

We will make use of lemma 5.1.

Lemma 5.1. If V^* is a non-substitution table of V, then $V^\top V^* = I$.

Proof. $(V^\top V^*)_{ij} = \sum_{k=1}^{m} v_{ki} v_{kj}^* = v_{i(j)i} v_{i(j)i}^* = v_{i(j)i} = 1$ if the column index $i = j$ and zero otherwise, since row $i(j)$ is a unit vector. □

If only the units identified by non-substitution table V^* are active, then an activity vector takes the format V^*x and gross output amounts $V^\top V^*x = Ix = x$, applying lemma 5.1. In other words, gross outputs and activity levels can be identified when there is only one production unit for each commodity.

A commodity vector y is feasible by means of non-substitution table V^* if it can be produced by an activity vector s which is not only feasible, but also of the form V^*x.

Definition. Commodity vector y is *feasible by means of a non-substitution table,* V^*, if:

$$y \le (V^\top - U)V^*x; x \ge 0, LV^*x \le N \qquad (5.15)$$

5.4   The substitution theorem

The substitution theorem claims that any feasible commodity vector is feasible by means of a fixed non-substitution table. In other words, some sub-set of production units, one for each commodity, is capable of supplying whatever is a feasible commodity bundle.

Theorem 5.1 (Substitution theorem). Consider a pure make table V, a use table U, an employment row vector L, and a force N. For some positive net output proportions, a_0, let the maximum consumption level, $c(a_0)$, exist and be positive. Then there exists a non-substitution table V^* of V such that any non-negative feasible commodity vector is feasible by means of this one table V^*.

Proof. The basic idea of the proof is to select production units, one for each commodity, from the set of active sectors that sustain the production of the positive net output, $a_0c(a_0)$. The selection may not be arbitrary. For example, if the first production unit has input vector e_1 (see (1.19)), which has no labor, then it can be active (as it does not influence the balance of commodity 1 or any other), but may not be selected (as it cannot provide net output for the other sectors or consumption). It is natural to think of a price test for the selection. Unfortunately, shadow prices are of no use, since they render all active sectors equally profitable (with a zero profit level). Instead, we will use the chapter 2 prices, which associate positive value-added with a net output-generating input-output matrix. The proof is organized as follows. In part 1 we investigate the production of $a_0c(a_0)$. For every commodity output j we construct input coefficients, a_{ij}, which each are a weighted average of u_{ik} over sectors k producing commodity j. The weights are determined by the outputs, v_{kj}. With matrix A we associate a price vector $p > pA$. In part 2 we select the cheapest among the active sectors (yielding $a_0c(a_0)$), valuing inputs by p. This defines non-substitution table V^*. In part 3 we investigate the consequent input coefficients matrix, UV^*, and consider any non-negative feasible commodity vector, y. The activity levels of the non-substitution sectors are equal to the gross output vector, x, which is the product of the Leontief inverse of UV^* with y. The economy-wide activity level vector is V^*x. Part 4 presents two key results: First, the value of the frontier point, $yc(y)$, under the shadow prices associated with $c(a_0)$ is less than or equal to $c(a_0)$. Second, the product of the slack variables and the non-substitution matrix is zero. Part 5 shows that the activity levels given by V^*x are feasible.

1. Let the activity vector $s(a_0)$ sustain $c(a_0)$. Then $V^\top s(a_0) \ge a_0c(a_0) + Us(a_0) \ge a_0c(a_0) > 0$ by assumption, so that we may divide by this vector and define $A = \widehat{Us(a_0)}VV^\top\widehat{s(a_0)}^{-1}$. (Incidentally, a_{ij} is the weighted average of u_{ik} with weights $v_{kj}s_j(a_0)/\sum_{k=1}^{m} v_{kj}s_j(a_0)$, the market shares of the producers of commodity j. This *industry technology model* of a technical coefficient will be analyzed further in

chapter 7.) Since $Ax < x$ for $x = V^{\top}s(a_0)$, theorems 2.1 and 2.2 yield $pA < p$ for some $p \geq 0$.

2. Among all sectors i producing commodity j ($s_i(a_0) > 0$ and $v_{ij} = 1$), let i (j) minimize costs, $pu_{\bullet i}$. (We know that $i(j)$ exists because $V^{\top}s(a_0)$ is positive.) By construction of these identifiers, $pu_{\bullet i} \geq pu_{\bullet i(j)}$ whenever $v_{ij} = 1$ and $s_i(a_0) > 0$. It is obvious that $a_{\bullet j}$ is a weighted average of such $u_{\bullet i}$:

$$a_{kj} = \frac{\displaystyle\sum_{i=1}^{m} u_{ki}s_i(a_0)v_{ij}}{\displaystyle\sum_{l=1}^{m} v_{lj}s_l(a_0)} = \frac{\displaystyle\sum_{i:v_{ij}=1,s_i(a_0)>0} u_{ki}s_i(a_0)}{\displaystyle\sum_{l:v_{lj}=1,s_l(a_0)>0} s_l(a_0)}$$

Hence also $pa_{\bullet j} \geq pu_{\bullet i(j)}$. Define V^* by $v_{ij}^* = 1$ if $i = i(j)$ and zero otherwise. Then V^* is a non-substitution table of V.

3. Moreover, $UV^* = (u_{\bullet i(1)} \cdots u_{\bullet i(n)})$. It follows that $p > pA \geq pUV^*$. By theorem 2.1, UV^* has a non-negative Leontief inverse, say B. Let commodity vector y be non-negative and feasible. Define $x = By$. It remains to show that V^*x is feasible.

4. Let $p(a_0)$, $w(a_0)$, $\sigma(a_0)$ solve the dual program (5.12). Then $p(a_0)yc(y) \leq c(a_0)$. This is trivial for $p(a_0)y = 0$. Otherwise

$$\left(\frac{p(a_0)}{p(a_0)y} \; \frac{w(a_0)}{p(a_0)y} \; \frac{\sigma(a_0)}{p(a_0)y} \right)$$

is feasible in the dual program of y, whence the inequality is:

$$\frac{c(a_0)}{p(a_0)y} = \frac{w(a_0)N}{p(a_0)y} \geq w(y)N = c(y)$$

where $w(y)N$ is the solution value and the equalities reflect theorem 4.1. By assumption, $c(a_0)$ is positive, and, therefore, so are $w(a_0)$ and N. V^* identifies sectors $i(j)$ for which $s_{i(j)}(a_0) > 0$, and, by corollary 4.5, $\sigma_{i(j)}(a_0) = 0$. In matrix notation, $\sigma(a_0)V^* = 0$.

5. Combination of the observations on the shadow prices completes the proof:

$$w(a_0)LV^*x = [p(a_0)(V^{\top} - U) + \sigma(a_0)]V^*x$$
$$= p(a_0)y \leq p(a_0)yc(y) \leq c(a_0) = w(a_0)N$$

by the dual constraint, lemma 5.1, and theorem 4.1. Division by $w(a_0)$ yields the feasibility of V^*x.

$\square$

Corollary 5.1. The PPF is given by $p(a_0)y = c(a_0)$ and the shadow prices are $p(a_0)/c(a_0)$ and $w(a_0)/c(a_0)$ everywhere. The relative commodity prices are the Leontief inverse of the labor coefficients.

Proof. Let commodity vector y be non-negative and feasible. Then $(I - UV^*)x = y$ for some $x \geq 0$. If y is on the frontier, there is full employment, $LV^*x = N$. By part 4 of the proof of theorem 5.1, $w(a_0) > 0$. It follows that in part 5 all the entries in the string of (in)equalities are equal. Consequently, $p(a_0)y = c(a_0)$ and

$$\left(\frac{p(a_0)}{c(a_0)} \ \frac{w(a_0)}{c(a_0)} \ \frac{\sigma(a_0)}{c(a_0)} \right)$$

is feasible in the dual program (5.12) (with $a = y$) and yields value

$$\frac{w(a_0)}{c(a_0)} N = 1$$

by application of theorem 4.1 to the problem with $a = y$. This is optimal in view of $c(y) = 1$ (another consequence of the string of equalities) and the application of theorem 4.1 to the problem with $a = y$.

The relative commodity prices must now be found. By the dual constraints (5.12), $p(a_0)(V^\top - U) = w(a_0)L - \sigma(a_0)$. Post-multiplication by the non-substitution table, V^*, yields, in view of lemma 5.1 and the fact $\sigma(a_0)V^* = 0$ (established in part 4 of the proof of theorem 5.1), that $p(a_0)(I - UV^*) = w(a_0)L$. Post-multiplication by the Leontief inverse B (part 3 of the proof) yields $p(a_0) = w(a_0)LV^*B$. Relative commodity prices are preserved by division by $w(a_0)$ and yield the stated result, since LV^* is the vector of labor coefficients when commodities are produced by the sectors identified by the non-substitution table V^*. □

Remark 5.1. A precise statement of the assumed condition is as follows. Some positive net output may be consumed if some sub-table of the use matrix has non-negative Leontief inverse (2.18) and the factor endowment is positive. This ensures the existence of a positive consumption vector a_0 with a positive level. The maximum consumption level, $c(a_0)$, exists if a_0 requires labor.[2] This is a weak condition on the economy, (V, U, L). Positivity of the labor coefficients, L, is sufficient but not necessary, since Ls has to be positive only for a sub-set of activity levels, s, namely those with net output a_0.

The substitution theorem revolves around the commodity prices that sustain the production of some positive net output vector. It was shown that the commodity prices also sustain the production of any other net output vector. The PPF is a plane of constant value under those prices. If some commodity price is zero, it may be supplied in infinite quantity. In this case, the frontier is parallel to the axis of such a commodity.

Let us finish the example of (5.2), (5.4), and $N = 1$. The production of a unit of the second commodity requires half a labor unit. One unit of the second commodity or a full labor unit is required to produce a unit of the first commodity. The first technique is more economic. Hence the pertinent non-substitution table is the one given in (5.14). This conclusion holds whatever the pattern of final demand.

---

[2] More precisely, $(V^\top - U)s \geq a_0$ implies $Ls > 0$.

5.5 A postscript

The most prominent statement of the substitution theorem is due to Johansen (1972). He calls the combination of input coefficients (UV^*, LV^*) identified by a non-substitution table (V^*) a *technology*. Then he proves the statement that if some technology V^* has a positive price vector $p^* = p^*UV + LV^* \leq p^*UV^{**} + LV^{**}$ for all technologies V^{**}, then any non-negative feasible commodity vector is feasible by means of V^*. A technology with such a price vector constitutes a competitive equilibrium since all other technologies are rendered unprofitable. Thus, a competitive equilibrium technology solves the substitution problem. An admitted shortcoming of the formulation is that the pertinent non-substitution table, V^*, must be identified *a priori* in order to verify the competitive price property. However, Johansen (1972, p. 388) notes that a competitive equilibrium will exist if the technologies form a closed set and one of them is productive in the sense that it can produce positive final consumption. Unfortunately, this is false.[3] Johansen (1972, p. 384) assumes implicitly that all activities require some labor input (L positive) and claims that this assumption could be dispensed with. This is also false.[4]

Our analysis, based on ten Raa (1995), advances in two ways. First, the intuition of Johansen that an economy must merely be capable of producing some positive final consumption has been confirmed. Second, the assumption of positive labor input has been limited to the macroeconomic requirement that the same positive final consumption vector has positive labor input. Our formulation of the substitution theorem is general. It does not appeal to preconceived competitive prices and constructs the dominant technology by specification of non-substitution table V^*. The trap in which Johansen fell has been avoided by a subtle identification of the non-substitution table. In the proof of theorem 5.1 we studied the efficient production of a net output vector with proportions given by vector a_0. The identification of winners proceeded in two steps. In the first step we considered the sectors which are active in the efficient production (activity levels $s_i(a_0) > 0$). By the phenomenon of complementary slackness (corollary 4.5), these sectors are the ones that break even with competitive prices. The competitive prices are of no help in identifying a non-substitution table, but it is also not allowed to pick an arbitrary sub-set of the active sectors. In the second step, however, we selected the sectors that are most profitable in terms of material costs, regardless of labor costs. In other words, we did not use the competitive price system, but the material price vector (2.12) that drives a wedge between all material revenues and costs, including those in sectors without labor costs.

5.6 An application

An application of the substitution theorem (theorem 5.1) is the international division of labor. Sectors of different countries can simply be stacked into one big system. Formally

---

[3] A counterexample is a single-output economy with $u_i = 1 - 1/i$ and $l_i = 1/i^2$. The price vector of technology i fulfills $p_i = p_i u_i + l_i$ or $p_i = 1/i$. The cost of the next technology, evaluated at p_i, is $p_i u_{i+1} l_{i+1} = (1/i)[1 - 1/(i+1)] + 1/(i+1)^2$, which is less then $p_i = 1/i$.

[4] Net output in the counterexample increases with i. The technologies have a perfect limit, $u^* = 1$ and $l^* = 0$, but it does not solve the substitution problem because it generates no surplus.

sectors are differentiated not only by output but also by country. Each commodity may be produced in a number of countries; there is no need for a given number of national sectors per commodity. In other words, a country may have a specific number of national sectors in the market of a commodity. Once all the sectors are stacked, the substitution theorem identifies for each commodity one sector and, thereby, one country. It may be that some countries are losers in that they will not produce any of the commodities. Those countries are technologically inferior and labor will migrate out. If the assumption of labor mobility is not fulfilled, factor inputs become region-specific, so that their number exceeds one and the substitution theorem no longer applies. The choice of technique (or country) will depend on the pattern of final demand.

The substitution theorem presumes not only a single factor input, but also a single commodity output, for each sector. Both restrictions are lifted in chapter 6, where we present a general framework to account for inputs and outputs.

Exercises

1. Show that positivity of net output need not imply positivity of all sectoral activity levels, not even when the number of sectors equals the number of commodities.
2. Determine the non-substitution table of an arbitrary economy with two commodities and three sectors.
3. Shows that the substitution theorem breaks down when there are two factor inputs. (*Hint*: a single output example will do.)

References

Johansen, L. (1972). "Simple and General Nonsubstitution Theorems for Input-Output Models," *Journal of Economic Theory* 5 (3), 383–94

ten Raa, Th. (1995). "The Substitution Theorem," *Journal of Economic Theory* 66 (2), 632–6; reprinted in Thijs ten Raa, *Structural Economics*, London and New York, Routledge (2004)

Samuelson, P. A. (1951). "Abstract of a Theorem Concerning Substitutability in Open Leontief Models," in Tjalling C. Koopmans (ed)., *Activity Analysis of Production and Allocation*, Monograph 13, Cowles Commission for Research in Economics, New York, John Wiley, 142–6

6   The System of National Accounts

6.1   Introduction

The power of input-output analysis is its capacity to analyze economies as they are given by a coherent set of data, namely the national accounts. The so-called System of National Accounts (SNA) was initiated by the United Nations (1968) and has since been revised (United Nations 1993). The main purpose of this chapter is to explain the system.

In section 6.2 some origins of the system of national accounts are identified and an outline is provided. Section 6.3 is long but rewarding: it provides a comprehensive treatment of the system of national accounts. Every account is balanced by a *residual item*. Because a system of national accounts is interdependent, the residual items are related: if all accounts except one are balanced, then the whole system, including the remaining account, must be balanced. Enlargements of input-output accounts are introduced in section 6.4. One of the main accounting problems is the valuation of *transactions*. Unlike textbook economics, transactions are not frictionless but involve margins. The measurement issues in national and international trade are resolved in section 6.5. Transactions may also be subject to taxation. To my knowledge the SNA is the only framework for a proper understanding of the value-added tax, the topic of section 6.6. In section 6.7 the concepts of national product and income are discussed. The conceptual distinction between the two – one measures *products* and the other *value-added* – is crucial. National income and product coincide on the national level, but not on a sectoral level. A significant implication of the simultaneous balance of national accounts is that certain missing information can be found by imputation. Section 6.8 shows how value-added taxes, which are recorded by commodity, can be traced back to the paying production units. Thus a gap, noted by the Central Bureau of Statistics (1992, p. 192), is filled by exploitation of the structure of the SNA instead of additional data collection. Section 6.9 extends the framework to Social Accounting Matrices (SAMs).

6.2   A bird's eye view

National accounts are organized in order to measure the national product or income of an economy. *Product* and *income* are different concepts and it takes a framework to relate the two through the economic activities of production, consumption, and distribution. If

Table 6.1 *National accounts of the Netherlands, 1989 (billion guilders)*

	1. Goods and services	2. Production	3. Factors	4. Capital	5. Financial	6. Foreign flows	7. Foreign stocks	Total
1. Goods and services	0 margins	460 U	284 + 72 $C + G$	109 I		268 E		1193
2. Production	904 V							904
3. Factors	40 VAT	389 + 55 $FC + CF$		1 VAT		61 from abroad		546
4. Capital			72 + 55 $S + R$				1 from abroad	128
5. Financial				16 surplus			51 new debt	67
6. Foreign flows	249 M		63 to abroad				17 surplus	329
7. Foreign stocks				2 to abroad	67 new claims			69
Total	1,193	904	546	128	67	329	69	

the framework is systematic, relationships between the various economic variables are suggested. Thus, the SNA may be used to model economic policies. Jan Tinbergen measured and organized national economic statistics so that economic ideas of crisis management could be assessed numerically. His work was macroeconomic in orientation and method. A systematic relationship of product and income statistics requires separate accounts for the items and, therefore, a microeconomic framework. Wassily Leontief was the first economist to make the *tour de force* of relating national accounts with the microeconomic general equilibrium framework. He divided the economy into sectors. Each sector has a commodity output and a multitude of inputs producing it. A "sector" consolidates two conceptually different entities, namely a production unit and its output. Two assumptions are implicit. First, there is a common classification for production units or firms on the one hand and for outputs or commodities on the other. Second, a firm in a particular sector produces "the" commodity of the sector it belongs to. Clearly, the concept of a sector is a rather demanding one, raising a number of issues. How do we embed the accounts of multi-product firms in sectors? Classify firms by production process or by nature of output? If the latter is chosen, which commodity of the products determines the classification?

To free national accounting from the rigid concept of an input-output sector, Stone (1961) introduced the idea of using separate accounts for separate entities, such as commodities and production units. His SNA was adopted by the United Nations (1968) and has since been revised (United Nations 1993). The system's very flexibility has ensured success in becoming the world standard. The basic idea will be presented in section 6.3. We will then present a system of seven accounts for the Netherlands. The treatment of trade margins and value-added tax will be highlighted. Concepts of product and income measurements will be identified and interrelated.

An SNA organizes various accounts into one table, making use of the fact that every transaction is both a receipt to one party and an expenditure to another. A credit item in one account must be a debit item in some other account and vice versa. A principle of the SNA is that every account comprises a row and a column. The *row* lists the *receipts* or credits and a *column* the *expenditures* or debts. The first account consists of the first row and the first column. Any credit entry (an element of the first row), is also a debit entry in some other account (the element of some column). Thus accounts are not written separately as pairs of columns but collapsed into each other by means of a matrix. The advantage of this organization is that it admits a bird's eye view of an entire system of national accounts. An example is given in table 6.1, the national accounts of the Netherlands.[1]

6.3   The System of National Accounts

The first account in table 6.1 is the commodities account. The first row shows the sales to the various other accounts of the economy: 460 billion guilders worth of commodities are sold to production units. It credits the commodities account, but debits the production account. This figure represents the material costs of production and is denoted by U, for (input) use.

---

[1] Table 6.1 is a simplified version of table E10 of the Central Bureau of Statistics (1992).

284 + 72 billion guilders of commodities are sold to households and the government for private and public consumption (C and G, respectively), 109 billion guilders of commodities are used for investment (I) and 268 billion guilders are exported (E), entering the foreign account. Total sales are 1193 billion guilders. All these receipts must be credited to the various accounts, which is done in the first column. The bulk of the goods and services is supplied by the production units (account 2), so the second entry is the main one: 904 billion guilders of commodity output, denoted by V. Foreign countries supply a fair share (imports M) and the government collects receipts in the form of product taxes such as the value-added tax (VAT). The latter figure is 40 billion guilders and includes excise and import duties. Since the recipients are creditors to the goods and services accounts, the payments in the first columns are debits from the perspective of the goods and services account.

The goods and services credits are the sales reported in the first row and represent the demand for commodities. The goods and services debits are the receipts reported in the first column and represent the supply of commodities. National accounting is accounting, not economics: in accounting, total credit equals total debit, or demand equals supply. This equality is always obtained retrospectively by properly accounting for the origin and the destination of every item in the account, every commodity in it, including items that have found no economic destination. If supply exceeds demand in an economic sense, some commodities will not be marketed. Accountants assign them to *inventory investment* and hence record the "transaction" as an investment. Every account has an entry, which absorbs any residual and thus balances the account; the residual items are printed in *italics*. The residual item of the first account is part of the fourth credit entry.[2]

The strength of matrix accounting is also its weakness. While it is theoretically correct that a credit in a receiving account equals a debit in an expending account, this need not hold in real-life accounts. The 72 billion guilders of commodity sales to the government are recorded by the selling suppliers (production units or importers) as well as by the buying demander (the government) and discrepancies may result from underreporting, overreporting, or errors. In a traditional account book comprising pairs of columns, one pair for every account, this would simply show as an inconsistency between a credit in one account and a debt in the associated entry in the other account. The SNA reserves only one space for this transaction and the national accountant is forced to decide what the "true" value of the transaction must have been and this single figure enters the matrix as both a credit to the row account and as a debit to the column account. The value is settled in a dialogue between representatives of the departments that handle the two accounts.

Such an adjustment is not easy, because it has ramifications. An SNA is a square matrix where the number of rows or columns equals the number of accounts. Since every account is balanced by a residual item, the row sum and the column sum must be equal. When a diagonal entry of an SNA is altered, the accounts continue to be balanced: if an entry which is not on the diagonal is changed, then one must not only restore balance in the account under consideration, but also in the other account to which the entry belongs. Moreover,

---

[2] It is not necessary that the residual item be located on the credit side, as we shall see in the presentation of the further accounts.

such revisions involve adjustments of other entries (possibly the balancing items), which do not reside on the diagonal and therefore disturb third accounts, etc. In short, an update of an account is a hard job that affects the whole SNA.

A way to a accommodate discrepancies explicitly is by introducing a separate account for errors. Any discrepancies between credits and debts can thus be allocated. However, this procedure does not overcome the accounting problems just discussed. Imagine adding a new account 8 for errors. The inclusion of an error account would, in a slightly artificial manner, balance all the "real" accounts. Let the latter be given by the following matrix:

$$\begin{pmatrix} x_{11} & \cdots & x_{17} \\ \vdots & \ddots & \vdots \\ x_{71} & \cdots & x_{77} \end{pmatrix} \tag{6.1}$$

In matrix (6.1) x_{ij} is the transaction from account i to account j, but row totals do not necessarily match respective column totals. The discrepancies are accounted for in the error account, by expanding matrix (6.1) to:

$$\begin{pmatrix} x_{11} & \cdots & x_{17} & \varepsilon_1 \\ \vdots & \ddots & \vdots & \vdots \\ x_{71} & \cdots & x_{77} & \varepsilon_7 \\ \delta_1 & \cdots & \delta_7 & \gamma \end{pmatrix} \tag{6.2}$$

In matrix (6.2) the accounts are balanced:

$$x_{11} + \cdots + x_{17} + \varepsilon_1 = x_{11} + \cdots + x_{71} + \delta_1$$
$$\vdots \tag{6.3}$$
$$x_{71} + \cdots + x_{77} + \varepsilon_7 = x_{17} + \cdots + x_{77} + \delta_7$$

Some magic can be made in the system of equations (6.3): Add the equations and subtract from either side the figure $\sum_{i,j=1}^{7} x_{ij}$:

$$\varepsilon_1 + \cdots + \varepsilon_7 = \delta_1 + \cdots + \delta_7 \tag{6.4}$$

Equation (6.4) shows that the error account *must* be balanced. The national accountant is restricted in his administration of errors. Accounting for errors accommodate discrepancies and balances the accounts, but the structure of the SNA reasserts itself. Only double-entry accounting, with possible different reports of transactions in the accounts of the parties involved, would accommodate a direct reflection of the raw statistics without any adjustments.

As we go down the accounts of the SNA, items we have encountered before reappear and fewer are novel. In the account 2 (production units) the 904 billion guilders of commodity outputs reappear on the credit side and no other receipts are present. The first expenditure is on material inputs: 460 billion guilders. The residual, 444 billion guilders, is *value-added* and credited to the factor inputs. In the interest of future discussion, it is broken down into two components: 389 factor costs (*FC*) and 55 billion consumption of fixed capital (*CF*).

The figure of 444 billion guilders expended on factor inputs enters the factor input account 3, as the main receipt. It is gross income, including taxes. Other income is generated by value-added taxes on goods and services as well as new capital (houses). The final item on the credit side is income from abroad. Income payments abroad are entered on the debit side of the account. The main expenditure is on consumption (public and private). The residual item on the account is *savings*, 127 billion guilders. This figure can be found on the capital entry and has been divided between net savings (*S*) and savings for the replacement of capital (*R*).

Transactions flow from origins to destinations. Origins are on the left-hand side of the SNA and destinations at the top. Thus, the first row shows the flows of goods and services to the various compartments of the economy and the second shows the outflow of the production units. The entries in the third row represent the services that flow from the factor inputs, labor, capital, and government. The 61 billion guilders accounts for the services that flow abroad.

As rows show the outflows, columns show the inflows into the accounts. The first column shows the inflow of goods and services, the second column the inputs of production, and the third column depicts how factor inputs, primarily households, are enabled to sustain their services. When the service suppliers take up foreign residence, the funds go abroad.

Savings form the main credit item on the capital account. It is augmented only by a small amount of capital transfers from abroad. Capital is expended on domestic investment and added to foreign stocks. The government takes a small amount and the *surplus* on the capital account enters the financial account.

The surplus of 16 billion guilders is caused by savings in excess of investment and finds it way abroad in the form of new net financial claims. New net claims are the difference between new claims (67 billion) and new debt (51 billion). Finance is raised by the surplus and new debt, which can be found in the row of account 5, and expended on new claims in the column of that account. In contrast to "real" accounts, representing tangibles as goods and services, factor inputs, and capital, finance is peculiar. New debt is a receipt to the finance account and therefore entered in the row, which generally lists the credits. The residual of the financial account is hidden in the *new claims*.

The account of foreign flows, also called the current account, is organized by collecting all the foreign flow items we have come across. In the column we find exports and factor income from abroad and in the row we find imports and factor income payments abroad. Since exports and factor income from abroad exceed imports and factor income outflow abroad, there is a *surplus* (17 billion guilders) on the current account; this figure augments the row elements at the foreign capital entry (account 7). This surplus is the common residual item to the foreign flows and stocks accounts. Many economies show the opposite picture, with more imports than exports. The difference between the two is called the *trade deficit*.

Although each account has its own residual item to balance the row and column totals, there is some dependency. A fascinating aspect of a system of accounts, say matrix (6.1), is the following. Let all accounts be balanced except one (say the last one):

$$x_{11} + \cdots + x_{17} = x_{11} + \cdots + x_{71}$$
$$\vdots \tag{6.5}$$
$$x_{61} + \cdots + x_{67} = x_{16} + \cdots + x_{76}$$

Then the remaining account *must* also be balanced. This result is obtained by adding the equations (6.5) and then subtracting $\sum_{i,j=1}^{6} x_{ij}$ from either side. We have seen above that the addition of an error account to balance the existing ones implies that the errors themselves must be balanced. Now, by the same logic, we may deduce that account 7, the foreign capital account, must be balanced. It is for this reason that the same surplus item that balances the current account also balances the foreign capital account. All the entries in the latter account have already been discussed.

Inspection of the financial and foreign stocks accounts (accounts 5 and 7) reveals a well-known relationship between the capital surplus and the current account surplus. The net new claims abroad match the capital surplus (in the financial account), but also the sum of the current account surplus and the net capital transfers from abroad (in the foreign stocks account). Since the net capital transfers are tiny (1 billion guilders in table 6.1), the *capital surplus is basically equal to the current account surplus.*

6.4   Enlargements

The degree of detail in an SNA depends on the availability of data and the purpose of analysis. In this book, the emphasis is on production and consumption, with little attention being paid to redistribution issues. The only income account is account 3, for the factor inputs. A fully fledged system has separate accounts for secondary incomes, to represent the redistribution that takes place in modern societies with income policies. The system is flexible and it is easy to add detail.

For our purpose, we must distinguish the various goods and services, as well as production units and other constituent accounts. We do so by disaggregating accounts into sub-accounts and blowing up the entries into sub-matrices. In the Netherlands, twenty-two goods and services are distinguished, sub-dividing account 1 into accounts 1a (food ingredients) – 1v (goods in process). Similarly, production is divided into ten units: accounts 2a (agriculture) – 2j (imputed bank services).

The cell on row 1 and column 2 of the SNA depicts the sales of commodities and services to the production units, $U = 460$ billion guilders. Since account 1 is divided into twenty-two goods and services accounts and account 2 into ten production accounts, U is blown up to a 22×10-dimensional matrix, the *use table* of the economy. U becomes a matrix of inputs with rows for the goods and services and columns for the production units. The use table is presented in table 6.2. If you added all the row or column totals, you would obtain the figure of 460. Thus, table 6.2 provides the detail of one entry in the SNA.

The cell on row 2 and column 1 of the SNA depicts the production of goods and services, $V = 904$ billion guilders. Figure V is blown up to a 10×22-dimensional matrix, the *make table* of the economy. V becomes a matrix of outputs with rows for the production units and columns for the goods and services. The make table is presented in table 6.3.

The dimensions of the use and the make tables are reversed because of their positions in table 6.1. Consequently, comparison of the two requires transposition of one of the two tables. The *net output table* of the economy is: $V^\top - U$. It has the same dimension as the use table: goods and services by production units. The net output table is the centerpiece of the national accounts.

Post-multiplication of the net output matrix by column vector e, defined by (2.7), amounts to summation over production units and yields a *commodity* vector of net outputs: the final demand vector of the economy. By the material balance (equating the column sums and the row sums of the goods and services accounts in table 6.1), final demand equals consumption (private as well as public) and investment minus value-added tax plus exports minus imports. Final demand is the national product and the breakdown holds for every commodity (the various goods and services). The value-added taxes (row 3, column 1 of the SNA) and imports can be found in the make table (table 6.3) and consumption, investment and exports in table 6.4. Thus, Tables 6.2, 6.3, and 6.4 form a complete set of enlargements of the goods and services account.

Pre-multiplication of the net output matrix by row vector $e^\top$, defined by (2.8), amounts to summation over commodities and yields a *production* vector of value-added: the income vector of the economy. Now for any matrix the sum of the row totals equals the sum of the column totals. This is the identity between the national product and income. It is a macroeconomic identity that does *not* hold at the micro level. For example, business services contribute zero to final demand (all their output is used as input), but add value, in fact quite a bit.

6.5   Trade

No presentation of national accounts is complete without an explanation of the treatments of trade and tax margins, both domestic and international. The accounts treat trade as follows. Domestic trade is included in production unit 2f. The main commodity input is business services (11 billion guilders, table 6.2). The main output is trade margins (73 billion guilders, table 6.3). Other production units also "produce" trade margins (commodity 1t) and the total figure is 89 billion guilders (the column total of the make table). Trade margins are not sold separately to firms, households, government, and foreign countries, but in conjunction with a carrier. Commodity 1t is therefore assigned to goods (accounts 1a – 1y) rather than to production units, etc. Thus row 1t of the SNA has entries in column 1 goods and services); see the top row of table 6.3. The negative of the total margins (minus 89 billion guilders) enters diagonal element (1t, 1t). In this way, trade margins contribute to the supply side of the commodity accounts only through the column totals of the carriers, commodities 1a – 1j;

Table 6.2 *Blow-up of U (billion guilders)*

	2a Agriculture	2b Mining	2c Industry	2d Utilities	2e Construction	2f Trade, hotel, repair
1a Food ingredients	13.120	0.000	42.831	0.000	0.022	0.077
1b Food	2.187	0.007	7.890	0.127	0.092	4.402
1c Textiles	0.081	0.002	3.904	0.000	0.102	0.572
1d Wood	0.298	0.018	6.809	0.002	11.216	0.589
1e Paper	0.101	0.048	16.977	0.059	0.328	5.438
1f Oil	0.609	0.192	21.244	0.069	1.092	0.355
1g Chemicals	1.350	0.158	26.285	0.211	2.388	1.103
1h Metals	1.178	0.558	35.499	0.673	10.262	2.787
1i Transport equipment	0.055	0.005	3.281	0.001	0.118	3.472
1j Utilities	1.196	0.645	6.506	8.132	0.129	1.501
1k Construction	0.371	0.063	1.546	0.186	15.569	0.814
1l Hotels, restaurant services	0.015	0.008	0.790	0.014	0.034	0.826
1m Repair tools	0.039	0.019	0.456	0.050	0.609	0.813
1n Transport services	0.043	0.296	0.691	0.004	0.291	0.326
1o Communication	0.184	0.054	1.211	0.142	0.139	1.611
1p Business services	1.150	0.326	10.339	0.747	2.694	11.263
1q Public services	0.005	0.000	0.000	0.000	0.000	0.000
1r Health services	0.332	0.072	0.667	0.119	0.123	0.249
1s Other goods and services	0.538	0.547	19.181	1.128	1.365	8.102
1t Trade and transport margins	0.000	0.000	0.000	0.000	0.000	0.000
1u Own investment goods	0.000	0.000	0.000	0.000	0.000	0.000
1v Goods in process	0.000	0.000	0.000	0.000	0.000	0.000
Total	22.852	3.018	206.107	11.664	46.573	44.300

Table 6.2 (cont.)

	2g Transport comm.	2h Other services	2i Government	2j Imputed bank services	Total
1a Food ingredients	0.000	0.095	0.112	0.000	56.257
1b Food	0.291	3.304	0.590	0.000	18.890
1c Textiles	0.094	0.303	0.154	0.000	5.212
1d Wood	0.036	0.926	0.487	0.000	20.381
1e Paper	0.999	6.133	1.703	0.000	31.786
1f Oil	1.985	0.723	0.797	0.000	27.066
1g Chemicals	0.085	3.068	0.879	0.000	35.527
1h Metals	1.194	2.804	3.712	0.000	58.667
1i Transport equipment	0.928	0.080	1.464	0.000	9.404
1j Utilities	0.433	1.732	0.820	0.000	21.094
1k Construction	2.157	5.304	4.666	0.000	30.676
1l Hotels, restaurant services	0.195	1.448	0.483	0.000	3.813
1m Repair tools	0.830	0.926	0.188	0.000	3.930
1n Transport services	1.880	0.363	0.468	0.000	4.362
1o Communication	0.584	3.213	0.766	0.000	7.904
1p Business services	2.517	16.724	7.587	18.028	71.375
1q Public services	0.000	0.061	0.208	0.000	0.274
1r Health services	0.172	3.015	1.091	0.000	5.840
1s Other goods and services	7.603	7.076	2.192	0.000	47.732
1t Trade and transport margins	0.000	0.000	0.000	0.000	0.000
1u Own investment goods	0.000	0.000	0.000	0.000	0.000
1v Goods in process	0.000	0.000	0.000	0.000	0.000
Total	21.983	57.298	28.367	18.028	

Table 6.3 *Blow-up of margins, V, VAT and M (billion guilders)*

	1a	1b	1c	1d	1e	1f	1g	1h	1i	1j	1k	1l
1t	4.703	18.596	9.918	8.605	3.879	2.869	11.272	24.029	4.847	0.173		
2a	26.848	16.216	0.152	0.016	0.000	0.000	0.000	0.050	0.000	0.000	0.034	0.000
2b	0.283	0.000	0.000	0.730	0.000	1.387	0.000	0.000	0.000	13.709	0.000	0.000
2c	20.115	54.402	9.767	16.042	25.943	20.175	50.382	60.304	16.441	0.467	2.603	0.000
2d	0.000	0.000	0.000	0.000	0.000	0.000	0.000	0.000	0.000	17.623	0.000	0.000
2e	0.000	0.000	0.000	0.059	0.000	0.000	0.000	0.063	0.047	0.000	70.622	0.000
2f	0.014	0.100	1.060	0.271	0.319	0.000	0.289	3.899	0.107	0.000	0.114	15.059
2g	0.000	0.014	0.000	0.001	0.110	0.000	0.000	0.000	0.440	0.000	0.192	0.051
2h	0.000	0.000	0.000	0.000	6.374	0.000	0.000	0.000	0.000	0.000	0.000	0.764
2i	0.009	0.078	0.000	0.000	0.213	0.000	0.000	0.018	0.132	0.000	1.451	0.185
2j	0.000	0.000	0.000	0.000	0.000	0.000	0.000	0.000	0.000	0.000	0.000	0.000
VAT	−0.283	5.055	3.778	1.615	1.211	6.202	1.869	5.392	4.506	1.630	7.262	1.500
M	17.122	14.594	15.550	11.678	9.106	20.795	28.578	72.594	21.874	2.584	0.010	0.000
Total	68.810	109.055	40.224	39.018	47.155	51.427	92.390	166.321	48.395	36.187	82.287	17.559

	1m	1n	1o	1p	1q	1r	1s	1t	1u	1v	Total
1t								−88.891			
2a	0.000	0.000	0.000	0.026	0.000	0.008	0.209	0.131	0.000	0.000	43.645
2b	0.000	0.000	0.000	0.001	0.000	0.000	0.062	0.000	0.133	0.000	16.305
2c	0.000	0.002	0.002	1.065	0.000	0.000	11.023	4.870	0.715	0.838	295.156
2d	0.000	0.000	0.000	0.530	0.000	0.000	1.001	0.000	0.661	0.000	19.815
2e	0.000	0.203	0.000	0.484	0.000	0.000	0.495	0.435	0.065	0.000	72.472
2f	8.903	0.128	0.000	5.053	0.000	0.067	6.240	73.015	0.043	0.000	114.681
2g	0.223	31.396	12.359	0.965	0.000	0.037	0.241	9.670	0.430	0.000	56.119
2h	0.071	0.055	0.009	117.825	0.000	56.956	24.624	0.770	0.036	0.000	207.502
2i	0.000	0.011	0.000	5.122	69.334	0.647	0.277	0.000	0.635	0.000	78.113
2j	0.000	0.000	0.000	0.000	0.000	0.000	0.000	0.000	0.000	0.000	0.000
VAT	1.056	−3.068	0.010	−0.421	0.000	0.529	2.242	0.000	0.000	0.000	39.885
M	0.000	0.000	0.000	0.000	0.000	0.012	34.261	0.000	0.000	0.000	248.758
Total	10.254	28.727	12.380	130.638	69.334	58.257	80.675	0.000	2.718	0.838	

Table 6.4 *Blow-up of final demand categories (billion guilders)*

	C	G	I	E	Total
1a	0.580	0.000	−0.279	12.252	12.553
1b	46.691	0.123	−0.168	43.520	90.166
1c	22.985	0.000	0.829	11.198	53.649
1d	8.062	0.000	4.697	5.878	18.637
1e	7.689	0.000	0.162	7.519	15.370
1f	8.267	0.000	−0.328	16.422	24.361
1g	10.495	0.000	1.518	44.849	56.862
1h	16.439	0.144	30.055	61.016	107.654
1i	9.743	0.000	15.107	14.141	38.991
1j	9.325	0.000	0.230	5.538	15.093
1k	1.871	0.000	48.432	1.308	51.611
1l	13.746	0.000	0.000	0.000	13.746
1m	6.324	0.000	0.000	0.000	6.324
1n	5.142	0.013	0.000	19.210	24.365
1o	3.963	0.000	0.000	0.513	4.476
1p	45.490	0.379	7.977	5.416	59.262
1q	0.864	68.196	0.000	0.000	69.060
1r	50.500	1.911	0.000	0.006	52.417
1s	14.373	0.999	−0.417	17.988	32.943
1t	0.000	0.000	0.000	0.000	0.000
1u	0.000	0.000	2.718	0.000	2.718
1v	0.000	0.000	0.838	0.000	0.838
Total	283	72	111	267	

see the top row of table 6.3, which contributes to column totals $1a - 1j$. Since the column total of $1t$ is zero, there is no double counting of trade margins. Thus zero enters the SNA in the very first cell of table 6.1.[3]

The column totals of table 6.3 constitute the total supply of commodities, including trade margins and value-added tax (rows $1t$ and 3 in the SNA). Table 6.3 identifies trade margins not only by commodity (row $1t$), but also by receiving production unit (column $1t$).

The bottom line of table 6.3 shows the value of imports by commodity as perceived by the domestic agents. Hence these values represent cost, insurance, freight (c.i.f.), including shipment and insurance costs but excluding import duties (which are included in the product taxes, primarily value-added tax). Exports are also valued from the viewpoint of domestic agents, and, therefore, do not exclude this cost. In other words, exports are subject to the free-on-board (f.o.b.) valuation. The treatment is best illuminated by the case of commodity quantities, which are not produced or used domestically, but imported and exported. The Netherlands processes significant amounts of throughput between Germany and the rest of

---

[3] The practice of inserting a negative in cell ($1t$, $1t$) is not essential. Any change of a diagonal entry of a system of accounts effects the balance of its own account in straightforward manner, without ramifications whatsoever for the other accounts. If the diagonal element ($1t$, $1t$) were left blank, the trade margin account would add to 89 billion guilders.

the world, since Rotterdam is a main port for Germany. Consider that 1 billion guilders worth of goods are imported from Germany and exported to America. The imports include the cost of insurance of the freight on the river Rhine, but are f.o.b. in the port of Rotterdam, excluding transatlantic insurance costs. The c.i.f. of imports and f.o.b. of exports measurement make the physical volumes of trade perfectly comparable and admit the extraction of the material balances from the national accounts.[4]

6.6   Value-added tax

The last item that deserves special attention is the treatment of value-added tax (VAT). VAT is used in Europe and contemplated in the United States. The great advantage of VAT over a sales tax is that it is deductible by business and, therefore, does not interfere with the free market mechanism of finding more roundabout yet cheaper modes of production. Sales taxes separate commodity markets into consumer products and commercial inputs, with business concentrating on the latter to escape the burden of taxation. Any restriction of the entrepreneurial search for the cheapest combination of inputs is bound to waste resources and, therefore, be inefficient. VAT, however, makes businesses a mere shifter of taxes from households to the government. Businesses receive VAT when they sell and pay VAT when they buy. When purchasing, businesses pay VAT like any other agent in the economy, but the payment is deductible when income is taxed. This has two consequences. First, VAT does not influence business decision-making. Second, since businesses are eager to report payments of VAT, the receipt by the other party of the transaction can be traced. In other words, the market mechanism is used to administer the tax. By providing an incentive to report VAT payments, it is difficult for the receiving party to avoid their transfer to the government.

Households may not deduct VAT and, therefore, face prices which differ from production costs and which may distort their consumption pattern and perhaps even induce them to withhold factor inputs, such as labor services. However, VAT can be introduced without a change of relative commodity prices. Moreover, while it is true that it increases the prices of consumption goods relative to those of factor inputs, such as leisure time forgone, alternative taxation schemes cannot escape an increase in the opportunity costs of factor inputs either.

How does it work? VAT must be paid on all sales except exports.[5] The commodity supply sector is $e^\top V + M$, where row vector $e^\top$ defined by (2.8) compresses the make table into a row vector by aggregation over production units. The bottom of table 6.3 displays the sum of the commodity supply vector and the trade margins. Let the tax rate on commodity i be t_i and let t denote the column vector comprising these rates. In the Netherlands t_i is 0.175 (or 17.5 percent) for most goods, but the rates are lower for basic necessities. Gross

---

[4] It may be puzzling that the same volume of the commodity is available for 1 billion guilders c.i.f. from Germany and 1 billion guilders f.o.b. from the Netherlands. Theoretically, it might be thought that the Americans would be better off buying goods directly in Germany, but this ignores geography and the consequent transport costs.

[5] The idea is that foreign customers do not benefit from the government services.

VAT payments are obtained by post-multiplication by $\hat{t}$ (the diagonal matrix derived from vector t):

$$(e^\top V + M - E^\top)\hat{t} \tag{6.6}$$

Expression (6.6) is the row vector of VAT payments by commodity.[6] When profits are assessed for corporate taxation, VAT payments by business are deductible. Businesses pay VAT on their purchases, which are given by the use table, U (table 6.2). The dimensions of this table are goods $\times$ production units. Aggregation over production units by post-multiplication with the e-vector defined in (2.7), we obtain the commodity input column vector for all businesses and pre-multiplication by the diagonal matrix of VAT rates yields the column vector of VAT payments by businesses: $\hat{t}Ue$. The net VAT payments accrued by the government are obtained by transposition and subtraction from the gross VAT payments (6.6):

$$VAT = (e^\top V + M - E^\top)\hat{t} - (\hat{t}Ue)^\top \tag{6.7}$$

Expression (6.7) can be simplified. The material balance, equating supply and demand of goods and services, reads:

$$margins + e^\top V + VAT + M = (Ue + C + G + I + E)^\top \tag{6.8}$$

The terms on the left-hand side are the row vectors in the column of the goods and services account (see tables 6.1 and 6.3), where for simplicity we ignore the non-VAT product taxes. The right-hand side contains the column vectors in the row of the goods and services account (see tables 6.2 and 6.4), transposed for dimensional consistency. Balance (6.8) can be rewritten as:

$$e^\top V + M - E^\top - (Ue)^\top = (C + G + I)^\top - margins - VAT \tag{6.9}$$

Substituting balance (6.9) in VAT-expression (6.7):

$$VAT = [(C + G + I)^\top - margins - VAT]\hat{t} \tag{6.10}$$

Equation (6.10) shows that VAT is in effect levied on *domestic final demand* (households, government, and business investment).[7]

As with trade, the SNA records transactions from the viewpoint of domestic users. Business inputs (U) are recorded excluding VAT, since that is the way they are considered in decision-making. Consumption and investment (C, G, and I) are recorded including VAT, since that is what the users face. Thus, to obtain the VAT base, $C + G + I$ must be netted prior to the application of the diagonal matrix with the VAT rates.[8] This explains the deduction

---

[6] Note that exports are exempted and since exports are a column vector – see the SNA in table 6.1 and the enlargements in table 6.4 – they must be transposed to make the dimensions compatible.

[7] If the VAT-deductible business purchases also encompass investment and rent r on capital outlays K, then the base is not $C + G + I$, but only $C + G - rK$.

[8] VAT must also be deduced from domestic final demand when the latter enters the material balances, – e.g. in linear programs that maximize the level of domestic final demand (chapter 9).

of VAT on the right-hand side of (6.10). The equation can now be solved for either the row vector *VAT* or the effective VAT rates:

$$VAT = [(C + G + I)^\top - margins]\widehat{\widehat{1 + t}}^{-1} \tag{6.11}$$

Indeed, (6.11) is equivalent to:

$$t_i = VAT_i/(C_i + G_i + I_i - margins_i - VAT_i) \tag{6.12}$$

For example, the first commodity (food ingredients) has a VAT-component of -0.283 (table 6.3, column $1a$), while $C_i + G_i + I_i - margins_i$ amounts to $0.580 + 0.000 - 0.279 - 4.703 = -4.402$ (table 6.4, row $1a$ and Table 6.3, column $1a$, first entry). The effective VAT rate on food ingredients is, therefore, $-0.283/(-4.402 + 0.283) = 0.07$ or 7 percent.[9]

6.7 Gross national product

Value-added taxes increase the prices of commodities, but this inflation is excluded from the so-called gross national product (GNP) at basic prices, which is a measure of the *net output of an economy*. GNP and income are equal and are usually introduced as the sum of wages, salaries, etc. Since the equality is not a definitional matter, it is best to introduce the concepts in separation as product and income entities. The GNP at basic prices measures *products*, namely consumption (private and public), investment, and net exports, net of value-added taxes:

$$GNP = C + G + I + E - M - VAT \tag{6.13}$$

Although expression (6.13) defines GNP as a scalar, taking the terms from the aggregated SNA (table 6.1), tables 6.2–6.4 can be used to disaggregate GNP by product. Expression (6.13) can be simplified by substituting the aggregated goods and services account balance given by the first row and column of table 6.1:

$$GNP = V - U \tag{6.14}$$

Expression (6.14) shows that GNP is the aggregated net output of the economy and explains why GNP is defined as the *final* product of the economy, excluding the output used in industry. If we included the intermediate product, U, in our measure of GNP, we would be double counting. To illustrate this, let us create a separate sector for the final stage of the production process in some sector. For example, let a licensing sector identify all transportation equipment by a number. Thus, in table 6.2 we would introduce sector $2k$ (licensing) and commodity $1w$ (registered transportation equipment). All the transportation equipment would be bought by sector $2k$ and resold to all other sectors as well as the final

---

[9] Equation (6.12) has been derived on the assumptions that all sales are taxed and all deductions are taken by business. If some rates are not taxed, the tax base may be smaller than $C_i + G_i + I_i$, and if some deductions are not taken, VAT_i may be excessive. This disclaimer is pertinent as the product taxes also have non-VAT components, which we ignore. In either case, the denominator may turn negative. For example, VAT on oil (6 billion guilders according to table 6.3, column f) exceeds consumption net of margins (8 billion guilders minus 3 billion guilders, see tables 6.4 (column C, entry f) and table 6.3 (row $1t$, entry f).

demand categories, in precisely the same amount as transportation equipment *per se* in the original accounts. There is no change in expression (6.13), since transportation equipment is out and registered transportation equipment is in. Inclusion of U would equate GNP to V instead of (6.14), and thus capture *two* commodity outputs: not yet licensed and licensed transportation equipment.

The production account relates GNP to income. From row and column 2 of the SNA, we see that net output $V - U$ equals factor costs plus the consumption of fixed capital (depreciation):

$$GNP = FC + CF \tag{6.15}$$

Both factor costs and depreciation in (6.15), are *income* components and can be disaggregated by production units, as table 6.5 shows. The equality of GNP and income holds only at the macroeconomic level. Strictly speaking the equality cannot be disaggregated at all, since goods and services classify GNP, while production units classify income and the two classifications need not have anything in common.[10] Even if there were a one-to-one relationship between commodities and sectors, disaggregation of the macroeconomic identity would be false. Consider the economy with:

$$V = \begin{pmatrix} 1 & 0 \\ 0 & 1 \end{pmatrix}, U = \begin{pmatrix} 0 & 1 \\ 0 & 0 \end{pmatrix} \tag{6.16}$$

Under (6.16) the commodity vector of net outputs is:

$$(V^\top - U)e = \begin{pmatrix} 0 \\ 1 \end{pmatrix} \tag{6.17}$$

Expression (6.17) shows that GNP comprises the second commodity only. Now look at value-added by production unit:

$$e^\top(V^\top - U) = (1 \quad 0) \tag{6.18}$$

Expression (6.18) shows that all income is earned in the first sector. GNP and the gross national income account for the row and column sums of the net output matrix, respectively. They are equal because both row sums and column sums add to the grand total, but there is no reason why specific terms should match.

Mention of a few variations on the GNP concept is in order. Exclusion of depreciation (CF) turns the G of gross into the N of net (as in *NNP*). In any of the concepts, the P of product may become the I of income, but this changes the dimension of disaggregations (from commodity to sector detail). The last variation is the concept of Gross Disposable Income (GDI): GDI is obtained by adding two items to GNP (or, equivalently, national income), namely indirect taxes (to return from basic prices to market prices) and net income from abroad (another source of purchasing power):

$$GDI = GNP + VAT + NetIncAbr \tag{6.19}$$

---

[10] The numbers of commodities and production units are generally different.

Table 6.5 *Blow-up of FC + CF (billion guilders)*

	2a	2b	2c	2d	2e	2f	2g	2h	2i	2j	Total
3a Wages and salaries	2.399	0.731	43.065	2.516	13.958	29.645	16.141	56.278	34.030	0.000	198.763
3b Employees premiums	0.636	0.164	11.302	0.502	5.064	7.097	3.679	13.686	11.961	0.000	54.091
3c Other income (gross)	17.024	12.321	34.626	5.130	6.888	32.916	13.907	78.742	3.367	−18.028	186.893
3d Non-product taxes minus subsidies	0.736	0.071	0.057	0.003	−0.011	0.721	0.410	1.498	0.387	0.000	3.872
Total	20.795	13.287	89.050	8.151	25.899	70.379	34.137	150.204	49.745	−18.028	

Table 6.6 *The non-zero items of an economy without production*

	1. Goods and services	3. Factors	6. Foreign flows
1. Goods and services		$C + G$	
3. Factors			Income from abroad
6. Foreign flows	M		

The disposal need not be at home, but may be on imports, as is shown by eliminating from (6.19) *VAT* and NetIncAbr, using (6.13) and the foreign flows account 6 in table 6.1 (*NetIncAbr = M − E + Surplus*):

$$GDI = C + G + I + Surplus \qquad (6.20)$$

Equation (6.20) shows that disposable income is domestic final demand plus the surplus on the foreign account. An extreme example is a resource-based economy such as Kuwait after it runs out of oil. The non-zero accounts in the SNA are goods and services, factors, and foreign flows, see table 6.6.

The three entries in table 6.6 are equal to each other as well as to GDI, while GNP is zero. All income is transfers of returns on investments from abroad, such as London real estate.

6.8   Imputation of VAT to industries

This section provides a policy exercise that shows the power of input-output analysis. Rearranging the definition of the net VAT payments (6.7):

$$VAT = [e^{\top}(V − U^{\top}) − (E^{\top} − M)]\hat{t} \qquad (6.21)$$

Equation (6.21) shows the VAT collected by commodity. Vector t lists the tax rates. The first component was calculated as 0.07 in section 6.6, a rate of 7 percent on food ingredients, and the other rates can be found in the same way.[11] Post-multiplication of expression (6.21) with the unit vector e reproduces the total VAT figure (see table 6.1):[12]

$$40 = [e^{\top}(V − U^{\top}) − (E^{\top} − M)]t \qquad (6.22)$$

The *National Accounts* of the Netherlands Central Bureau of Statistics (1992, p. 192) mention that it is unknown which production units pay the tax. Input-output analysis gives the answer. Since exports are exempt, production units catering for domestic final demand contribute more. Thus, let Z be the matrix of net exports (production units × commodities). Then $e^{\top}Z = E^{\top} − M$ and the total figure, (6.22), reads:

$$40 = e^{\top}(V − U^{\top} − Z)t \qquad (6.23)$$

---

[11] We ignore the non-VAT components of the product taxes.
[12] We continue to ignore the other product taxes.

The matrix in the middle on the right-hand side of (6.23) is of the dimension production units × commodities. Post-multiplication by vector t makes it a vector with one element for each sector.[13] These elements are precisely contributions to the government. Pre-multiplication by $e^\top$ adds them up. Exports erode the tax base. If certain levels of tax revenues are targeted, commodities that are exported must be taxed heavily at home.

Leers, Nijssen, and Pruis (1992) have carried out the disaggregation (by sector of production) of the vector of net exports, $E^\top - M$, into matrix Z and thus determined the sectoral *burden* vector of VAT:[14]

$$b = (V - U^\top - N)t$$
$$= (6.3 \quad 0.5 \quad 12.9 \quad 2.1 \quad 9.7 \quad 4.7 \quad -2.3 \quad 3.3 \quad 2.2)^\top \qquad (6.24)$$

Result (6.24) shows that the main burden falls on industry, sector 3. Sector 7, transportation and communication, is a negative contributor of indirect taxes. This finding reflects the subsidies extended to these services in the Netherlands.

If there are as many production units as commodities, (6.21) may be used to determine the commodity VAT rates that sustain an alternative burden vector. The solution t is determined by the Leontief inverse of the input-output coefficients implicit in the use, make, and net exports tables. The extraction of such coefficients from the national accounts is the subject of chapter 7.

6.9 Social Accounting Matrices

Social Accounting Matrices (SAMs) extend the logic of input-output analysis from production to income distribution. This pays attention to the redistribution of factor income to the domestic institutions. Pyatt (2001) divides the latter into urban households, rural households, estate households, private companies, and public companies. One creates a SAM by insertion of a *domestic institutions account* between the factors account (table 6.1, account 3) and the capital account (table 6.1, account 4).

The row of the domestic institutions current account shows the receipts. There are no receipts from the goods and services account and the production account (the first two cells are zero), but the main source is factor income, the third cell. If the factor account is disaggregated (by the various types of labor and capital), then in this cell we find a matrix that allocates the different types of factor income to the various types of households and other institutions. The structure of this sub-matrix is determined by the distribution of ownership of all real assets (including the various types of human capital) that provide factor services. Columns of this sub-matrix show that distribution of ownership. In economic analysis it is standard to assume that the distribution of ownership is given. In other words, the proportions of the cells of a column in the income redistribution table are fixed. Clearly, this is precisely analogous to the assumption that input proportions in production are given (fixed proportions of the column cells in the use table).

---

[13] Vector t has the dimension of a commodity vector.
[14] Imputed bank services are excluded from their analysis.

The next element in the row of the domestic institutions current account is the diagonal element. It represents all the transfers between the various households and companies. The last entry in this row will be the transfers from abroad, previously allocated to the factors (the 61 billion guilders figure in table 6.1) and thus shifted down to the new account.

The same applies to the transfers abroad. The 63 billion guilders figure in table 6.1 is shifted right into the domestic institutions account. In a SAM, factor income is allocated to the domestic institutions account and the foreign account. The domestic institutions spend their income (recorded in the row) on goods and services and capital. The column 3 entries of table 6.3 are thus shifted right into the newly inserted account. This completes the description of the modification of an SNA to a SAM.

The critical data requirement is the distribution of factor ownerships by households and other domestic institutions. The information is not readily available and one must combine economic and demographic statistics with sensible assumptions to interpolate gaps.

It is customary to extend input-output analysis to SAMs by assuming that proportions within columns remain fixed, at least of the components that vary in (scenario) analysis. This is reasonable for the use table in the SNA part and for the distribution of income by institution in the extended SAM. The indiscriminate application of this principle is problematic in other cases, for example the make table. To assume fixed proportions in columns of the make table is tantamount to assuming fixed shares of industries in commodity markets. This assumption underlies the so-called "industry technology model." In chapter 7 we will reveal some serious shortcomings of this approach.

Anyway, the extension amounts to an inclusion of consumption effects in multiplier analysis, along the lines we have seen in chapter 3. And in efficiency analysis, of the type that will be undertaken in chapter 9, it amounts to an inclusion of the distributional effects of competitive policies.[15]

Exercises

1. Encircle T (true) or F (false) in each case.

National product is the value of output	T	F
National product equals national income	T	F
Business services contribute directly to the national product	T	F
Business services contribute directly to the national income	T	F
The contribution of agriculture to national income may be negative	T	F
If there is unemployment, the wage rate is zero	T	F
The consumers are net payers of VAT	T	F
The producers are net payers of VAT	T	F
Savings must be equal to investment	T	F

---

[15] A very recent application is an analysis of the income inequality that comes with competition in the Chinese economy (ten Raa and Pan, 2005).

Table 6.7 *Example of a small open economy*

	Good 1	Good 2	Good 3	Production sector 1	Production sector 2	Production sector 3	Factors	Capital	Foreign flows
Good 1				0	0	0	9	?	1
Good 2				0	10	0	9	?	1
Good 3				0	0	20	9	?	0
Production sector 1	10	0	0						
Production sector 2	0	20	0						
Production sector 3	0	0	30						
Factors	1	1	3	6 + 3 + 1	3 + 5 + 2	2 + 8 + 0		0	0
Capital	0	0	?				?	0	
Foreign flows	0	0	?				0	0	0

2. For an economy with as many commodities as sectors, determine the VAT rates that sustain a given sectoral burden vector. Discuss the cases with, respectively, more or less commodities than sectors.

3. A small open economy, with all goods tradable, has the following SNA (billion dollars) (table 6.7).

   In this SNA, the sum $6 + 3 + 1$ represents the capital costs + wage bill + profit in sector 1 (respectively) and a similar breakdown of factor costs holds for sectors 2 and 3. Explain your answers to the following questions:

   (a) Complete the capital account. Are savings and investment always equal?
   (b) Show the trade deficit is zero. Is this always so?
   (c) Show that GNP and income are equal, sector by sector. Is this always so?
   (d) What are the VAT rates?

4. Consider the following 1992 economy. All figures are in million dollars. Manufacturing produces 6 of a material good. Costs are 3 for capital, and 2 for labor. The service sector produces 6 of a service, as well as 1 of the (same) good. Costs are 3 for materials, 1 for capital, and 2 for labor. There are no margins, taxes, depreciation, or investment. Domestic consumption of the good and the service are equal. Trade is free and balanced. You may assume full employment.

   Determine the constituent terms of GNP and income, also by product and income categories, including profits.

5. The Minister of Economic Affairs wants to reduce the VAT contribution by one sector without increasing the burden of the other sectors. The Minister of Finance objects, as it would erode the tax base. The Minister of Economic Affairs argues, however, that the product of the sector under consideration would be cheaper and that, therefore, the products of the other sectors can be taxed at a higher rate. Who is right?

References

Central Bureau of Statistics (1992). *National Accounts 1991* I, 's-Gravenhage, SDU (in Dutch)

Leers, Th., S. Nijssen, and C. Pruis (1992) "Specification of the VAT Contribution by Sector," Universiteit van Tilburg, unpublished paper

Pyatt, G. (2001). "Some Early Multiplier Models of the Relationship between Income Distribution and Production Structure," *Economic Systems Research* 13 (2), 139–64

ten Raa, Th. and H. Pan (2005). "Competitive Pressures on China: Income Inequality and Migration," *Regional Science & Urban Economics* 35 (0)

Stone, R. (1961). *Input-Output and National Accounts*, Paris: OECD

United Nations (1968). *A System of National Accounts*, Studies in Methods, Series F, no. 2, rev. 3 (1993). *Revised System of National Accounts*, Studies in Methods, Series F, no. 2, rev. 4

7 The construction of technical coefficients

7.1 Introduction

Technical coefficients were defined in chapter 2 as the input requirements (amounts of commodities) per unit of output (for each commodity). The technical coefficients for output 1 were written in a column vector, (2.1), and placement of all the "recipes" next to each other yields the matrix of technical coefficients, (2.2). The matrix of technical coefficients is a function of the input and output data of the economy, which were presented in section 6.4. For every pair of a use and a make table, (U, V), we face the task of constructing the associated matrix of technical coefficients: $A(U, V)$. It is important to distinguish a function, such as A, and a value it can take, $A(U, V)$. A *value* is a matrix of technical coefficients that is associated with a given pair of data. The *function* itself represents the association or the rule by which the coefficients are constructed. The latter is the topic of this chapter.

If there are as many commodities as production units and the make table, V, is a diagonal matrix, the situation is simple. Every sector would use an input vector, a column of U, and make a single output. There is a one-to-one relationship between commodities and sectors. Each commodity is produced by precisely one sector and division of the input vector by the quantity of output determines its technical coefficients:

$$a_{ij}(U, V) = u_{ij}/v_{jj}, i, j = 1, \ldots, n \tag{7.1}$$

In matrix notation, (7.1) reads:

$$A(U, V) = U(V^\top)^{-1} \tag{7.2}$$

Although the transposition in (7.2) is redundant for diagonal matrices (whence $V = \hat{V} = V^\top$), it has been inserted for dimensional considerations, as is explained now. Multiplying through (7.2) by matrix $V^\top$, we obtain:

$$A(U, V)V^\top = U \tag{7.3}$$

In (7.3) $A(U, V)$ is of the dimension commodity $\times$ commodity, V commodity $\times$ sector and U commodity $\times$ sector. This consistency would not have been obtained without transposition of the make table. Moreover, formulas (7.2) and (7.3) will be shown to hold for non-diagonal make tables V and (7.3) even for rectangular matrices.

The purpose of this chapter is to extend the construction of technical coefficients to make tables that are not diagonal or not even square. The off-diagonal entries in a make table are secondary products and rectangular make tables are used in the estimation of technical coefficients.

7.2   Secondary products

In this section we study economies with the same number of sectors as of commodities, but without a one-to-one relationship between sectors and commodities. The make table is no longer diagonal. Most of the commodity outputs will be produced by the so-called "primary sectors," but not all of them. Sectors may also produce each other's commodities as so-called "secondary products." Formally, we write:

$$V = \hat{V} + \check{V} \tag{7.4}$$

In decomposition the first term of (7.4) contains the diagonal elements of make table V and the second term the off-diagonal elements. The two terms are the primary output table and the secondary output table. Empirically, secondary output is smaller than primary output. In the light of this stylized fact we assume that primary output dominates secondary output, for every commodity. The commodity vectors of primary and secondary outputs are obtained by aggregation of the primary and secondary output tables across sectors. Since output tables are of the dimension sectors $\times$ commodities, aggregation across sectors is effected by pre-multiplication by the unit row vector, $e^\top$. Following McKenzie (1960) we say that primary output *dominates* if and only if:

$$e^\top \hat{V} > e^\top \check{V} \tag{7.5}$$

In the presence of secondary products, technical coefficients must be derived indirectly. Following van Rijckeghem (1967), the strategy is to set up an equation for the matrix of coefficients and to solve it. Thus, let $a_{ik}(U, V)$ be the requirements of commodity i per unit of commodity k. As sector j produces v_{jk} units of commodity k, where $k = 1, \ldots, n$, the commodity input requirements are $a_{ik}(U, V)v_{jk}$. Summing over products, sector j requires $\sum_{k=1}^{n} a_{ik}(U, V)v_{jk}$ of commodity i as input. The observed purchase of commodity i by sector j is u_{ij}. Equating the theoretical and empirical inputs, we obtain:

$$\sum_{k=1}^{n} a_{ik}(U, V)v_{jk} = u_{ij} \tag{7.6}$$

In matrix notation, the equations (7.6) reproduce (7.3) with V no longer a diagonal matrix, but given by (7.4). The determination of technical coefficients is, therefore, the problem of solving (7.3).

The consequent coefficients are called *commodity technology* coefficients, as they are derived on the assumption that every commodity has its own input structure, irrespective the sector of fabrication. United Nations (1993) is a relevant reference for the commodity technology model.

Theorem 7.1(Commodity technology coefficients). Let the use and make tables be square. If primary output dominates, then the inverse of $V^\top$ exists and the unique solution to (7.3) is given by $A(U, V) = U(V^\top)^{-1}$.

Proof. $V^\top = \hat{V} + \breve{V}^\top = \hat{V}(I + \hat{V}^{-1}\breve{V}^\top)$. By dominance, $e^\top \hat{V} > e^\top \breve{V} \geq 0$, hence $v_{ii} > 0$ and $\hat{V}^{-1}$, the diagonal matrix with elements v_{ii}^{-1}, exists. Also, $\hat{V}^{-1}\breve{V}^\top e = \hat{V}^{-1}(e^\top \breve{V})^\top < \hat{V}^{-1}(e^\top \hat{V})^\top = e$. Hence $\sum_{k=0}^{\infty} (-\hat{V}^{-1}\breve{V}^\top)^k$ exists and is the inverse of $I + \hat{V}^{-1}\breve{V}^\top$, precisely as $\sum_{k=0}^{\infty} A^k$ is the inverse of $I - A$ (theorem 2.1). In short, $V^\top$ is the product of two invertible matrices, hence invertible.   □

The presence of secondary products has a problematic consequence for the sign of the technical coefficients (ten Raa 1988). To illustrate the problem, consider an economy with two production units – one pure, producing one unit of commodity 1, and the other producing one unit of commodity 2 *plus* v units of commodity 1, the secondary product. The make table is:

$$V = \begin{pmatrix} 1 & 0 \\ v & 1 \end{pmatrix} \tag{7.7}$$

Substituting (7.7) in theorem 7.1:

$$A(U, V) = U \begin{pmatrix} 1 & -v \\ 0 & 1 \end{pmatrix} = (u_{\bullet 1} \quad u_{\bullet 2} - u_{\bullet 1} v) \tag{7.8}$$

In expression (7.8) the technical coefficients of commodity 1 are given by the input structure of sector 1, because that sector is pure. The technical coefficients of commodity 2 are given by the inputs of sector 2 after deduction of the input requirements of the secondary product, v. Since vector $u_{\bullet 1}$ lists the input requirements of one unit of commodity 1, $u_{\bullet 1} v$ lists the input requirements of v units of commodity 1. The residual inputs in sector 2, given by vector $u_{\bullet 2} - u_{\bullet 1} v$, must be allocated to product 2. As only one unit of product 2 is produced, this yields the input coefficients vector for product 2. The deduction may cause a negative. If u_{11} is big, but u_{12} is small, then $a_{12} = u_{12} - u_{11} v$ will be negative.

Commodity technology coefficients are independent of the sector of fabrication, as if all sectors employ the same technology. However, if sector 2 used no amount of the input of which the primary producer used a positive amount ($u_{11} > 0$, but $u_{12} = 0$), then it is hard to believe that sector 2 would employ the same technique as sector 1 in the production of commodity 1.

An alternative construction of technical coefficients, the industry technology model is based on the assumption that sectors have specific input structures, irrespective of the commodity composition of their outputs. In this approach, sector 1 uses u_{i1} of input i for the production of output $v_{11} + \cdots + v_{1n}$. The input is thought to be allocated proportionally. Output is $u_{i1} v_{1j}/(v_{11} + \cdots + v_{1n})$, hence $u_{i1}/(v_{11} + \cdots + v_{1n})$ per unit. Output j gets similar but different amounts of input i per unit in the other sectors. The technical coefficient is now taken to be the weighted average of these industry coefficients, where the weights are the shares of the industries in the market of commodity j, $v_{kj}/(v_{1j} + \cdots + v_{nj})$:

$$\tilde{a}_{ij}(U, V) = \sum_{k=1}^{n} u_{ik}(v_{k1} + \cdots + v_{kn})^{-1} v_{kj}(v_{1j} + \cdots + v_{nj})^{-1} \tag{7.9}$$

Input-output coefficients based on formula (7.9) are called the *industry technology* coefficients, as it is assumed that every industry has its own input structure. To avoid confusion with the commodity technology coefficients, a tilde ($\sim$) is attached to these input-output coefficients. The matrix version of formula (7.9) reads:

$$\tilde{A}(U, V) = U\widehat{Ve}^{-1}V\widehat{V^{\top}e}^{-1} \tag{7.10}$$

Unlike the commodity technology coefficients, the industry technology coefficients are not plagued by the problem of negativity. In formula (7.10) all factors on the right-hand side are non-negative and, therefore, so are those on the left-hand side. The weakness of the industry technology coefficients, however, is the reliance on a concept of industry output, $v_{kl} + \cdots + v_{kn}$, the second factor in formula (7.9) or (7.10). Inputs are allocated to outputs in proportion to the output shares. If the make table is reported in current values and some relative price happens to be high, that commodity will be assigned a lot of input and, therefore, a high technical coefficient. In other words, the allocation of inputs depends on the units of measurement of the outputs. A change of the units of measurement or the price system ought to affect the technical coefficients in the straightforward way described in formula (2.15): If the current price system $e^{\top}$ becomes p, then the technical coefficients a_{ij} must be multiplied and divided by prices p_i and p_j, respectively. In matrix notation this is transformation is given by (2.26). Example (7.7) shows that this invariance of measurement units is not observed by the industry technology coefficients. By formula (7.10) the industry technology coefficients are:

$$\tilde{A}(U, V) = U \begin{pmatrix} 1 & 0 \\ 0 & (v+1)^{-1} \end{pmatrix} \begin{pmatrix} 1 & 0 \\ v & 1 \end{pmatrix} \begin{pmatrix} (1+v)^{-1} & 0 \\ 0 & 1 \end{pmatrix} \tag{7.11}$$

Post-multiplication of expression (7.11) by

$$\begin{pmatrix} 0 \\ 1 \end{pmatrix}$$

yields the second column:

$$\tilde{a}_{\bullet 2}(U, V) = \frac{u_{\bullet 2}}{v+1} \tag{7.12}$$

According to expression (7.12) the input coefficients of commodity 2 equal the sectoral coefficients of industry 2, which indeed is the unique producer of this product. Focus on the second coefficient in expression (7.12):

$$\tilde{a}_{22}(U, V) = \frac{u_{22}}{v+1} \tag{7.13}$$

The coefficient (7.13) must measure the input units of commodity 2 required per output unit of commodity 2. This number ought to be independent of the unit of measurement of commodity 2, or its price. If you need half a pound of food ingredients to produce a pound of food ingredients, you also need half a kilogram per kilogram. The same holds for a price change. If you need half a guilder per guilder, you also need half a euro per euro of food ingredients. Now imagine that the price of commodity 2 is constant but commodity 1 features 10 percent price inflation. The use of base-year prices deflates the secondary product and, therefore, reallocates input to the primary product. This increases the technical coefficient (7.13) to:

$$\frac{u_{22}}{0.9 * v + 1} \tag{7.14}$$

Less input of commodity 2 is required per unit of commodity 2 if units are measured in base-year prices than in current prices.

To rule out such anomalies, we must stick to formula (2.26): If commodities are priced by vector p and the use and make tables are consequently replaced by $\hat{p}U$ and $V\hat{p}$, respectively, then the technical coefficients must be pre-multiplied and post-multiplied by $\hat{p}$ and $\hat{p}^{-1}$, respectively. Following Stone (1961, formula VIII.37), technical coefficients are declared *price invariant* if for all $p > 0$:

$$A(\hat{p}U, V\hat{p}) = \hat{p}A(U, V)\hat{p}^{-1} \tag{7.15}$$

Example (7.14) showed that the industry technology coefficients (7.10) are not price invariant. The commodity technology coefficients are fine.

Lemma 7.1. The solution of theorem 7.1 is price invariant.

Proof. By (2.10) and lemma 4.2 we have $A(\hat{p}U, V\hat{p}) = \hat{p}U[(V\hat{p})^{\top}]^{-1} = \hat{p}U(\hat{p}V^{\top})^{-1} = \hat{p}U(V^{\top})^{-1}\hat{p}^{-1} = \hat{p}A(U, V)\hat{p}^{-1}$. $\qquad\qquad\square$

Price invariance is an important requirement. It ensures that technical coefficients do not depend in an essential way on the units of measurement. Technical coefficients are a way to model the *production possibilities* – that is the supply side of an economy. In interaction with demand, one may then proceed to explain scarcities and prices. Such a supply–demand analysis of prices requires that the building bricks of the economic model, including the technical coefficients, depend on physical relationships only. If the measurement of technical coefficients depends on prices, they can no longer be used in economic analysis. It is not said that the observed technical coefficients are independent of market prices. On the contrary, one of the interesting questions we shall address is the choice of technique as a function of price. But the *measurement* of these techniques must be independent of prices.

Not only commodity technology coefficients are price invariant. Another example are the technical coefficients defined by $A(U, V) = 0$. This example is peculiar because it violates the material balance, as all intermediate demand is suppressed. Let us express the material balance requirement in terms of the data, (U, V), and the method of construction, A.

The *material balance* equates supply and demand for all commodities. Supply is total output by commodity and is given by the column totals of the make table, $V^\top e$. Demand comprises intermediate demand and final demand. Final demand is a residual, namely the difference between supply and intermediate demand. Intermediate demand is the commodity input vector that feeds industry. It is proportional to the output, where the proportions are given by the input-output coefficients, $A(U, V)$. Intermediate demand is, therefore, $A(U, V)V^\top e$. However, intermediate demand can also be observed directly through the use table. The commodity input vector is given by the row totals of the use table, Ue. Consequently, the material balance reads:

$$A(U, V)V^\top e = Ue \tag{7.16}$$

By theorem 7.1, commodity technology coefficients solve (7.3) and simple post-multiplication with vector e proves they fulfill the material balance, (7.16). Industry technology coefficients are given by (7.10) and also fulfill the material balance:

$$\tilde{A}(U, V)V^\top e = U\widehat{Ve}^{-1}V\widehat{V^\top e}^{-1}V^\top e = U\widehat{Ve}^{-1}Ve = Ue \tag{7.17}$$

Commodity technology coefficients are not the only ones that are price invariant and fulfill the material balance. Another example follows.

The European System of Integrated Economic Accounts (ESA) coefficients (EUROSTAT, 1979) are determined by dividing inputs by commodity outputs:

$$\overline{A}(U, V) = U\widehat{V^\top e}^{-1} \tag{7.18}$$

Coefficients matrix (7.18) fulfills price invariance, (7.17),

$$\overline{A}(\hat{p}U, V\hat{p}) = \hat{p}U\widehat{\hat{p}^\top V^\top e}^{-1} = \hat{p}U\widehat{V^\top e}^{-1}\hat{p}^{-1} = \hat{p}\overline{A}(U, V)\hat{p}^{-1} \tag{7.19}$$

and the material balance, (7.16):

$$\overline{A}(U, V)V^\top e = U\widehat{V^\top e}^{-1}V^\top e = Ue \tag{7.20}$$

However, the coefficients of formula (7.18) have another shortcoming. Parallel to the material balance in the quantity system, the value system features a financial balance and the "European" coefficients do not observe it.

The *financial balance* equates revenues and costs for all sectors. Revenues are the value of sectoral output and are given by the row totals of the make table, Ve. Costs comprise material costs and value-added. Value-added is defined residually as the difference between revenues and material costs. The material costs per units of commodities are given by the column total of the input-output coefficients matrix, $e^\top A(U, V)$. The material costs of sector j are, therefore, $e^\top A(U, V)v_{j\bullet}^\top$ (where row vector $v_{j\bullet}$ lists the outputs of sector j). The sectoral material costs can be aligned in row vector $e^\top A(U, V)V^\top$. However, they can also be observed directly through the use table; the sectoral material costs are given by the column totals of the use table, $e^\top U$. Consequently, the financial balance reads:

$$e^\top A(U, V)V^\top = e^\top U \tag{7.21}$$

By theorem 7.1, commodity technology coefficients solve (7.3) and, therefore, fulfill the financial balance, (7.21), trivially, as pre-multiplication with vector $e^\top$ confirms. The industry technology coefficients do *not* observe the financial balance, as a simple example shows. Consider the economy with:

$$U = \begin{pmatrix} 1/2 & 0 \\ 0 & 1/2 \end{pmatrix}, \; V = \begin{pmatrix} 1 & 0 \\ 1/2 & 1 \end{pmatrix} \tag{7.22}$$

The industry technology coefficients (7.10) of data (7.22) are given by:

$$\tilde{A}(U, V) = \begin{pmatrix} 1/3 & 0 \\ 1/9 & 1/3 \end{pmatrix} \tag{7.23}$$

Substitution of matrix (7.23) in the financial balance (7.21), yields:

$$(1 \quad 1) \begin{pmatrix} 1/3 & 0 \\ 1/9 & 1/3 \end{pmatrix} \begin{pmatrix} 1 & 1/2 \\ 0 & 1 \end{pmatrix} = (1 \quad 1) \begin{pmatrix} 1/2 & 0 \\ 0 & 1 \end{pmatrix} \tag{7.24}$$

Working out products (7.25) reads:

$$(4/9 \quad 1/3) \begin{pmatrix} 1 & 1/2 \\ 0 & 1 \end{pmatrix} = (1/2 \quad 1/2) \tag{7.25}$$

Equation (7.25) is nonsense, proving that the industry technology coefficients contradict the financial balance. Example (7.22) also shows that the ESA does *not* observe the financial balance. The coefficients (7.18) are given by:

$$\bar{A}\left(\begin{pmatrix} 1/2 & 0 \\ 0 & 1/2 \end{pmatrix}, \begin{pmatrix} 1 & 0 \\ 1/2 & 1 \end{pmatrix} \right) = \begin{pmatrix} 1/2 & 0 \\ 0 & 1/2 \end{pmatrix} \overline{\begin{pmatrix} 1 & 1/2 \\ 0 & 1 \end{pmatrix} \begin{pmatrix} 1 \\ 1 \end{pmatrix}}^{-1}$$

$$= \begin{pmatrix} 1/3 & 0 \\ 0 & 1/2 \end{pmatrix} \tag{7.26}$$

Substitution of coefficients (7.26) into the financial balance, (7.21), yields:

$$(1/3 \quad 1/2) \begin{pmatrix} 1 & 1/2 \\ 0 & 1 \end{pmatrix} = (1/2 \quad 1/2) \tag{7.27}$$

Again, (7.27) is nonsense, completing the demonstration.

In fact, the commodity technology coefficients are the *only* ones that are price invariant and fulfill the material and financial balances. For square economies this result is due to Kop Jansen and ten Raa (1990). A general demonstration is in section 7.3.

7.3   Different numbers of commodities and sectors

Care must be exercised in the construction of technical coefficients when the numbers of commodities and sectors differ. The ESA coefficients were obtained by dividing sectoral inputs by commodity output totals. Coefficients constructed in this way cease to exist in the absence of a one-to-one relationship between commodities and sectors. The industry technology model is more robust. It was obtained by dividing sectoral inputs by sectoral output totals and, for each commodity, by taking a weighted average of such sectoral input coefficients. This is still doable when the numbers of sectors and commodities differ. Industry coefficients (7.10) are indeed well defined for rectangular matrices U and v of dimensions $n \times m$ and $m \times n$, respectively, where n is the number of commodities and m the number of sectors.

At first sight, commodity technology coefficients cease to exist when the numbers of commodities and sectors differ. The explicit expression of the coefficients given by theorem 7.1 is no longer applicable, since it involves the inverse of a matrix. It is, however, very instructive to investigate the equation that underlies the commodity technology coefficients, (7.3). Let us first discuss some properties of the technology coefficients in a rectangular framework. The requirements of price invariance and of material and financial balance are given by conditions (7.15), (7.16), and (7.21). These conditions continue to make perfect sense for rectangular use and make tables. Moreover, we will prove that only commodity technology coefficients fulfill them. In fact, two of the conditions are sufficient to prove this claim.

Theorem 7.2. Only commodity technology coefficients are price invariant and financially balanced.

Proof. Let coefficients $A(U, V)$ be price invariant and financially balanced. By the latter, (7.21):

$$e^\top A(\hat{p}U, V\hat{p})(V\hat{p})^\top = e^\top \hat{p}Ue$$

Substituting the former, (7.15):

$$pA(U, V)V^\top = pU$$

for all $p > 0$. Now let p tend to $e_i^\top$. Then the last equation shows that the ith row of $A(U, V)V^\top$ equals the ith row of U. Since this is true for every row, the matrices must be equal. Hence $A(U, V)$ fulfills (7.3), the equation that defines the commodity technology coefficients. □

Theorem 7.2 shows that price invariance and financial balance characterize the commodity technology coefficients. The material balance may also be used to characterize the commodity technology model, but the characterization is *not* in combination with price invariance.[1] The pertinent property is now scale invariance.

Input-output coefficients are *scale invariant* if they are constant for constant input-output proportions. If all inputs and outputs of sector i are multiplied by a factor s_i, keeping their proportions constant, the use and make tables turn $U\hat{s}$ and $\hat{s}V$ (where s is the vector with elements si). Scale invariance is given by the condition:

$$A(U\hat{s}, \hat{s}V) = A(U, V) \qquad (7.28)$$

for all $s > 0$. Scale invariance does *not* require that input-output coefficients are constant. It requires such a thing only when use and make tables have the same input and output

---

[1] Remember that the ESA coefficients were also seen to fulfill this pair of requirements.

proportions per sector. In other words, if an economy has constant proportions, then it is required to have constant technical coefficients. Conversely, a change of a technical coefficient must be ascribable to a change in the returns to scale or the proportions of a table. Although scale variance is not as strong a requirement as one might suspect at first sight, it has a powerful implication. □

Theorem 7.3. Only commodity technology coefficients are scale invariant and materially balanced.

Proof. Let coefficients $A(U, V)$ be scale invariant and materially balanced. By the latter, (7.16):

$$A(U\hat{s}, \hat{s}V)(\hat{s}V)^\top e = U\hat{s}e$$

Substituting the former, (7.28):

$$A(U, V)V^\top e = Ue$$

for all $s > 0$. Now let s tend to unit column vector e_j. Then the last equation shows that the jth column of $A(U, V)V^\top$ equals the jth column of U. Since this is true for every column, the matrices must be equal. Hence $A(U, V)$ fulfills (7.3), the equation that defines the commodity technology coefficients. □

Theorems 7.2 and 7.3 do not require that the numbers of commodities and of sectors be equal. Thus, the commodity technology coefficients are the only ones fulfilling conditions (7.15), (7.16), (7.21), and (7.28), whatever the dimensions. Now let us turn to the existence issue. We shall discuss two cases.

Case I: more commodities than sectors

This case is encountered when input-output data are aggregated into national accounts. In the case of the Netherlands (section 6.4), there are $n = 22$ commodities but only $m = 10$ sectors. Because the equation defining the commodity technology coefficients has a component for every input flow, there are 220 equations. On the other hand, the number of technical coefficients is $22*22 = 484$. Consequently there are not enough equations to determine all the commodity coefficients. It is simply impossible to infer the technical coefficients from a single macroeconomic observation with fewer sectors than commodities. This does not disbar economic analysis. In chapter 8 we will analyze national accounts using linear programming.

Case II: more sectors than commodities

This case is encountered when input-output data are in raw form. Business establishment reports of inputs and outputs are organized in worksheets, which are essentially disaggregated use and make tables. The number of columns of the use table and the number of rows of the make table are equal to the number of reporting establishments. The SNA does not force the statistician to aggregate the rows and the columns into macroeconomic sectors. In fact, for the purpose of estimation of technical coefficients it is preferable to preserve the raw data in the use–make framework with separate sectors for all the reporting units.

If the number of commodities is $n = 22$, but the number of reporting units is, say, $m = 100$, the system defining the commodity technology coefficients, (7.3), comprises 2200 scalar equations (one for each input flow), while the number of unknown technical coefficients is 484. It would be a coincidence if any matrix of technical coefficients balanced all the equations. There are so many equations that some of them will be fulfilled only approximately. In other words, an *error term* must be introduced:

$$U = A(U, V)V^\top + \varepsilon \tag{7.29}$$

Equation (7.29) renders the determination of technical coefficients an estimation problem. Basically, the technical coefficients are chosen so as to minimize the error term. For example, if the errors are independent and identically distributed, the sum of squares is minimized. If the errors are not identically distributed, but proportional to output, then establishments may be aggregated into sectors, one for each primary output, and theorem 7.1 may be applied.[2]

The estimation framework illuminates the problem of *negative coefficients*. The problem that the equation defining the commodity technology coefficients yields negatives persists when the numbers of commodities and sectors differ. However, it is possible to estimate the coefficients subject to non-negativity constraints. Moreover, the hypothesis that the non-negativity constraints are true can be tested. The intuition is as follows. Roughly speaking, the imposition of the non-negativity constraints should not push the error terms into a tail of the error distribution. Such an event is considered unlikely and constitutes a basis for the rejection of the hypothesis of non-negativity. Ten Raa (1988) has rejected non-negativity. A problem manifests itself: The imposition of commodity input-coefficients common to all production units seems unwarranted.[3]

7.4   Other inputs

A practical aspect of technical coefficients is that they can be determined on a piecemeal basis, input by input. The commodity technology coefficients for input i, a_{i1}–a_{in}, are determined by the system of equations (7.6), where j runs from 1 to n. This system of equations is specific for input i. The situation is the same for other methods of construction. The industry technology coefficients for input i are determined by the ith row of matrix equation (7.10). This involves the ith row of the use table (representing input i) and multiplication by an expression which depends only on the make table,

$$\widehat{Ve}^{-1}V\widehat{V^\top e}^{-1} \tag{7.30}$$

[2] Econometricians call this "heteroskedasticity of the first degree."
[3] Mattey and ten Raa (1997) provide a rigorous statistical analysis of the problem, and confine it to a small sub-set of inputs.

The same techniques can be applied to determine other technical coefficients, as for capital and labor inputs. Instead of considering the use of input i, given by row vector $u_{i\bullet}$, we now take capital and labor input vectors, K and L, and subject them to the same manipulations. We handle the commodity and industry technology models.

The commodity technology *capital coefficients* are obtained in the same way as the commodity coefficients, given by (7.2) or (7.3). The inputs are divided by the transposed make table:

$$k(K, V) = K(V^\top)^{-1} \tag{7.31}$$

In the same way, the *labor coefficients* are determined by:

$$l(K, V) = L(V^\top)^{-1} \tag{7.32}$$

If we use the industry technology model, (7.10), we multiply by expression (7.30) and obtain the following capital coefficients:

$$\tilde{k}(K, V) = K\widehat{Ve}^{-1}V\widehat{V^\top e}^{-1} \tag{7.33}$$

In the same way, the industry technology labor coefficients are determined by:

$$\tilde{l}(L, V) = L\widehat{Ve}^{-1}V\widehat{V^\top e}^{-1} \tag{7.34}$$

All the coefficients (7.31), (7.32), (7.33), and (7.34) are *direct coefficients* as they measure the amount of factor input per unit of gross output. The labor and capital requirements embodied in the commodity inputs are not accounted. Total coefficients measure the factor input requirements per unit of commodity, directly or indirectly through the production of the commodity inputs. The total coefficients can be calculated as follows. Take commodity 1. How much capital is required to produce one unit? The direct requirement is k_1. However, the commodity inputs, listed in vector $a_{\bullet 1}$, require $ka_{\bullet 1}$ units of capital as well as $Aa_{\bullet 1}$ commodities, which in turn require $kAa_{\bullet 1}$ units of capital, etc. The total requirements are $k_1 + ka_{\bullet 1} + kAa_{\bullet 1} + kA^2 a_{\bullet 1} + \cdots = k(I + A + A^2 + A^3 + \cdots)e_1$. The row vector of *total capital coefficients*, one for each commodity, is therefore given by $k(I + A + A^2 + A^3 + \cdots)$. In other words, *total coefficients are obtained by inflating direct coefficients through the Leontief inverse* (2.18). The total coefficient captures not only the direct requirements, but also all the multiplier effects (chapter 3).

The analysis for labor is completely analogous. If the direct labor coefficients are given by l, then the total labor coefficients are given by:

$$\lambda = l(I - A)^{-1} \tag{7.35}$$

In construct (7.35) l and A can be constructed according to any model, but for consistency it is better to stick to one model and, because of its nice properties, there is much to say in favor of the commodity technology model, although the limitations of this model also appear in the context of factor inputs. The problem of negatives was due to the inversion of the make table and, therefore, may also plague the factor input coefficients. The imposition of common capital and labor coefficients on all producers of a particular commodity is stringent. Chapter 8 analyzes variations of factor input coefficients across production units.

Exercises

1. Consider exercise 3 of chapter 6. What are the capital and labor coefficients, both direct and total?

2. The lump-sum model of technical coefficients simply divides inputs by sector outputs. Write up the formula. Prove that the lump-sum coefficients are scale invariant. Show, by example, that none of the other axioms holds.

3. The by-product technology model treats secondary products as negative inputs. Write up the formula for the technical coefficients. Prove that the by-product technology coefficients fulfill the invariance axioms, but not the balance axioms.

References

EUROSTAT (1979). *European System of Integrated Economic Accounts (ESA)*, 2nd edn., Brussels, Office of the Official Publications of the European Communities

Kop Jansen, P. S. M. and Th. ten Raa (1990). "The Choice of Model in the Construction of Input-Output Coefficients Matrices," *International Economic Review* 31 (1), 213–27; reprinted in Thijs ten Raa, *Structural Economics*, London and New York, Routledge (2004)

Mattey, J. and Th. ten Raa (1997). "Primary versus Secondary Production Techniques in US Manufacturing," *Review of Income and Wealth* 43 (4), 449–64; reprinted in Thijs ten Raa, *Structural Economics*, London and New York, Routledge (2004)

McKenzie, L. W. (1960). "The Matrix with Dominant Diagonal and Economic Theory," *Symposium on Mathematical Methods in the Social Sciences*, Palo Alto, Stanford University Press

ten Raa, Th. (1988). "An Alternative Treatment of Secondary Products in Input-Output Analysis: Frustration," *Review of Economics and Statistics* 70 (3), 535–8; reprinted in Thijs ten Raa, *Structural Economics*, London and New York, Routledge (2004)

van Rijckeghem, W. (1967). "An Exact Method for Determining the Technology Matrix in a Situation with Secondary Products," *Review of Economics and Statistics* 49, 607–8

Stone, R. (1961). *Input-Output and National Accounts*, Paris: OECD

United Nations (1993). *A System of National Accounts*, Studies in Methods, Series F, no. 2, rev. 4

8 From input-output coefficients to the Cobb–Douglas function

8.1 Introduction

The macroeconomic production function of an economy summarizes the maximum level of net output that is possible for any combination of factor inputs. It is customary to consider two factor inputs, *capital* and *labor* (Solow 1957). The disaggregation and extension to more factor inputs is conceptually straightforward (Johansen, 1972). The macroeconomic concept of a level of net output is more problematic. The net output of an economy is a commodity vector and the measurement of a "level" requires a price system. But which price system? This problem of value has puzzled economists for centuries. Classical economists consider capital a produced commodity and labor the ultimate factor input. For each commodity they calculate the labor costs. In chapter 5 we saw that the consequent price system is invariant with respect to the composition of final demand. It could be used to measure the level of net output. If there are two factor inputs, the situation is more complicated. The PPF is no longer straight, but curved. A simple example may be used to illuminate the issue. Consider an economy with two commodities but no material inputs. For commodity 1 we need one unit of labor plus one unit of capital. For commodity 2 we need two units of labor plus one unit of capital. Let the economy be endowed with three units of labor and two units of capital. The production possibilities are plotted in figure 8.1.

The flat line connects all points that are producible with the three units of labor, ignoring the capital constraint. The steep line connects all points that are producible with the two units of capital, ignoring the labor constraint. The production possibility points must be under either line and, therefore, the kinked line gives the frontier. In this situation, neoclassical economists would reason as follows. If final demand for commodity 1 is stronger, then the capital constraint is binding and the marginal productivity of labor is zero. Hence the commodity prices are determined by the capital costs. They would be equal by the symmetry of the capital input structure. If final demand for commodity 2 is stronger, then the labor constraint is binding and commodity 2 gets twice as expensive as commodity 1. The measurement of net output varies with the *location in the commodity space*. A metric that is consistent with the neoclassical reasoning is the distance from the origin to a commodity bundle relative to the distance from the origin to the frontier point on the same ray in output space. By construction, any frontier point would have measure one. If the technology and

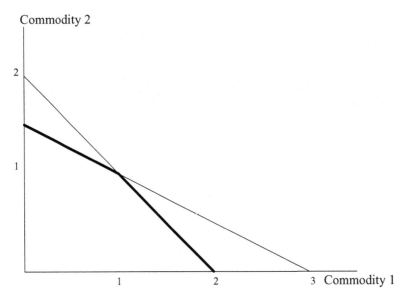

Figure 8.1   A production possibility frontier. (PPF)

the endowment composition remain constant, the metric would suffice to measure the level of any output bundle. If the proportions of output remain constant, it would still be possible to measure the level. However, if we have simultaneous changes in the technology or the endowment composition, on the one hand, and the net output composition, on the other, we have a problem. Such a situation is depicted in figure 6.2.

In figure 8.2, the new PPF reflects the economy with the same input-output coefficients but with more capital and labor. The labor endowment has become four and the capital endowment three. Moreover, assume final demand has shifted from commodity 1 to commodity 2. What happened to the level of output? If we stick to the original metric, the level of the new output (0   2) is a third more than what was previously feasible, namely output (0   1.5). However, if we base the metric on the new technology, the level increases by one-half. Some arbitrariness remains unresolved in the measurement of the national product.

8.2   Derivation of the macroeconomic production function

For a small open economy the situation is brighter, as a natural measure for the level of net output is available. If all commodities are tradable, the world terms of trade determine the opportunity value of each of them. So, if the world terms of trade are given by a row vector p, the value of net outputs is py where commodity vector $y = (V^{\mathsf{T}} - U)s$ is the net output, see definition (5.9). Here matrices U and V are the use and the make tables of the economy (see section 6.4) and vector s is the sectoral activity vector. The national product is $py = \underline{v}s$

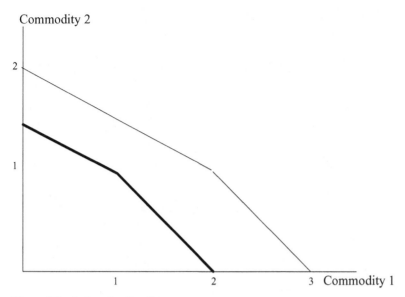

Figure 8.2 A changing frontier

where row vector $\underline{v}$ is given by:[1]

$$\underline{v} = \underline{p}(V^\top - U) \tag{8.1}$$

Vector (8.1) lists value-added. By definition, the macroeconomic production function, F, determines the maximum level of the national product or income that can be attained with a given combination of capital and labor inputs – M and N, say. The question is how to allocate activity such that value-added is maximized subject to the capital and labor constraints. Denoting the capital and labor employment row vectors by K and L, respectively:

$$F(M, N) = \max_{s \geq 0} \underline{v}s : Ks \leq M, Ls \leq N \tag{8.2}$$

The solution to problem (8.2) is determined as in section 4.7. Analogous to program (4.28) the dual program is:

$$\min_{r,w \geq 0} rM + wN : rK + wL \geq \underline{v} \tag{8.3}$$

Only sectors that break even ($rK_i + wL_i = \underline{v}_i$) are active and contribute to the national product. In section 4.7 we have seen that two sectors are active with full employment of capital and labor. The capital/labor ratio of the endowment must be in between the capital/labor ratios of the active sectors. If the endowment were to coincide with the dot indicated in figure 8.3, there would be full specialization in the corresponding sector and

---

[1] Value-added is underscored to distinguish it from value-added coefficients.

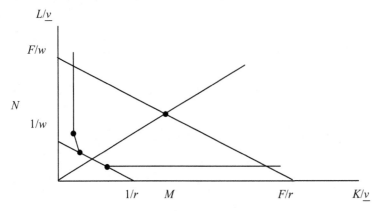

Figure 8.3 Solving the dual program

value-added would be equal to one. Two sectors combine in the generation of one unit of value-added if the endowment is on a line segment between two dots.[2]

The kinked curve in figure 8.3 is the isoquant of capital/labor endowments, which produce one unit of national income or product. All the other isoquants are similar and obtained by multiplication of all the distances from the origin to the isoquant points by a constant. The consequent family of isoquants characterizes the macroeconomic production function.

To implement the derivation of the macroeconomic production function, three data must be available for each sector: value-added, capital employment, and labor employment.

8.3   Substitution

Even when the observed input-output proportions are fixed for every sector, the macroeconomic production function features a lot of substitutability between capital and labor. The substitution does not take place within, but *between*, sectors. From a macroeconomic point of view, the reallocation of activity to a more capital-intensive sector amounts to the substitution of capital for labor. Now, as we saw in chapter 7, the appropriate sectoral units are not broad industries or other groupings of economic activities, but individual production units. The number of "sectors" equals the number of reporting establishments and is very large. Instead of three points, we must have many dots in figure 8.3.[3]

The situation can be summarized by imposition of an establishment density function, $f(K/\underline{v}, L/\underline{v})$, over the plane of figure 8.3 (see figure 8.4, p. 104). Thus, establishments are identified by their capital and labor coefficients, per unit of value-added, and the density function counts them.[4] The isoquant in figure 8.3 approaches a smooth curve. Not all establishments will earn a place on the isoquants. From the solution to the dual program

---

[2] As we have seen in section 4.7, only one sector will be active if the endowment ratio is extreme. For example, if capital were added to the endowment given by the lower dot (figure 8.2), it could not be employed in any sector.

[3] See Hildenbrand (1981).

[4] Warning: The notation F remains reserved for the production function and is *not* the distribution function associated with density function f in mathematical statistics.

it is clear that only the points relatively close to the origin will be selected. The isoquant is the lower envelope of the cloud of production units. A segment of the lower envelope determines the relative factor rewards (through its slope, see figure 8.3) and higher points are inefficient.

As usual we have assumed that an establishment can be operated at any level of activity. In other words, there are constant returns to scale. In section 8.4, we introduce capacity constraints.

8.4 Returns to scale

If there are constraints to the expansion of establishments, capital and labor can no longer be concentrated in just two activities, but must be distributed over a more substantial subset. The involvement of less efficient units implies that the economy features decreasing returns to scale. The analysis is essentially the same. Establishments are to be identified by their capital and labor coefficients, $K_i/\underline{v}_i$ and $L_i/\underline{v}_i$, where $\underline{v}_i$ are the components of the vector (8.1). The density of establishments is given by function f. An additional constraint limits expansion to a full capacity level: $s_i \leq S_i$. The positive level s_i summarizes establishment specific limitations. These qualitative constraints may be of a technical or an organizational nature. The classical example of the limit to production is entrepreneurship – or, more generally, *knowledge*. To expand production you not only need inputs, but also an entrepreneur. If entrepreneurial skills are process-specific, then there is a constraint for each activity.

Definition. The *macroeconomic production function* is given by the solution to:

$$F(M, N) = \max_{s \geq 0} \underline{v}s : Ks \leq M, Ls \leq N, s \leq S \tag{8.4}$$

The macroeconomic production function is conditioned by the capacities, listed in vector S, and determined by the solution to the dual program (4.20):

$$\min_{r,w,\sigma,\tau \geq 0} rM + wN + \tau S : \underline{v} = rK + wL - \sigma + \tau \tag{8.5}$$

Dividing the constraint components by value-added:

$$\min_{r,w,\sigma,\tau \geq 0} rM + wN + \tau S : 1 = r\frac{K_i}{\underline{v}_i} + w\frac{L_i}{\underline{v}_i} - \frac{\sigma_i}{\underline{v}_i} + \frac{\tau_i}{\underline{v}_i} \tag{8.6}$$

The situation is depicted in figure 8.4.

The production units are identified by their capital and labor intensities, $(K_i/\underline{v}_i, L_i/\underline{v}_i)$: the points plotted in the ground plane of figure 8.4. Their capacity density is given by the unimodal surface plotted in the vertical direction. As before, the units with low input requirements will be active. However, since the most efficient units run into capacity constraints, there remains capital and labor to be utilized by other production units. By the phenomenon of complementary slackness (corollary 4.5), only units with zero slack, σ_i, are active. Some of them may even turn out a profit, when the capacity constraint is met. This is indicated by $\tau_i > 0$. By the dual constraint in (8.6), $\tau_i = \underline{v}_i - rK_i - WL_i$ (σ_i is zero for

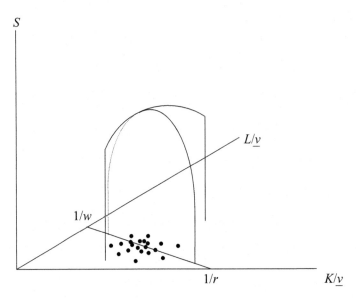

Figure 8.4 Production units at full, partial, and zero capacity

active sectors) or value-added minus factor costs (per unit of activity level). In other words, τ_i is profit per unit of activity.

Note that the non-negativity constraint, $s_i \geq 0$, and the capacity constraint, $s_i \leq S_i$, cannot be simultaneously binding. The production units with σ_i positive reside over the straight line in figure 8.4 and those with τ_i positive are under the line. The (three) units on the line in figure 8.4 are those for which:

$$r\frac{K}{\underline{v}} + w\frac{L}{\underline{v}} = 1 \qquad (8.7)$$

They are active, but the capacity constraint is not binding effectively by theorem 4.2 (the strong form of the phenomenon of complementary slackness).

Since the units above the line are inactive and the units below the line operate at full capacity by the phenomenon of complementary slackness (corollary 4.5), national income amounts to:

$$\sum_{r\frac{K_i}{\underline{v}_i}+w\frac{L_i}{\underline{v}_i}<1} \underline{v}_i S_i + \sum_{r\frac{K_i}{\underline{v}_i}+w\frac{L_i}{\underline{v}_i}=1} \underline{v}_i S_i \qquad (8.8)$$

In the discrete case, *capacity density function f* is concentrated in the observed points $(K_i/\underline{v}_i, L_i/\underline{v}_i)$, where it takes the values S_i. When the number of establishments is large, capacity density f may be approximated by a continuous function, as suggested by the surface in figure 8.4, and the expression for the national income – say, Y – becomes the integral:

$$Y = \int\limits_{r\frac{K}{\underline{v}}+w\frac{L}{\underline{v}}\leq 1} \underline{v}f\left(\frac{K}{\underline{v}}, \frac{L}{\underline{v}}\right) \tag{8.9}$$

The integration is with respect to the identifiers of the production units, $(K/\underline{v}, L/\underline{v})$. We have increased the activity levels of the break-even production units (8.7) to their full capacity values. This change is limited to the boundary of the region of integration, a sub-set of measure zero, and, therefore, does not affect the value of national income. Another simplifying consequence of this observation is as follows. Although the data of the economy consist of the value-added, capital employment, labor employment, and capacity distributions across establishments, or their identifying factor input coefficients $(K/\underline{v}, L/\underline{v})$, we have only to know the product of the value-added and the capacity distribution – that is, value-added at full capacity.

Definition.   The full-capacity *value-added density*, $\underline{v}f$, is a function of the factor input intensities:

$$(\underline{v}f)(K/\underline{v}, L/\underline{v}) \tag{8.10}$$

The full-capacity employment densities are obtained by multiplying (8.10) with the factor input intensities:

$$\frac{K}{\underline{v}}(\underline{v}f) = Kf, \quad \frac{L}{\underline{v}}(\underline{v}f) = Lf \tag{8.11}$$

If the full-capacity value-added density is positive for positive factor input intensities, then any capital/labor endowments ratio can be accommodated and there will be full employment in the determination of the value of the macroeconomic production function:

$$\int\limits_{r\frac{K}{\underline{v}}+w\frac{L}{\underline{v}}\leq 1} \frac{K}{\underline{v}}(\underline{v}f)\left(\frac{K}{\underline{v}}, \frac{L}{\underline{v}}\right) = M, \quad \int\limits_{r\frac{K}{\underline{v}}+w\frac{L}{\underline{v}}\leq 1} \frac{L}{\underline{v}}(\underline{v}f)\left(\frac{K}{\underline{v}}, \frac{L}{\underline{v}}\right) = N \tag{8.12}$$

Equilibrating demand and supply of capital and labor, equations (8.12) determine the factor input prices, r and w. Substitution in the national income expression yields GNP as a function of the factor inputs, M and N. The following result is due to Houthakker (1956).

Theorem 8.1.   Let the full-capacity value-added density be a Pareto function with positive parameters μ, κ, and λ:

$$(\underline{v}f)\left(\frac{K}{\underline{v}}, \frac{L}{\underline{v}}\right) = \mu\left(\frac{K}{\underline{v}}\right)^{\kappa-1}\left(\frac{L}{\underline{v}}\right)^{\lambda-1}$$

Then the macroeconomic production function is Cobb–Douglas:

$$F(M, N) = AM^\alpha N^\beta; A, \alpha, \beta > 0; \alpha + \beta < 1$$

Proof. The density function is positive for positive factor inputs. Hence equations (8.12) are valid. The left-hand side of the capital component becomes:

$$
\mu \int_0^{1/r} \int_0^{[1-r(K/\underline{v})]/w} \left(\frac{K}{\underline{v}}\right)^\kappa \left(\frac{L}{\underline{v}}\right)^{\lambda-1} d\frac{K}{\underline{v}} d\frac{L}{\underline{v}}
$$

$$
= \frac{\mu}{\lambda} \int_0^{1/r} \left(\frac{K}{\underline{v}}\right)^\kappa \left[\left(1 - r\frac{K}{\underline{v}}\right) \Big/ w\right]^\lambda d\frac{K}{\underline{v}} \tag{8.13}
$$

$$
= \frac{\mu}{\lambda} r^{-\kappa-1} w^{-\lambda} \int_0^1 t^\kappa (1 - t)^\lambda dt
$$

We changed variable $t = r\dfrac{K}{\underline{v}}$ in (8.13). Substituting the equation into the capital component of (8.12) and taking the logarithm:

$$
\log M = -(\kappa + 1)\log r - \lambda \log w + c_1(\mu, \kappa, \lambda) \tag{8.14}
$$

In (8.14) the last term is a constant dependent on the Pareto parameters, but not r or w. Similarly:

$$
\log N = -\kappa \log r - (\lambda + 1)\log w + c_2(\mu, \kappa, \lambda) \tag{8.15}
$$

Recalling national income Y, similarly from (8.9):

$$
\log Y = -\kappa \log r - \lambda \log w + c_3(\mu, \kappa, \lambda) \tag{8.16}
$$

It is handy to rewrite (8.16) as:

$$
(\kappa + \lambda + 1)\log Y = -\kappa(\kappa + \lambda + 1)\log r - \lambda(\kappa + \lambda + 1)\log w + c_4(\mu, \kappa, \lambda) \tag{8.17}
$$

Substituting (8.14) and (8.15) into (8.17):

$$
(\kappa + \lambda + 1)\log Y = \kappa \log M + \lambda \log N + c_5(\mu, \kappa, \lambda) \tag{8.18}
$$

Divide (8.18) by $\kappa + \lambda + 1$ and take exponents:

$$
Y = AM^\alpha N^\beta \tag{8.19}
$$

The constants in (8.19) are:

$$
A = e^{c_5(\mu,\kappa,\lambda)/(\kappa+\lambda+1)} > 0, \alpha = \frac{\kappa}{\kappa + \lambda + 1} > 0, \beta = \frac{\lambda}{\kappa + \lambda + 1} > 0 \tag{8.20}
$$

Expression (8.20) immediately implies that $\alpha + \beta < 1$. $\square$

Since the sum of the exponents is less than one, the Cobb–Douglas function features decreasing returns to scale. As the economy expands, the capacity of efficient production units gets exhausted and less efficient units must be activated. The marginal products of capital and labor are diminishing. As they determine the factor rewards, the interest and the wage bills do not exhaust the national product. In fact, the main theorem of linear programming (theorem 4.1) yields that the national product, $\underline{v}s$ equals $rM + wN + \tau S$ – that is interest plus wages plus profit. Entrepreneurial skill earns a profit when it is short.

The Cobb–Douglas function with increasing returns to scale cannot be explained in a competitive framework. With increasing returns to scale, marginal costs are less than average costs. In a competitive economy, prices are equated with marginal costs. Hence prices would be less than average costs, rendering activity unprofitable.

Exercises

1. The marginal rate of substitution of capital for labor of a production function at a point $F(M, N)$, is the amount of capital, ΔM, needed to compensate a unit reduction of labor, $\Delta N = -1$, such that $F(M + \Delta M, N - 1) = F(M, N)$. Show that an economy with a finite number of production units has a marginal rate of substitution that decreases with the labor force, from infinity to zero. Show that the result holds for an economy with a Cobb–Douglas production function.

2. Show that cost minimization in an economy with a smooth production function yields that the marginal rate of substitution equals w/r, the wage rate relative to the rental rate of capital.

3. Argue why this macroeconomic equality does *not* hold for the individual production units with their fixed input proportions.

References

Hildenbrand, W. (1981). "Short-Run Production Functions Based on Microdata," *Econometrica* 49 (5), 1095–1125

Houthakker, H. S. (1956). "The Pareto-Distribution and the Cobb–Douglas Production Function in Activity Analysis," *Review of Economic Studies* 23, 27–31

Johansen, L. (1972). *Production Functions*, Amsterdam, North-Holland

Solow, R. M. (1957). "Technical Change and the Aggregate Production Function," *Review of Economics and Statistics* 39 (3), 312–20

9 The diagnosis of inefficiency

9.1 Introduction

The macroeconomic production function measures the maximum value-added that can be earned by appropriate allocation and utilization of given amounts of capital and labor. In reality, the allocation is not optimal. Consequently, economies are not on, but *within*, their PPFs. The degree by which a net output vector could be extended until the PPF was hit is a measure of the *inefficiency* of the economy. One might view this as the application of the mathematical programming approach to macroeconomic efficiency analysis. The approach has been surveyed by Seiford and Thrall (1990). This measure of inefficiency will be presented in section 9.2 and is related to the macroeconomic production function of chapter 8. Inefficiency may be due to different misallocations. The net exports vector may be sub-optimal given the terms of trade. The amount of inefficiency that can be ascribed to this source is the trade inefficiency. If we take the net exports vector for granted, there may still be room for improvement. In other words, there is also domestic inefficiency. Part of it may be ascribed to the wrong allocation of capital and labor across production units, the so-called "allocative inefficiency," and part to the underutilization of the observed sectoral stocks, the so-called "X-inefficiency." The latter distinction can be traced back to Leibenstein (1966) and Comanor and Leibenstein (1969). The full decomposition into trade, allocative, and X-inefficiencies is presented in section 9.3 and applications to the Canadian and Dutch economies follow in sections 9.4 and 9.5.[1]

9.2 Inefficiency

The informational requirements for the determination of the inefficiency of an economy are basically the same as for the determination of the PPF. We need the use and the make tables, U and V, the capital and labor employment row vectors, K and L, the available stocks of capital and labor, M and N, and a price vector that reflects the terms of trade. In this chapter, only a sub-set of the commodities, T, is tradable. A $|T|$-dimensional row vector, $\underline{p}$, gives the terms of trade. The other commodities are non-tradable. We may assume that the tradable

---

[1] For a review of the input-output literature on decompositions I refer to Rose and Casler (1996).

commodities are listed up front. The net output of the economy comprises domestic final demand plus net exports:

$$(V^\top - U)e = a + \begin{pmatrix} d \\ 0 \end{pmatrix} \tag{9.1}$$

In (9.1) vector d is $|T|$-dimensional (only the T-components of net exports are non-zero). The value of net exports, $\underline{p}d$, is denoted by $-D$, where D is the deficit on the trade balance.

Domestic final demand comprises consumption and investment. Investment is a means to facilitate future consumption. This is why it is included in the objective function.[2] The purpose of this section is to determine by how much we could expand domestic final demand through a reallocation of activity.

Activity levels are normalized by their observed levels. If we consider an alternative activity vector, s, the components greater than unity indicate the production units with increased activity, and the components smaller than unity indicate the production units with decreased activity. The allocation is *feasible* if the capital and labor requirements do not exceed the available quantities: $Ks \leq M$ and $Ls \leq N$. The net output is given by the commodity vector $(V^\top - U)s$ and must be divided between domestic final demand and net exports . As we want to measure by how much domestic final demand can be increased, we consider the decomposition:

$$(V^\top - U)s \geq ac + \begin{pmatrix} z \\ 0 \end{pmatrix} \tag{9.2}$$

In inequality (9.2) scalar c is the *expansion factor* and vector z is the new net exports vector. Domestic final demand cannot be increased by importing unlimited amounts; the trade balance stipulates that $\underline{p}z \geq -D$.

Summarizing, the following linear program determines the maximum expansion of domestic final demand:

$$\max_{s,c,z} e^\top ac : (V^\top - U)s \geq ac + \begin{pmatrix} z \\ 0 \end{pmatrix}, Ks \leq M, Ls \leq N, \underline{p}z \geq -D, s \geq 0 \tag{9.3}$$

If the solution value of program (9.3) is $c = 1.1$, for example, it means that only a fraction 1 of 1.1 feasible final demand is realized, that is 0.91 or 91 percent. In general, $1/c$ measures the efficiency of an economy:

Definition. The *efficiency* of an economy comprising a use and a make table, a domestic final demand vector, capital and labor employment vectors and stocks, and given the terms of trade, is the inverse of the optimal expansion factor in linear program (9.3):

$$1/c^* \tag{9.4}$$

---

[2] More precisely, Weitzman (1976) has shown that domestic final demand is the appropriate measure for the present discounted value of future consumption, at least for competitive economies.

As usual, we write linear program (9.3) in the standard format (4.15):

$$\max_{s,c,z} (0 \quad e^{\top}a \quad 0) \begin{pmatrix} s \\ c \\ z \end{pmatrix} : \begin{pmatrix} U - V^{\top} & a & \begin{pmatrix} I_T \\ 0 \end{pmatrix} \\ K & 0 & 0 \\ L & 0 & 0 \\ 0 & 0 & -\underline{p} \\ -I & 0 & 0 \end{pmatrix} \begin{pmatrix} s \\ c \\ z \end{pmatrix} \leq \begin{pmatrix} 0 \\ M \\ N \\ D \\ 0 \end{pmatrix} \qquad (9.5)$$

Program (9.5) features the $|T|$-dimensional unitary matrix I_T. If we denote the shadow prices of the commodities, capital, labor, the deficit, and the non-negativity constraints by p, r, w, ε, and σ, respectively, dual program (4.20) becomes:

$$\min_{p,r,w,\varepsilon,\sigma \geq 0} (p \quad r \quad w \quad \varepsilon \quad \sigma) \begin{pmatrix} 0 \\ M \\ N \\ D \\ 0 \end{pmatrix} :$$

$$(p \quad r \quad w \quad \varepsilon \quad \sigma) \begin{pmatrix} U - V^{\top} & a & \begin{pmatrix} I_T \\ 0 \end{pmatrix} \\ K & 0 & 0 \\ L & 0 & 0 \\ 0 & 0 & -\underline{p} \\ -I & 0 & 0 \end{pmatrix} = (0 \quad e^{\top}a \quad 0) \qquad (9.6)$$

Writing out the components of program (9.6) and eliminating variable $\sigma \geq 0$, we obtain:

$$\min_{p,r,w,\varepsilon \geq 0} r \geq 0M + wN + \varepsilon D : p(V^{\top} - U) \leq rK + wL, \ pa = e^{\top}a, \ p_T = \varepsilon \underline{p} \quad (9.7)$$

Let us first explain the dimensions of the last equation in program (9.7). p_T is the $[T]$-dimensional vector of prices of the tradable commodities. The terms of trade, listed in row vector $\underline{p}$, are denoted in the world trade currency, typically the dollar. The price vector, p, is given in the domestic currency unit, say the guilder. Hence the dimension of ε is guilders per dollars and ε is the exchange rate. It is also the shadow price of the deficit constraint. Consequently, recalling theorem 4.5, ε measures the increase of domestic final demand per dollar of international debt. Foreign currency is rewarded its marginal productivity. The dual program (9.7) indicates that a low rate of interest, a low wage rate, and a low exchange rate support an efficient allocation of resources. Since the exchange rate is expressed as domestic currency units per foreign currency unit, this means that the currency must be strong.

The first equation in dual program (9.7) explains why the optimal allocation, supported by shadow prices, is an *equilibrium* allocation. Value-added equals factor costs minus slack. By the phenomenon of complementary slackness (corollary 4.5), active sectors have zero-value slack, hence zero profit. By the same token, if profit were negative (positive slack), the sector would be inactive. In short, the prices are such that profits are maximized. Profits are zero, but would be negative in other sectors. The efficient allocation of resources induces specialization in resource-extensive activities.

Theorem 9.1 reveals the relationship between the efficiency measure and the macroeconomic production function.

Theorem 9.1. If all commodities are tradable, the allocation that sustains the value of the macroeconomic production function (8.2) with $\underline{v} = \underline{p}(V^\top - U)$, also solves the linear program that maximizes the level of final demand, (9.3).

Proof. Denote the solution to the macroeconomic production frontier program (8.2) by s^* and define

$$c^* = \frac{\underline{v}s^* + D}{\underline{p}a} \tag{9.8}$$

and

$$z^* = (V^\top - U)s^* - ac^* \tag{9.9}$$

Then (s^*, c^*, z^*) fulfills the constraints of linear program (9.3). Let (s, c, z) be any other feasible point. Then, using (9.3) and (9.8),

$$\underline{p}ac \le \underline{p}(V^\top - U)s - \underline{p}z = \underline{v}s - \underline{p}z \le \underline{v}s^* + D = \underline{p}ac^* \tag{9.10}$$

Hence also $e^\top ac \le e^\top ac^*$. Consequently, (s^*, c^*, z^*) solves linear program (9.3). $\square$

To maximize the level of domestic final demand, it is best to allocate activity such that value-added at world prices is maximized, *irrespective* of the pattern of domestic final demand. In addition to the substitution theorem (theorem 5.1), theorem 9.1 is another result where the supply side of the economy dictates its efficient organization. The capital and labor productivities are independent of the pattern of demand. Linear program (9.3) is therefore a good device to measure the productivities, a line of research that will be pursued in chapter 12.

The relationship between the efficiency measure and the macroeconomic production function value is completed by a comparison of the values of the constituting programs. If trade is balanced, the expansion factor becomes the ratio of the potential GNP (given by the production function) to the observed GNP (given by the national accounts). This statement is easy to demonstrate. The expansion factor is given by (9.8). Here, by (9.1), the denominator reads $\underline{p}a = \underline{p}(V^\top - U)e - \underline{p}d = \underline{v}e + D$, using the expression for $\underline{v}$ given by theorem 9.1. Hence (9.8) reduces to

$$c^* = \frac{\underline{v}s^* + D}{\underline{v}e + D} \tag{9.11}$$

In expression (9.11), s^* supports the value of the macroeconomic production function, $\underline{v}s^*$. Now, if trade is balanced, the deficit is zero, and by definition (9.4) efficiency amounts to $1/c^* = \underline{v}e/\underline{v}s^*$, which is the observed/potential GNP ratio.

9.3   Decomposition

There are three sources of inefficiency – namely, misorientation of the economy *vis-à-vis* the rest of the world, misallocation of activity between sectors, and underutilization of factor inputs within sectors. The decomposition of inefficiency proceeds by a residual analysis. Departing from the optimal, domestic final demand maximizing organization of the economy, we first isolate the trade inefficiency through replacement of the optimal net exports vector by the observed one. The consequent reduction of the expansion factor can be ascribed to the sub-optimal trade position of the economy. The remainder of the reduction of the expansion factor must, therefore, be ascribed to domestic sources of inefficiency: allocative inefficiency and X-inefficiency. A second residual analysis separates the two. Replacing the optimal activity vector by the one that is so close to the actual one that no reallocations between sectors are required, we identify the allocative inefficiency. The residual must be X-inefficiency, the loss of domestic final demand due to the underutilization of endowments at the sectoral level that would be eliminated without reallocations.

If we fix the trade position of the economy in program (9.3), but organize it efficiently otherwise, we face the restricted linear program:

$$\max_{s,c} e^\top ac : (V^\top - U)s \geq ac + \begin{pmatrix} d \\ 0 \end{pmatrix}, Ks \leq M, Ls \leq N, s \geq 0 \qquad (9.12)$$

If we denote the expansion factor of (9.3), involving free trade, by c^{***} and the expansion factor of program (9.12), involving observed trade, by c^{**}, then

$$1 \leq c^{**} \leq c^{***} \qquad (9.13)$$

In (9.13) the first inequality stems from the fact that $s = e$ and $c = 1$ is feasible with respect to program (9.12) and the second inequality reflects the fact that the addition of a constraint ($z = d$) reduces the maximum value of the objective function, or at least keeps it at the same level.

By definition (9.4), the total efficiency of the economy is $1/c^{***}$. It ranges from zero to one. If it is one, the expansion factor is one, and there is no way to boost the level of domestic final demand: The economy is totally efficient. In general, the difference between one and the efficiency level measures the inefficiency of the economy. Thus, the total *inefficiency* is defined by $1 - 1/c^{***}$. Inefficiency can be decomposed as follows:

$$\frac{c^{***} - 1}{c^{***}} = \frac{c^{***} - c^{**}}{c^{***}} + \frac{c^{**} - 1}{c^{***}} \qquad (9.14)$$

In decomposition (9.14) the first term measures *trade inefficiency* and the second term *domestic inefficiency*. If the imposition of the observed trade position has a great effect on the solution to the linear program, then c^{**} is low and most of the inefficiency can be ascribed to the poor trade position of the economy. If the imposition of the constraint has little effect, then most of the inefficiency can be ascribed to the domestic organization of the economy.

Now we pour in additional constraints to rule out reallocations of endowments between sectors. Recall that K was defined as the capital employed in sector i. Let $\overline{K}_i$ be the capital present in sector i. Then the stock of capital is given by:

$$\sum_{i=1}^{m} \overline{K}_i = M \tag{9.15}$$

and $K_i/\overline{K}_i$ is the capacity utilization rate of sector i. The following constraint ensures that the sector operates without the need to reallocate capital from other sectors:

$$s_i \leq \overline{K}_i/K_i \tag{9.16}$$

The next constraint eliminates the need for labor reallocations between sectors, by letting sectors hire additional labor from the pool of the unemployed:

$$\sum_{s_i > 1} L_i(s_i - 1) \leq N - \sum_{i=1}^{m} L_i \tag{9.17}$$

Labor reallocation constraint (9.17) can be rewritten as follows:

$$\sum_{s_i > 1} L_i s_i + \sum_{s_i \leq 1} L_i \leq N \tag{9.18}$$

The reallocation constraints (9.16) and (9.18) can be summarized in matrix notation. Denoting the vector with elements $\overline{K}_i/K_i$ by $\overline{K}/K$, we obtain:

$$s \leq \overline{K}/K, \, L\max(s, e) \leq N \tag{9.19}$$

The restrictions in (9.19) rule out any endowment reallocations between sectors. The second constraint in (9.19) is non-linear, but a trick reduces it to a combination of linear constraints: A number (N, in this case) is an upper bound to a maximum if and only it is an upper bound to each argument of the maximum. It is easy to explain the trick for an economy with two sectors, where the second constraint in (9.19) reads:

$$L_1 \max(s_1, 1) + L_2 \max(s_2, 1) \leq N \tag{9.20}$$

Inequality (9.20) is equivalent to the quadruple of inequalities, where in each case one of the arguments of a max is selected:

$$L_1 s_1 + L_2 s_2 \leq N, \, L_1 s_1 + L_2 1 \leq N, \, L_1 1 + L_2 s_2 \leq N, \, L_1 1 + L_2 1 \leq N \tag{9.21}$$

Similarly, when the number of sectors is not 2 but m, the second inequality of (9.19) is replaced by a system of 2^m linear inequalities.

The addition of the reallocation-barring constraints to the last linear program yields the expansion factor that can be achieved by sheer elimination of waste at the sectoral levels, c^*. We have:

$$1 \leq c^* \leq c^{**} \tag{9.22}$$

The first inequality in (9.22) stems from the fact that the additional constraints do not affect the feasibility of the allocation with $s = e$ and $c = 1$. The second inequality in (9.22) reflects the fact, noted before for (9.13), that a solution value does not increase when constraints are added. Inequalities (9.22) amounts to a decomposition of the domestic inefficiency term in formula (9.14):

$$\frac{c^{**} - 1}{c^{***}} = \frac{c^{**} - c^*}{c^{***}} + \frac{c^* - 1}{c^{***}} \tag{9.23}$$

The last term in the further decomposition (9.23) captures the *X-inefficiency*, since it reveals the expansion that can be brought about without reallocations. The first term in (9.23) measures the *allocative inefficiency*.

9.4   Diagnosis of the Canadian economy

The determination of the efficiency of the Canadian economy requires the following data: the use and the make table, the domestic final demand vector, the capital and labor employment vectors and stocks, and the terms of trade. The capital employment vector is derived from the capital stocks and utilization rates by sector. Ignoring export subsidies, it is assumed that commodities can be sold at current prices $p = e^{\top}$. Then the formal data requirements can be summed up by the list U, V, a, $\overline{K}$, K, L, and N. Here, $\overline{K}$ is the row vector of capital employed by sector while row vector K displays the utilized amounts. The use and the make table and the domestic final demand vector can be taken from the national accounts of the Canadian economy (Statistics Canada 1987). At least in principle, it is also possible to extract the labor employment by sector from the accounts, using the salaries and wages as a proxy. As regards the capital stocks, the use of capital earnings would be problematic, since the cost of capital and profit are not separated in the national accounts. Fortunately, Statistics Canada has separate capital and labor accounts for the sectors. Capital stock and labor employment by sector are listed in table 9.1. Table 9.1 also features the utilization rates of capital, $K_i/\overline{K}_i$, which have been constructed by ten Raa and Mohnen (1994, 2001). Application to the capital stocks yields the levels of employment of capital by sector. The capital endowment equals the total of the gross capital stocks. The labor force is supplied separately. All data concern the year 1980.[3]

The total efficiency of the Canadian economy is determined by c^{***}, the solution to the free trade program, (9.3). The result yields a value of 1.47. By definition (9.4), the efficiency is $1/c^{***} = 0.68$ and the inefficiency is its complement: 0.32 or about 30 percent.

To decompose the inefficiency in X-inefficiency, allocative inefficiency, and trade inefficiency, we must fix the net exports at their observed levels and constrain the activity vector. The first step is to isolate the gain to free trade that comes with the solution of the linear program, c^{***}. However, when the observed net exports values are imposed, the linear program gets stuck at the initial point ($s = e$). The Canadian economy may be so open that any increase of activity requires imports. To investigate this possibility, let us check if

$$(V^{\top} - U)s \geq ac + \binom{d}{0} \Rightarrow c \leq 1 \tag{9.24}$$

---

[3] The analysis is joint work with Pierre Mohnen.

Table 9.1 *Current price capital stock, January 1990 (000 dollars)*

	Beginning of year 1980 gross stock	Capacity utilization	Utilized gross stock	Persons-hours in Canada 1980
1. Agricultural and related services	50,577,600	83.2	42,080,563	1,124,983
2. Fishing and trapping	1,670,800	83.2	1,390,106	66,419
3. Logging and forestry	3,931,200	93.0	3,656,016	120,356
4. Mining, quarrying and oil wells	63,862,324	75.4	48,152,192	300,593
5. Food	9,314,027	83.2	7,749,270	365,415
6. Beverage	3,446,768	83.2	2,867,711	59,430
7. Tobacco products	522,200	86.8	453,270	13,594
8. Plastic products	766,144	86.4	661,948	63,033
9. Rubber and leather products	2,039,415	85.5	1,743,700	97,570
10. Textile and clothing	4,086,015	90.0	3,677,414	324,883
11. Wood	5,554,700	91.7	5,093,660	223,070
12. Furniture and fixture	623,291	86.9	541,640	92,960
13. Paper and allied products	20,067,366	95.4	19,144,267	241,631
14. Printing, publishing and allied	2,847,308	99.5	2,833,071	196,813
15. Primary metals	19,106,100	83.2	15,896,275	238,713
16. Fabricated metal products	5,005,801	82.3	4,119,774	306,132
17. Machinery	1,892,946	94.7	1,792,620	175,533
18. Transportation equipment	8,691,460	67.0	5,823,278	347,822
19. Electrical and electronic products	3,245,277	78.0	2,531,316	252,551
20. Non-metallic mineral products	5,812,500	75.4	4,382,625	103,837
21. Refined petroleum and coal	9,673,900	69.7	6,742,708	32,548
22. Chemical and chemical products	14,795,815	92.2	13,641,741	155,668
23. Other manufacturing	1,054,440	97.5	1,028,079	121,633
24. Construction	8,453,300	66.3	5,604,538	1,295,175
25. Transportation and communication	106,648,160	83.8	89,371,158	1,266,184
26. Electric power and gas	103,986,408	88.4	91,923,986	167,958
27. Wholesale and retail trade	24,009,392	83.8	20,119,870	3,056,772
28. Finance insurance and real estate	30,897,500	83.8	25,892,105	931,097
29. Community, business, personal services	50,818,092	83.8	42,585,561	2,563,001

In terms of *increases* of activity, $s' = s - e$ and $c' = c - 1$, inequality implication (9.24) reads:

$$(V^\top - U)s' \geq ac' \Rightarrow c' \leq 0 \tag{9.25}$$

In matrix notation, inequality implication (9.25) reads:

$$(V^\top - U - a) \geq \begin{pmatrix} s' \\ c' \end{pmatrix} \Rightarrow (0 \quad -1)\begin{pmatrix} s' \\ c' \end{pmatrix} \geq 0 \tag{9.26}$$

By lemma 4.1, inequality implication (9.26) is true if and only if

$$(0 \quad -1) = p(V^\top - U - a) \tag{9.27}$$

for some non-negative vector p. The second component of condition (9.27) merely normalizes the vector. The first component states that the economy cannot expand without increasing imports if and only if the net output table is valued zero by some non-negative vector p:

$$p(V^\top - U) = 0 \tag{9.28}$$

In other words, the economy is not self-reliant if and only if there were a competitive commodity price system, so that all activities break even, with no payments for capital or labor. The way to check condition (9.28) of the net output table is to solve the linear program

$$\min_{p,\mu} \mu : p(V^\top - U) = \mu e^\top (V^\top - U), \ pe = 1, \ p \geq 0, \ \mu \geq 0 \tag{9.29}$$

The combination $p = e$, $\mu = 1$ is feasible in program (9.29). For the Canadian net output table $(V^\top - U)$ the minimal μ turns out to be zero and the first constraint in (9.29) yields the commodity price system fulfilling (9.28). We may conclude that the Canadian economy is not self-reliant. This makes it impossible to separate domestic and trade inefficiencies.

Input-output analysis assumes that input and output proportions are constant at the activity level. When there are many production units, there is a lot of scope for substitution. In chapter 8, we were even able to derive the Cobb–Douglas production function for such an economy. In this application, however, the situation is reversed. The number of sectors is far fewer than the number of commodities. There are so many more commodities that an increase of activity always sparks off a flurry of commodity net input increases. Some of these commodities may not be produced domestically and must be imported. The fixing of the net exports vector is not tenable. The problem is removed when commodities within sectors are modeled as substitutes, as in traditional input-output analysis, allowing the fulfillment of the demand for the imported goods by domestically produced substitutes. This is a first step towards an analysis of the economy where production units enter the account separately, ensuing more scope for efficient improvements.[4]

Table 9.2 gives the aggregation of commodities to the level of sectors. The use and the make tables become square. The solution is given by $c^{***} = 2.20$. Fixing z at its observed level, we now obtain $c^{**} = 1.18$. Reallocations of capital and labor are barred by the imposition of restrictions (9.19). The solution to the linear program with reallocations barred is $c^* = 1.004$.

The expansion leaps are $c^* - 1 = 0$, $c^{**} - c^* = 0.18$, and $c^{***} - c^{**} = 1.02$. Hence the inefficiency of the Canadian economy consists of 0 percent X-inefficiency, 15 percent allocative inefficiency, and 85 percent trade inefficiency. This result confirms that the central problem of the Canadian economy is its misorientation on the world markets.

---

[4] Mattey and ten Raa (1997) investigate the US economy with almost 100,000 manufacturing plants.

Table 9.2 *Sector and commodity aggregations*

Statistics Canada (1990a, 1990b) 29 sectors[a]	Statistics Canada (1987) M-classification	
	50 sectors	92 commodities
1. Agricultural and related services	1	1–3
2. Fishing and trapping	2	5, 6
3. Logging and forestry	3	4
4. Mining, quarrying and oil wells	4–7	7–12, **13**
5. Food	8	14–22
6. Beverage	9	23, 24
7. Tobacco products	10	25, 26
8. Plastic products	12	29
9. Rubber and leather products	11, 13	27, 28, 30
10. Textile and clothing	14, 15	3–35
11. Wood	16	36–38
12. Furniture and fixtures	17	39
13. Paper and allied products	18	40–42
14. Printing, publishing and allied	19	43, **44**
15. Primary metals	20	45–49
16. Fabricated metal products	21	50–52
17. Machinery	22	53, 54
18. Transportation equipment	23	55–57
19. Electrical and electronic products	24	58, 59
20. Non-metallic mineral products	25	60, 61
21. Refined petroleum and coal	26	62, 63
22. Chemical and chemical products	27	64–67
23. Other manufacturing	28	68, 69
24. Construction	29	**70–72**
25. Transportation and communication	30–33	73–77
26. Electric power and gas	34	78, **79**
27. Wholesale and retail trade	35, 36	80, **81**
28. Finance, insurance and real estate	37–40	**82**, 83
29. Community, business, personal services	41–50	84–87, **88**, 89, 90, **91, 92**

Note: [a] The industry codes adopted here are slightly different from those in Statistics Canada (1990a, 1990b), where sector 26 is missing for reasons of confidentiality so that the last sector is indexed by number 30. Non-tradable commodities and the sectors declared non-tradable are shown in **bold print**.

Perhaps more interesting than the macroeconomic measures of the gains to full utilization of sectoral stocks, allocation of activity, and free trade is the identification of the sectors that would bring about the efficiency. These sectors accommodate the comparative advantage of the Canadian economy. From table 9.3 the comparative advantage can be seen to reside in mining, tobacco, and machinery. The commodity composition of the net exports can be found in table 9.4, which in fact has been calculated using the full, disaggregated, use and make data.

The dual constraints in program (9.7) determine the Lagrange multipliers to the material balance, the capital, labor, and the balance of payment constraints. The consequent

Table 9.3 *Sectoral activity levels*

Sector	X-efficient	Allocatively efficient	Totally efficient Square case	Rectangular case
1	1.00	1.14	0.00	0.00
2	1.00	1.18	0.00	0.00
3	1.00	1.08	0.00	0.00
4	1.00	1.19	2.63	5.80
5	1.00	1.18	0.00	0.00
6	1.00	1.18	0.00	0.00
7	1.00	1.18	803.21	30.65
8	1.01	1.24	0.00	0.00
9	1.01	1.26	0.00	0.00
10	1.01	1.25	0.00	0.00
11	1.00	1.08	0.00	0.00
12	1.00	1.18	0.00	0.00
13	1.00	1.07	0.00	0.00
14	1.01	1.20	1.21	1.45
15	1.00	1.18	0.00	0.00
16	1.01	1.23	0.00	0.00
17	1.01	1.43	0.00	14.87
18	1.01	1.22	0.00	0.00
19	1.01	1.27	0.00	0.00
20	1.01	1.21	0.00	0.00
21	1.00	1.15	0.00	0.00
22	1.01	1.27	0.00	0.00
23	1.01	1.31	0.00	0.00
24	1.00	1.18	2.20	1.60
25	1.00	1.17	0.00	0.00
26	1.00	1.16	0.00	1.10
27	1.00	1.16	0.00	1.46
28	1.00	1.18	2.21	1.47
29	1.00	1.18	0.00	1.45

commodity prices, rental rate of capital, wage rate, and exchange rate are reported in table 9.5; these values would prevail under competitive conditions. The first dual constraint in program (9.7) equates revenue and cost for the active sectors (of which $\sigma_i = 0$ according to the phenomenon of complementary slackness, corollary 4.5). The primal program drives the distribution of activity. As we add constraints, the imposition of the observed pattern of trade, and the exclusion of endowment reallocations, to carry out the decomposition analysis, more sectors are activated. The price of their primary outputs must be increased to equate revenue with cost. Since prices are normalized (by the second dual constraint) this must be at the expense of the price of commodities that were produced under free trade conditions, such as the items exported by the sectors that have a comparative advantage. If a factor input price decreases as constraints are added, it means that such a factor would be

Table 9.4 *Net exports (million dollars)*

Commodity	Actual net exports	Net exports under free trade
1. Grains	3,764	654
2. Live animals	169	−993
3. Other agricultural products	−288	−11,035
4. Forestry products	10	−210
5. Fish landings	55	−61
6. Hunting and trapping products	−3	0
7. Iron ores and concentrate	879	**9,150**
8. Other metallic ores and concentrates	−3,015	**28,975**
9. Coal	−328	**4,065**
10. Crude mineral oils	−4,974	**55,776**
11. Natural gas	3,776	**31,904**
12. Non-metallic minerals	733	**9,365**
13. Services incidental to mining	0	10,258
14. Meat products	293	−8,578
15. Dairy products	74	−5,035
16. Fish products	−320	−2,200
17. Fruits and vegetables preparations	−402	−2,856
18. Feeds	42	−427
19. Flour, wheat, meal and other cereals	−30	−472
20. Breakfast cereal and bakery products	5	−2,715
21. Sugar	3	−391
22. Miscellaneous food products	−512	−4,041
23. Soft drinks	−11	−1,368
24. Alcoholic beverages	23	−2,876
25. Tobacco processed unmanufactured	26	**2,256**
26. Cigarettes and tobacco manufacturing	−16	**26,407**
27. Tyres and tubes	−170	−249
28. Other rubber products	−199	−2,862
29. Plastic fabricated products	−436	−2,144
30. Leather and leather products	−449	−1,677
31. Yarns and man made fibres	−330	−57
32. Fabrics	−782	−483
33. Other textile products	−316	−2,209
34. Hosiery and knitted wear	−348	−1,871
35. Clothing and accessories	−456	−5,588
36. Lumber and timber	3,091	−1,085
37. Veneer and plywood	110	−675
38. Other wood fabricated materials	368	−2,458
39. Furniture and fixture	−91	−3,471
40. Pulp	3,571	139
41. Newsprint and other paper stock	3,976	2,378
42. Paper products	−328	−6,443
43. Printing and publishing	−584	−761
44. Advertising, print media	0	0
45. Iron and steel products	417	−13,621
46. Aluminum products	−424	−3,240

(cont.)

Table 9.4 (cont.)

Commodity	Actual net exports	Net exports under free trade
47. Copper and copper alloy products	903	−504
48. Nickel products	1,039	−461
49. Other non-ferrous metal products	999	232
50. Boilers, tanks and plates	−24	−990
51. Fabricated structural metal products	148	−3,354
52. Other metal fabricated products	−1,678	−8,132
53. Agricultural machinery	−1,209	**13,692**
54. Other industrial machinery	−5,535	**31,548**
55. Motor vehicles	924	−11,476
56. Motor vehicle parts	−3,795	−3,527
57. Other transport equipment	90	−4,233
58. Appliances and receivers, household	−1,466	−2,177
59. Other electrical products	−1,693	−8,159
60. Cement and concrete products	95	−2,538
61. Other non-metallic mineral products	−638	−3,120
62. Gasoline and fuel oil	326	−13,529
63. Other petroleum and coal products	1,271	5,107
64. Industrial chemicals	−2,039	−4,047
65. Fertilizers	−64	4,386
66. Pharmaceuticals	−301	−1,643
67. Other chemical products	−1,158	−5,654
68. Scientific equipment	−1,807	−3,966
69. Other manufactured products	−296	−3,971
70. Residential construction	0	1,861
71. Non-residential construction	0	3,785
72. Repair construction	0	0
73. Pipeline transportation	154	−865
74. Transportation and storage	610	−27,322
75. Radio and television broadcasting	−10	−1,991
76. Telephone and telegraph	−49	−8,325
77. Postal services	15	−1,811
78. Electric power	808	−1,081
79. Other utilities	0	0
80. Wholesale margins	2,171	3,093
81. Retail margins	0	0
82. Imputed rent owner-occupied dwellings	0	0
83. Other finance, insurance, real estate	−754	−20,307
84. Business services	−1,205	−3,015
85. Education services	33	34
86. Health services	−17	−136
87. Amusement and recreation services	−150	22
88. Accommodation and food services	0	0
89. Other personal and miscellaneous services	−91	2,425
90. Transportation margins	3,413	7,224
91. Supplies for office, laboratory and cafetaria	0	809
92. Travel, advertising and promotion	0	0

Note: Figures in **bold print** locate comparative advantages.

Table 9.5 *Shadow prices*

Commodity	X-efficient	Allocatively efficient	Totally efficient
1	0.31	1.68	1.03
2	0.18	1.70	1.03
3	0.50	0.93	1.03
4	0.28	0.43	1.03
5	0.58	1.32	1.03
6	0.97	0.88	1.03
7	0.66	0.98	1.03
8	0.79	1.13	1.03
9	0.55	1.17	1.03
10	0.43	1.38	1.03
11	0.50	1.08	1.03
12	0.41	1.36	1.03
13	0.28	0.83	1.03
14	44.60	1.04	1.43
15	0.44	0.72	1.03
16	0.36	0.87	1.03
17	0.30	0.92	1.03
18	0.63	1.05	1.03
19	0.35	0.96	1.03
20	0.55	0.89	1.03
21	0.41	0.59	1.03
22	0.76	0.78	1.03
23	0.60	1.25	1.03
24	0.43	0.97	1.16
25	0.45	1.02	1.03
26	0.10	0.41	1.03
27	0.02	1.48	1.03
28	0.25	0.44	0.69
29	2.69	1.22	1.03
Capital	44%	0%	30%
Labor ($/hr)	0.00	17.30	22.00
Debt	0.00	0.00	1.03

more productive and hence better off under conditions of free trade. Table 9.4 shows that free trade is in the interest of all factor inputs. This is not always the case.

9.5   Diagnosis of the Dutch economy

In this section, the circle comes to a close. In chapter 6 the SNA was presented for the Netherlands. Can we infer the efficiency of the Dutch economy from the accounts? To answer this question, we must determine the potential output of the Dutch economy by maximizing the level of domestic final demand subject to the material balances, the capital and labor constraints, and the balance of payments – i.e. the linear program of section 9.2. As we have seen in section 9.4, the formal data requirements can be summed up by U, V, a,

$\overline{K}$, K, L, and N, where $\overline{K}$ is the row vector of capital employed by sector and K the utilized amount.[5] To extract all these from the accounts, Heberle and van Loon (2003) make some assumptions.

The accounts (section 6.4) featured twenty-two goods and services and ten production sectors, but of the latter "imputed bank services" is deleted, being an accounting construct. Capital employment is approximated by "Other income (gross)" plus "Non-product taxes minus subsidies" and labor employment is approximated by "Wages and salaries" plus "Employees premiums." (This is reasonable if the capital return and wage rates vary little between sectors.) To determine the available stocks of capital and labor, we need the utilization or unemployment rates. We use the readily available statistics of a capital utilization rate of 85 percent and an unemployment rate of 6.9 percent, although the former applies to the year 2000 (Statline, www.CBS.nl). This means that the use of capital could have been 15 percent higher. Applying this argument indiscriminately to all sectors yields the available stocks by sector, and summing these figures yields the capital endowment. The labor force is obtained similarly, by inflating the labor employment figures by 6.9 percent. The linear program will eliminate all this slack and reallocate capital and labor between sectors. Six of the twenty-one commodities are non-tradable, namely "hotels, restaurant services," "repair tools," "public services," "trade and transport margins," "own investment goods," and "goods in process." We assume that the terms of trade are unity. As part of the European Union, the Dutch economy is extremely open indeed.

The overall expansion factor is 1.08. Hence the Dutch economy is $1 - 1.08^{-1}$ or 7 percent inefficient. All sectors would continue to remain active in the optimum, except "mining, quarrying and oil wells" (table 9.1). The greatest expansion would be in "agriculture and related services." Fixing the net exports vector at its observed level reduces the expansion factor to 1.03. Hence the inefficiency consists of 4 percent trade inefficiency and 3 percent remains in the form of domestic inefficiency. Imposition of the reallocation-barring constraints reduces the expansion factor further, down to 1.025. Hence the allocative inefficiency is 0.4 percent and the X-inefficiency is 2.4 percent.

The main lesson of this section is pedagogical. It shows how the accounts can be used to determine the efficiency of an economy, by using additional statistics (factor utilization rates) or assumptions (such as uniform factor rewards). Additional statistics are preferred. In section 9.4 we used sectoral capital and labor employment statistics for the Canadian economy, while in this section we assumed that gross other income and the wage/salary bills were proxies for the Dutch capital and labor statistics. This assumption is crude. The "shut-down" of Dutch mining in the optimal allocation reflects the high gross other income in this sector. The latter includes a huge profit component though, which had better not be treated as a capital statistic.

9.6   Robustness of the efficiency measure

The efficiency of an economy measures its proximity to the PPF. It would be nice if the measure were independent of the demand side of the economy. Our efficiency measure is

---

[5] Recall from section 6.6 that VAT must be deduced from domestic final demand.

defined by linear program (9.3), which maximizes the level of domestic final demand, given its proportions. So it remains to be seen if the maximum level of domestic final demand is sensitive with respect to the pattern of consumption – that is, vector a. The latter is a column in the matrix of constraint coefficients, (9.5). Consequently, the sensitivity of the solution of the linear program can be investigated by formula (4.33). The rate of change of the solution was seen to be given by $-\lambda^*(dC)x^*$ where x and λ are the primal and dual variables and * denotes their optimal values. Confining coefficients changes to changes in a, we obtain $-p^*(da)/c^*$, where p^* is the commodity price vector. This expression can always be made equal to zero, because any change of proportions can be realized by a new vector, a', with the same value, p^*a'.[6] Hence, without loss of generality, we may put $p^*da = 0$ and conclude that the solution of the linear program has a zero rate of change with respect to a. Consequently, our measure of efficiency is insensitive with respect to the assumed proportions of domestic final demand. It should be mentioned that this is a local result, as it is based on formula (4.33), which holds for perturbations, but not for big, discrete changes.

The solution value is sensitive with respect to the other constraint coefficients. In chapter 10 we investigate the role of the terms of trade. In chapter 12 on technical change we investigate the role of the inputs and the outputs, U, V, K, and L.

Exercises

1. Consider exercise 3 of chapter 6. You may assume full employment.
   (a) What is the efficient allocation of activity? *Hint*: Plot the sectors and the endowments in the (labor/value-added, capital/value-added) plane.
   (b) Show that the wage rate would be up by a factor 10/7 and the interest rate down by a factor 20/21. How much does the inefficiency of the economy amount to?
   (c) By immigration, the labor force goes up by 25 percent. What is the effect on the allocation and the factor rewards?
2. Consider exercise 4 of chapter 6. Show that the (marginal) productivities of capital and labor are 1 and 3/2, respectively. What is the efficiency of the economy?

References

Comanor, W. S. and H. Leibenstein (1969). "Allocative Efficiency, X-Efficiency and the Measurement of Welfare Losses," *Economica* 26, 304–9

Heberle, W. and L. van Loon (2003). "The Efficiency of the Dutch Economy in 1989," unpublished paper, Tilburg University

Leibenstein, H. (1966). "Allocative Efficiency vs. X-Efficiency," *American Economic Review* 56, 392–415

Mattey, J. and Th. ten Raa (1997). "Primary versus Secondary Production Techniques in US Manufacturing," *Review of Income and Wealth* 43 (4), 449–64; reprinted in Thijs ten Raa, *Structural Economics*, London and New York, Routledge (2004)

---

[6] The argument is as follows. As a preliminary, note that replacement of a by αa, where α is a positive scalar, yields replacement of c^* by $(1/\alpha)c^*$ and, therefore, keeps the solution value intact. So, instead of $a + da$ we may just as well consider $\alpha(a + da)$. Then the change of proportions is $\alpha(a + da) - a = (\alpha - 1)a + \alpha da$ instead of da and its value is $p^*[(\alpha - 1)a + \alpha da] = (\alpha - 1)p^*a + \alpha p^*da = (\alpha - 1)e^\top a + \alpha p^*da$. This value is zero for $\alpha = e^\top a/(e^\top a + p^*da)$.

ten Raa, Th. and P. Mohnen (1994). "Neoclassical Input-Output Analysis," *Regional Science & Urban Economics* 24 (1), 135–58; reprinted in Thijs ten Raa, *Structural Economics*, London and New York, Routledge (2004)

    (2001). "The Location of Comparative Advantages on the Basis of Fundamentals Only," *Economic Systems Research* 13 (1), 93–108; reprinted in Thijs ten Raa, *Structural Economics*, London and NewYork, Routledge (2004)

Rose, A. and S. Casler (1996). "Input-Output Structural Decomposition Analysis: A Critical Appraisal," *Economic Systems Research* 8 (1), 33–62

Seiford, L. M. and R. M. Thrall (1990). "Recent Developments in DEA, the Mathematical Programming Approach to Frontier Analysis," *Journal of Econometrics* 46, 7–38

Statistics Canada (1987). *The Input-Output Structure of the Canadian Economy*, Catalogue 15–510 Occasional, Minister of Supply and Services Canada, Ottawa

    (1990a). Input-Output Division, "Persons-hours 1961–89," unpublished paper

    (1990b). Input-Output Division, "Current and Constant Price Capital Stock for 1980," unpublished paper

Weitzman, M. L. (1976). "On the Welfare Significance of National Product in a Dynamic Economy," *Quarterly Journal of Economics* 90, 156–62

10 Input-output analysis of international trade

10.1 Introduction

Our approach to international trade is in the tradition of computable general equilibrium modeling. A nice point of departure is the theoretical introduction of Ginsburgh and Waelbroeck (1981, pp. 30–1). They consider the maximization of consumption subject to commodity and factor input constraints. In the empirical part of their book, however, Ginsburgh and Waelbroeck (1981, p. 176) note that such a model could not be handled by available means. In the 1990s progress was made, and the goal achieved.

The key assumption of competitive analysis is that producers make decisions on the basis of the prices of the inputs and the outputs. In small markets, with few producers, this assumption is not applicable and one must take into account the strategic interactions. On big markets, competitive analysis is more relevant. The most appropriate application of competitive analysis is to the world economy, the realm of international trade. In this input-output study prices are competitive, derived from the material balance and resource constraints by means of the theory of linear programming. Production units that would remain active under an efficient organization of the economy break even while the production units failing this test are rendered unprofitable.

The logic is perfectly applicable to the division of economic activity between countries. Roughly speaking, one may pool the sectors of all the countries into an extended system with a make and a use table featuring many production units, and a linear program may be used to locate the activities which would best support the net output of the world economy. This approach is not common, however. International trade theorists have no fundamental objections, but circumvent the data requirements and substitute assumptions. A widely used but bad assumption is that of the availability of a state-of-the-art technology to all national economies. This presupposition removes an important source of the international division of activity from the analysis.

Competitive analysis ought to explain the trade in goods and services between national economies on the basis of the so-called "fundamentals": the endowments, the technologies, and the preferences of the consumers (Woodland 1982). In theory, supply and demand relations can be determined for all goods and services and for all countries, and the equilibrium between supply and demand determines the prices. For this purpose, three assumptions are required. Production units must be price takers; they must be cost minimizers, and, lastly, prices must be flexible. In short, the national economies must be *perfectly competitive*.

However, in reality countries have monopolistic sectors, protect industries, distort prices by taxation, etc. Consequently, the neoclassical prediction of the pattern of international trade will not match the data. The discrepancy between the actual and optimal patterns of specialization can be determined, *if* the neoclassical prediction is truly based on all three fundamentals of the economies: endowments, technologies, and preferences. However, if one element is missing – which is typically the case for technologies – it is no longer possible to predict the pattern of trade independently of the observed values. How do neoclassical economists proceed in such a situation? They basically estimate a model of trade that explains the observed pattern of trade conditional on the available fundamentals, such as endowments and preferences (Leamer 1984). Then the model is specified in such a way that supply and demand are consistent with pure competitive behavior.[1]

Customs authorities collect trade statistics, endowments are documented by employment and other agencies, and preferences are revealed by consumption statistics, but technology data are hard to get. The gap is usually filled by an estimated production function. However, the macroeconomic device of an aggregate production function that associates an amount of "output" with capital and labor inputs is too meager to explain the pattern of trade. The production function should at least reveal the commodity composition of output. A better device, is, therefore, a production function that associates with every factor input combination the set of commodity net output vectors that can be produced with it. Typically, it is estimated by regressing net exports on factor inputs. However, this procedure is justified only if the economy operates efficiently. If the assumption of competition is not fulfilled, the economy will be somewhere within the frontier. To make things worse, the entire concept of a "national production function" need not be the appropriate tool for the analysis of international trade. It presumes that the bill of final goods is produced using domestic technology, but international trade in intermediate inputs may render it irrelevant, as a simple example will illustrate.

Imagine we estimate the production function of Hong Kong to detect its comparative advantage. Suppose there are three commodities: rice, processed food, and electronics. It requires prohibitive amounts of factor inputs to grow rice in Hong Kong. Since rice is an intermediate input into processed food, the factor inputs of the latter are also extremely high using Hong Kong technology. Hence the prediction would be that the comparative advantage of Hong Kong does not rest in rice or processed food, but electronics. This is the original, Ricardian analysis of the comparative advantage of an economy. It is clear, however, how rice trade could nullify the conclusion. Hong Kong could import all the rice it needs and then produce processed food. This situation could be handled by a production function mapping the Hong Kong factor inputs into a net output vector with a huge negative entry for rice. In fact, the negative entry would fulfill all the intermediate demand for rice and the first sector of the economy (rice) would be suppressed. In applied work, however, domestic contributions to intermediate demand are included in the estimation process.

---

[1] An example of this methodology is the work of Diewert and Morrison (1986).

Because the net output comprises many commodities, the regression of net exports as a function of factor inputs is typically cross-sectional. The implicit assumption is that the function is the same across economies. Comparative advantages cannot be ascribed to a technological edge, but to the abundance of resources embodied in the pertinent commodities.[2] Unfortunately, one cannot tell if one tests the prediction of the pattern of trade or the hypothesis that technology is the same for all economies.

Leontief (1953) determined the capital and labor contents of the US export and import bundles and found that exports were more labor-intensive than imports. This is not what one expects of an economy abundant in capital. Leontief believed that the explanation of this paradox is the inefficient operation of capital in many other countries. In his words, an Indian tractor has a driver and another worker "who just sits there." One could say that US technology requires relatively *little* labor and, as we noted in section 9.2, it is efficient to specialize in resource-extensive activities.

A fully fledged account of the factor and commodity inputs and outputs in the different economies is required to determine the technological relations independently of the observed pattern of trade. Input-output analysis fulfills this task. We ground the analysis in the detailed use–make framework developed in section 6.4. Our methodology permits the modeling of technology and a determination of the efficient pattern of trade. The analysis extends Leontief's (1953) analysis of the factor intensity of exports and imports to the determination of the commodity composition of the efficient net trade vector. The latter need not match the observed pattern of trade. In fact, all the fun is in the differences. The true comparative advantages are based on the fundamentals of the economy – resources, technology, and consumption preferences, but not trade statistics – and detected by competitive economic analysis. The latter reveals how an idealized market form would function. The difference between the hypothetical economy and the observed economy captures the gains to full capacity utilization, reallocation, and free trade.

10.2 Partial equilibrium analysis

Partial equilibrium analysis studies the position of an economy *vis-à-vis* the rest of the world given the terms of trade. The analysis of chapter 9 is perfectly applicable and yields the vector of net exports that would be supplied if the economy were organized efficiently, with a focus on high value-added activities. To accommodate full employment of the factor inputs, the number of active sectors will be the number of factor inputs plus a number of sectors producing the non-tradable commodities. For an analysis, see example 4.1. The extreme pattern of specialization has been ascribed to the fixed input-output proportions of activity analysis. For example, Krueger (1984, p. 545) states that:

Programming models which assume a fixed-coefficients production technology are subject to the difficulty that there will generally be no more tradable goods produced than there are primary factors of production in the model.

---

[2] The names associated with this version of the neoclassical theory of international trade are Heckscher and Ohlin.

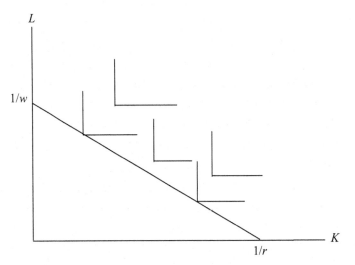

Figure 10.1 Solving the dual program

However, the mechanism of input substitution with its varying coefficients does *not* make specialization less likely. The program can be analyzed via its dual where we minimize the value of the endowments subject to the constraints that value-added is less than or equal to factor costs. As we saw in chapter 4, this amounts to the determination of the (value-added) isoquants in factor input space that just touch the $1 budget line (see figure 10.1).

The L-shape of the isoquants reflects the assumption of fixed proportions: one-sided expansions of either capital or labor yield no additional net output. Now, if we were to replace these isoquants by hyperboles or other smooth declining curves reflecting substitution, the conclusion would not be altered. By the same dual program we still have to find the sectors that just break even. As we saw in example 4.1, this can be done by pushing up the unit budget line in the direction of the endowments of the economy. Note, however, that even when the isoquants are smooth, only two points will be hit again.

In fact, substitution offers *more* scope for specialization in the greatest value-added-generating sectors, as they can adjust their input mix more freely to accommodate the factor inputs. All in all, specialization is not a feature of a fixed-proportions technology, but a consequence of free trade. In other words, if specialization is not observed, one may guess that some sectors are protected. Staunch neoclassical economists who go so far as to reconcile observed net outputs with competitive conditions must take pains to avoid specialization within their model.[3]

---

[3] Diewert and Morrison (1986) assume that activities producing the various observed export items are to be undertaken jointly. They use hyperbole-shaped isoquants not in input space but in output space. This unusual construct is a brute force device to exclude net output bundles with zero components. It also hinges on an *a priori* division between exports and imports, while in my view the big apple on the tree is to explain the directions of trade. The hyperbole shape of the isoquants in output space also violates the so-called convexity assumption of production theory, rendering the whole approach rather shaky.

The determination of activity in a small, open economy under conditions of free trade has been undertaken in chapter 9. When the terms of trade fluctuate, so does the performance of the economy. Price increases of export items boost the earning capacity of the economy, while price increases of import items are detrimental. The analysis of the terms of trade effect is an application of the sensitivity analysis of the linear program examined in chapter 4. The maximum attainable level of final demand is the solution to the linear program (9.3) and the terms of trade enter the balance of payments constraints, $pz \geq -D$. The *terms of trade*, p, constitute the last column of the matrix of coefficients, (9.5). According to formula (4.33), a small change in this matrix, say by dC, changes the solution of the program by $-\lambda^*(dC)x^*$ (where x and λ are the primal and dual variables and $*$ indicates optimal values). If we confine the change in C to the last column, this expression reduces to $\varepsilon^*(d\underline{p}z^*)$, the value change of the optimal net exports vector. Hence the change of the attainable consumption level is positive if the terms of trade increase the value of the net exports and negative otherwise. The result is illustrated by the balance of payments constraint. Since it is binding at the solution, we have $pz^* = -D$. Taking the differential, we see that $(d\underline{p})z^*$ is equal to $-\underline{p}dz^*$. This leakage of net exports measures the reduction of domestic final demand.

The above investigation of the response of an efficient economy to changing terms of trade is partial equilibrium analysis. At least in principle, it permits the construction of the net exports vector for all conceivable terms of trade, and thus of the net supply function. When markets are in general equilibrium, all the net supplies cancel out and this condition can be used to determine the general equilibrium prices for the tradable commodities. The mechanism of general equilibrium analysis is best explained in the case of a world with two countries.

10.3 General equilibrium analysis

Let us consider a pair of economies. The first economy comprises a use and a make table, U and V, respectively. The commodity net output vector is:

$$(V^{\top} - U)e = a + \begin{pmatrix} d \\ 0 \end{pmatrix} \tag{10.1}$$

In expression (10.1) vector a represents domestic final demand and (lower-dimensional) vector d net exports. (Net exports are available only for the tradable commodities; the other components are zero.) Capital and labor employment by sector are given by the row vectors K and L. Their total stocks are M and N. Instead of the observed net exports, d, we are interested in the competitive net exports, z. It will call for a different vector of activity levels – s instead of e. The new allocation is *feasible* if

$$(V^{\top} - U)s \geq ac + \begin{pmatrix} z \\ 0 \end{pmatrix}, \; Ks \leq M, Ls \leq N, s \geq 0 \tag{10.2}$$

for some non-negative level of domestic final demand, c. The latter constitutes the objective of the first economy. The feasibility constraints do not include a debt constraint. In general equilibrium analysis, the world prices are not known, but are to be determined, and it is, therefore, impossible to specify a debt constraint *a priori*.

The (similar) data of the second economy are denoted with tildes: $\tilde{U}$, $\tilde{V}$, $\tilde{a}$, $\tilde{d}$, $\tilde{K}$, $\tilde{L}$, $\tilde{M}$, $\tilde{N}$. The commodity classification is the same as in the first economy, but the sector classification may differ (ten Raa 1995). Even the number of sectors may be different. Trade links the two economies and the net exports of the one equal the net imports of the other: $d = -\tilde{d}$. The variables of the economies are s, c, z, $\tilde{s}$, and $\tilde{c}$, where z controls the net exports of the second economy as well, as these are equal to $-z$. The material balance of the second economy reads

$$(\tilde{V}^\top - \tilde{U})\tilde{s} \geq \tilde{a}\tilde{c} - \begin{pmatrix} z \\ 0 \end{pmatrix} \tag{10.3}$$

The material balances of the tradable commodities, (10.2) and (10.3), may be pooled. By summation:

$$(V^\top - U)s + (\tilde{V}^\top - \tilde{U})\tilde{s} \geq_T ac + \tilde{a}\tilde{c} \tag{10.4}$$

Subscript T restricts the inequality (10.4) to its first components, namely those of the *tradable* commodities. Conversely, if the pooled material balance holds, (10.4), then the country-specific balances, (10.2) and (10.3), hold by appropriate choice of net exports, namely $z = [(V^\top - U)s - ac]_T$, where T again selects the tradables. Consequently, there will be one shadow price vector for the tradable commodities, p_T, and we may use variables s and c to control trade variable z.

The capital and/or labor constraints may or may not be pooled. If there is no mobility of factor inputs, they must remain separate, and the shadow prices will be country-specific. If some factor is mobile, then its constraints may be pooled. As in the case of tradable commodities, there would be one shadow price if the factor input were mobile.

To summarize, we have material and factor input constraints, pooled for tradable or mobile inputs and separate for the two countries when the input is non-tradable or immobile. The objective is the consumption level $-c$ for one economy and $\tilde{c}$ for the other. There is a conflict of interest. If all sources of inefficiency are eliminated, it may still be possible to increase a level of domestic final demand, but only at the expense of the level in the other economy, so that we have a trade-off between the economies. The way to model this is to scan all possible directions in $(c, \tilde{c})$-space by letting $\tilde{c} = \gamma c$. For example, if $\gamma = 1$, we expand the two economies at a common rate. If $\gamma = 2$, we value improvements in the second economy twice as much as in the first economy. If $\gamma = 0$ we attach no weight at all to the second economy; any net output will be shipped to the first economy. Conversely, if γ tends to infinity, we put all the weight on the second economy.

For every non-negative value of γ we now have a well-defined linear program to determine the domestic sectoral activity levels, s and $\tilde{s}$, the trade vector, z, and the levels of domestic final demand, c and $\tilde{c}$ $(= \gamma c)$. The shadow prices yield the commodity prices (world-wide in case of tradables and country-specific otherwise) and the rental rate(s) of capital and the wage rates. The solutions will depend on the scan parameter, γ. If $\gamma = 0$, no importance is ascribed to country II, and its net output is used to feed country I. Country I imports a lot

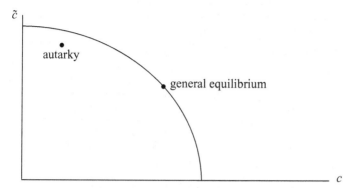

Figure 10.2 The world production possibilities set

and the value of its net export vector, $p_T z$, is negative. Conversely, if γ becomes big, all net output of country I is used to feed country II, and $p_T z$ is positive. In general equilibrium analysis, one assumes that there is a balance of payments. In other words, γ is increased until the value of net exports, $p_T z$, becomes zero – or, more generally, the observed trade balance, $p_T d$, where d is the actual vector of net exports given in (10.1). (The balance of payments can be non-zero in the period under consideration – e.g. to repay accumulated debt.) The allocation of activity and the shadow prices that are then obtained constitute the general equilibrium. In both countries, active production units break even and the others are unprofitable.

It is instructive to map the domestic final demand solution values as a function of γ. It yields the country utility frontier in the $(c, \tilde{c})$ -plane (figure 10.2). Points to the East are unfavorable to country II and correspond to low values of γ.

Points to the North correspond to high values of γ. All points on or under the frontier are feasible. The ones on the frontier correspond to the solutions of the linear program for different values of γ and the ones under it can be thought of as being brought about by disposal of commodities. (The material balances are inequalities and c and $\tilde{c}$ may always be lowered.) The allocation with actual net exports, d, is feasible with respect to some linear program, namely that associated with $\gamma = 1$, and therefore within the frontier. An interesting question is if the general equilibrium point dominates the observed point. At least in principle, it would be conceivable that the situation is as in figure 10.2. Here the observed point is within the frontier and the general equilibrium is on the frontier, but the latter is worse for one country (country II). If this is the case, free trade would be efficient, but not fair.

Trade could improve the observed allocation, by a move to the Northeast, but the balance of payments constraint would shift the allocation of utility on the frontier in a Southeastern direction and leave country II worse off; the value of γ would be so low that it offsets the expansion gains. However thinkable, this situation can and will be ruled out. In other words, free trade is mutually beneficial. In fact, in the remainder of this section we demonstrate the astounding result that the free trade equilibrium is beneficial to both economies compared not only to the observed allocation, but compared to *any* allocation achievable without changing their trade position.

For this purpose, we consider the general equilibrium program explicitly:

$$\max_{s,c,\tilde{s},z} c : \begin{pmatrix} U - V^\top & a & 0 & \begin{pmatrix} I_T \\ 0 \end{pmatrix} \\ K & 0 & 0 & 0 \\ L & 0 & 0 & 0 \\ -I & 0 & 0 & 0 \\ 0 & \tilde{a}\gamma & \tilde{U} - \tilde{V}^\top & \begin{pmatrix} -I_T \\ 0 \end{pmatrix} \\ 0 & 0 & \tilde{K} & 0 \\ 0 & 0 & \tilde{L} & 0 \\ 0 & 0 & -I & 0 \end{pmatrix} \begin{pmatrix} s \\ c \\ \tilde{s} \\ z \end{pmatrix} \leq \begin{pmatrix} 0 \\ M \\ N \\ 0 \\ 0 \\ \tilde{M} \\ \tilde{N} \\ 0 \end{pmatrix} \tag{10.5}$$

where γ is determined *ex post* so as to balance trade:

$$p_T z = p_T d \tag{10.6}$$

Let row vector $(p \quad r \quad w \quad \sigma \quad \tilde{p} \quad \tilde{r} \quad \tilde{w} \quad \tilde{\sigma})$ list the shadow prices associated with the eight constraints in program (10.5). The dual constraints are set up in the usual way. By the dual program, (4.20), pre-multiplication of the coefficients matrix in program (10.5) by the row vector of shadow prices yields the row vector of objective function coefficients:

$$(p \quad r \quad w \quad \sigma \quad \tilde{p} \quad \tilde{r} \quad \tilde{w} \quad \tilde{\sigma}) \begin{pmatrix} U - V^\top & a & 0 & \begin{pmatrix} I_T \\ 0 \end{pmatrix} \\ K & 0 & 0 & 0 \\ L & 0 & 0 & 0 \\ -I & 0 & 0 & 0 \\ 0 & \tilde{a}\gamma & \tilde{U} - \tilde{V}^\top & \begin{pmatrix} -I_T \\ 0 \end{pmatrix} \\ 0 & 0 & \tilde{K} & 0 \\ 0 & 0 & \tilde{L} & 0 \\ 0 & 0 & -I & 0 \end{pmatrix} = (0 \quad 1 \quad 0 \quad 0)$$

$$\tag{10.7}$$

The last component of vector equation (10.7) confirms that the prices of the tradable commodities are equal across the two countries:

$$p_T = \tilde{p}_T \tag{10.8}$$

The general equilibrium value of γ is chosen as to meet (10.6). Let us analyze the general equilibrium level of final demand in country I, c^*, and the sustaining activity vector, s^*. The main constraint is feasibility, the first constraint in program (10.5):

$$ac^* \leq (V^\top - U)s^* - \begin{pmatrix} z \\ 0 \end{pmatrix} \tag{10.9}$$

Pre-multiplying vector inequality (10.9) with price and invoking the phenomenon of complementary slackness (corollary 4.5):

$$pac^* = p(V^\top - U)s^* - p_T z = p(V^\top - U)s^* - p_T d \qquad (10.10)$$

The last step in (10.10) is the general equilibrium condition (10.6). The right-hand side of (10.10) can be simplified using the first component of dual constraint (10.7), which is given by the first equation of dual program (9.7):

$$pac^* = (rK + wL - \sigma)s^* - p_T d = rM + wN - p_T d \qquad (10.11)$$

The second step in (10.11) is by application of the phenomenon of complementary slackness (corollary 4.5) to the factor inputs and the non-negativity constraints in program (10.5).

We claim that the free trade solution, c^*, is better than any other final demand level c that is attainable under the observed trade vector, d. To substantiate our claim we must show that pac is less than pac^* or the right-hand side of (10.11). Notice that in the expression pac the price vector, p, that supports the *equilibrium* allocation s^* is used to value the level of final demand, c, associated with the *arbitrary* allocation, s. By the material and factor constraints of (arbitrary) allocation, s (see program (10.5)), but invoking properties of the general equilibrium prices (see the first component of dual constraint (10.7)), and mere non-negativity of σ and s,

$$pac \leq p(V^\top - U)s - p_T d = (rK + wL - \sigma)s - p_T d$$
$$\leq (rK + wL)s - p_T d \leq rM + wN - p_T d \qquad (10.12)$$

Comparison of inequality (10.12) with equality (10.11) shows that any final demand level, c, achievable by the first economy without changing its trade position, d, is dominated by the level under free trade, c^*.[4]

The result and argument for the other economy is completely analogous. Free trade is not only good for the whole, but for each and every participant.

10.4 The gains to free trade

The linear program that determines the free trade equilibrium takes the pair (or system) of economies to its frontier. If the allocation were within the frontier, it would be possible to have more output and to allocate it to domestic final demand in both economies. In other words, the level of domestic consumption would not be maximized. Each economy must operate on its frontier *and* the division of labor must be rational. This is where the principle of *comparative advantage* enters the scene.

Let us illustrate our analysis with a simple example. Two economies have equal endowments but different technologies. One economy has an absolute advantage over the other. Yet

---

[4] Strictly speaking, this argument is valid only if we can divide (10.11) and (10.12) by pa, hence if we can rule out $pa = 0$. A way of doing this is to assume that domestic final demand, a, is positive. Then $pa = 0$ only if $p = 0$, but this would mean, by the strong form of complementary slackness discussed in chapter 4, that all material balances have slack, hence that domestic final demand could be expanded, contradicting the maximization in program (10.5).

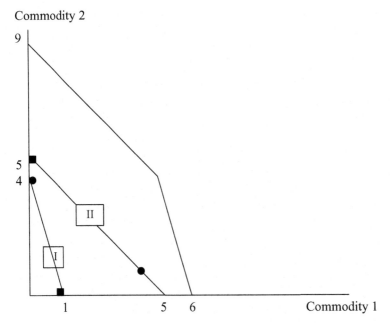

Figure 10.3 The production possibilities frontier (PPF) of two countries
Note: Square dots denote the autarky allocation, round dots denote the free trade allocation.

there will be trade, as the latter is driven by comparative advantages. Initially, we consider only one factor input – say, labor. The first economy can produce one unit of commodity 1, 4 units of commodity 2, or any linear combination of the two. The second economy has the absolute advantage and can produce 5 units of either commodity. The first economy has a comparative advantage in commodity 2, as the opportunity cost of a unit of commodity 2 is only a quarter-unit of commodity 1, while it is a full unit in the second economy. For simplicity, the use tables are assumed to be zero. Domestic final demand is different in the two economies. The first economy consumes commodity 1 and the second economy commodity 2 (both exclusively). Notice that in autarky the first economy can consume only one unit of commodity 1 but the second economy can consume five units of commodity 2.

In figure 10.3 the autarky points are given by the square dots. The lower, steep line is the PPF of country I and the middle line (with a 45 degree slope) is the frontier of country II. If you sum all the possible frontier outputs, you get the upper, kinked line. This is the world PPF.

The maximum output of commodity 1 is obtained when both countries produce it: $1 + 5 = 6$. Starting from this point, how could some commodity 2 be produced, forgoing as little of commodity 1 as possible? The answer is: by reallocating some labor in country I as it has the steeper frontier, yielding more commodity 2 per unit of commodity 1 forgone. This argument also implies that the costs in country I will determine the commodity prices, until we reach the kink in the world production frontier. At that point, country I produces commodity 2 and country II produces commodity 1. (This is the exact opposite of the autarky allocation.) From there on, the world PPF is obtained by also engaging country II in the production of commodity 2. Now country I is specialized (in commodity 2) and country II produces both commodities. The relative prices are now determined by the costs of country II, and hence are equal.

Where is the equilibrium? First we show that it cannot be a point on the first, Southeastern segment of the world PPF. Here country I produces $1 - \theta$ units of commodity 1 and 4θ units of commodity 2, where $0 \le \theta \le 1$. The opportunity cost of commodity 2 is a quarter of that of commodity: $p_2 = \frac{1}{4}p_1$. Since country I is not interested in consuming commodity 2, it is all for export. The value of export of country I is $p_2 4\theta$. Country II produces 5 units of commodity 1. Since it does not want to consume it, it is all for export. The value of export of country II is $p_1 5 = 4p_2 5$. In equilibrium, the payments must balance, hence $\theta = 5$, a contradiction with $0 \le \theta \le 1$.

It follows that the equilibrium must reside on the second, Northwestern segment of the world PPF. Here, the relative commodity prices are determined by the (one-to-one) trade-off in country II: $p_1 = p_2$. Country II produces $5 - \theta$ units of commodity 1 and θ units of commodity 2. The former are for export. Country I produces 4 units of commodity 2, all for export. Since the prices are equal, it must be, in equilibrium, that $\theta = 1$. It follows that country II produces 4 units of commodity 1 and 1 unit of commodity 2. The equilibrium allocation is denoted by round dots in figure 10.3.

So, what is the effect of free trade on the well-being of the consumers? The example has been set up so as to make the answer exceedingly simple yet surprising. The simplicity comes with the observation that the total output of commodity 1 (2) measures the level of final demand in country I (II). Under autarky, the figures were $1 + 0$ and $0 + 5$, respectively, where terms represent country contributions. Under free trade, the figures are $0 + 4$ and $4 + 1$, respectively. It follows that the expansion factors of the last section are $c = 4$ and $\tilde{c} = 1$. (Hence the equilibrium value of the scan parameter γ in $\tilde{c} = \gamma c$ is only 0.25.)

The message of the example is that the gains to trade may be very uneven. In fact, country II has zero gains to trade. The reason is that this, big economy produces both commodities. Its own costs determine the relative prices and hence the terms of trade. Trade does not offer an advantage over home production. The small economy, however, has a comparative advantage in the commodity, 2, that happens to be in great demand. This commodity is cheap in terms of autarky prices but expensive in the other country.

The distribution of the gains to free trade with respect to functional income is even more ambiguous. The straight lines in figure 10.1 represent the labor constraints. If we introduce capital, we would have similar straight lines representing the capital constraint, and the production possibility sets would be the kinked sets under two lines, as in figure 10.4.

The analysis is basically the same; the general equilibrium allocation points are positioned slightly closer to the origin, as the other factor constraints (than in the autarky points) become binding. This example shows that the gains to trade can have an extremely uneven distribution within countries. In figure 10.4 one constraint is binding under autarky and the other under free trade. The rewards would completely shift from one factor to another. A factor that is binding under autarky but no longer under free trade would stand

Commodity 2

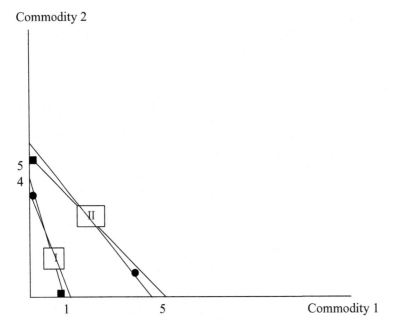

Figure 10.4 The production possibilities of two countries with two factors
Note: Square dots denote the autarky allocation, round dots denotes the free trade allocation

to lose. Free trade may redistribute national income sharply, and not necessarily in an equitable way.

10.5   Distortions

Although the resulting level of domestic consumption is higher, politicians get scared by the distributional consequences that surround the transition to free trade and hamper the process by protecting vested interests. Quotas or tariffs restrict imports. The purpose of this section is to estimate the inefficiency that comes with political interference in free, competitive markets.

The extreme case of protection is a return to autarky, with net exports given by $z = 0$. The general case of quotas can be modeled by constraints on z. From a formal point of view we have already handled partial protection cases. In the preceding analysis, some commodities were tradable and others non-tradable. We have shown that the elimination of all trade was detrimental to all parties. Note that it is immaterial to the analysis if the non-tradability was for physical or institutional reasons. For example, if the government restricts trade in some commodities, then further restrictions would be detrimental. In this way, we can argue that any partial limitation to free trade is detrimental. The drop in the objective value of the general equilibrium program measures the inefficiency.

A simple example is as follows. Suppose country II sets import quotas. Then the net exports vector, z, is bounded – say, by Z. This restriction is modeled by augmenting the constraint coefficients

$$\begin{pmatrix} 0 & 0 & 0 & \begin{pmatrix} I_T \\ 0 \end{pmatrix} \end{pmatrix}$$

to the matrix in program (10.5) and Z to the vector of bounds. Denote the shadow price of the added constraint by t. Then t is a row vector of the dimension of the tradable commodities and the last component of the dual constraint becomes $p_T - \tilde{p}_T + t = 0$. Consequently $\tilde{p}_T = p_T + t$. In the quota-imposing country, the prices of the tradable commodities go *up*, at least for the commodities where the quotas are effective. The costs of the quotas are given by the shadow prices, t, using the marginal productivity interpretation given in theorem 4.5.

The analysis reveals the implicit tariffs of quotas. By the dual constraints, the tariff is such that the domestic industries producing the protected output are no longer unprofitable, but break even. Thus, the price of a quota is expressed in the shadow tariff. In this way, non-tariff restrictions to free trade can be represented by tariff equivalents and addition to the tariffs yields an overall measure of protection for each commodity.

Although quotas and tariffs have equivalent effects on the allocation of resources across sectors, they differ as regards their income effects. When trade is restricted by quota, the tariff is implicit and merely appears as a price increase reflecting the cost of import substitution. The new high price applies to all units, including those within the quota. Suppliers collect the implicit tariff. The domestic suppliers need them to defray the costs of home production. The foreign suppliers reap a windfall profit. Where the tariff is imposed through customs in the importing country, the government of the latter at least collects it. Either policy is bad, though, because the national consumption levels are reduced. On top of this, quota policies have the added disadvantage of letting the rents associated with the restrictions leak abroad. As a matter of fact, it raises the earnings of foreign suppliers above competitive levels. A good example is the US protection of automobiles by quota. It reduces the level of consumption in the world, including the United States, and shifts income to the Japanese automobile suppliers who prospered in periods of American quotas. A tariff would have the same distortionary effects, but at least it would not transfer income abroad. Non-tariff quotas are irrational. The General Agreement on Trade and Tariffs (GATT) prohibits them, but governments try to negotiate them "under the counter."

10.6 Application

A predecessor of this study is Williams (1978) who, however, sticks to the observed pattern of trade, as do Diewert and Morrison (1986) and Chipman and Tian (1992). An application with the direction of trade endogenous is by ten Raa and Mohnen (2001). They calculate the efficient allocation of activity between Europe and Canada and locate the Canadian comparative advantage in minerals, machines, and clothing and footwear. In Europe, the other sectors (primarily manufacturing) would benefit from free bilateral trade. In autarky, labor is scarcer in Europe and capital is scarcer in Canada, according to the respective shadow prices. Free markets, however, would produce neither migratory pressure nor capital movements, as the factor input prices are nearly equalized. This result hinges on the observed structures of the economies and not on the theory of international trade where such equalization is predicted on the assumption of equal technologies.

Exercises

1. Consider exercise 9 of chapter 4. In which sector would this economy specialize under free trade with given terms of trade?
2. Trace the effects of inflation of the world trade currency unit on the allocation of activity and the prices of commodities and factor inputs (including the exchange rate) of the economy that maximizes the level of consumption.

References

Chipman, J. S. and Tian, G. (1992). "A General-Equilibrium Intertemporal Model of an Open Economy," *Economic Theory* 2 (2), 215–46

Diewert, W. E. and C. J. Morrison (1986). "Adjusting Output and Productivity Indexes for Changes in the Terms of Trade," *Economic Journal* 96, 659–79

Ginsburgh, V. and J. Waelbroeck (1981). *Activity Analysis and General Equilibrium Modelling*, Amsterdam, North Holland

Krueger, A. O. (1984). "Trade Policies in Developing Countries," in R. W. Jones and P. B. Kenen (eds.), *Handbook of International Economics* I, Amsterdam, Elsevier Science Publishers

Leamer, E. E. (1984). *Sources of International Comparative Advantage*, Cambridge, MA, MIT Press

Leontief, W. (1953). "Domestic Production and Foreign Trade: The American Capital Position Re-examined," *Proceedings of the American Philosophical Society* 97 (4), 332–49

ten Raa, Th. (1995). "Commodity and Sector Classifications in Linked Systems of National Accounts," in E. Giovannini (ed.), "Social Statistics, National Accounts and Economic Analysis," *Annali di Statistica*, Serie X, 6, 31–6; reprinted in Thijs ten Raa *Structural Economics*, London and New York, Routledge (2004)

ten Raa, Th. and P. Mohnen (2001). "The Location of Comparative Advantages on the Basis of Fundamentals Only," *Economic Systems Research* 13 (1), 93–108; reprinted in Thijs ten Raa, *Structural Economics*, London and New York, Routledge (2004)

James R. Williams (1978). *The Canadian–United States Tariff and Canadian Industry: A Multisectoral Analysis*, Toronto, University of Toronto Press

A. D. Woodland (1982). *International Trade and Resource Allocation*, Amsterdam, North-Holland

11 Environmental input-output economics

11.1 Introduction

In this chapter we analyze two types of environmental items: natural resources and pollutants. Natural resources are consumed "goods" and pollutants are produced "bads."[1] The consumption of natural resources will be analyzed in section 11.4 and the production of pollutants in section 11.5. Fundamentally, there is little difference. Instead of recording a pollutant such as smoke, we could just as well account for a natural resource such as clean air.

The main problem of the environment is that property rights are not specified. Overfishing occurs because neither the fish nor the sea belongs to anyone. Pollution takes place and affects the air, which belongs to no one particular. If there were an owner of the fish, he or she could charge a price for their extraction. If the right to clean air were specified, polluters could be fined. There are three policies which address environmental problems. The first is to impose *quantity limits* on destructive activities, such as a fish quotas or an emission standard. The second is to discourage environmentally harmful activities by *taxation*. The third is to specify particular *property rights*. The policies will be introduced and compared in section 11.2 by means of a simple example. Section 11.3 embeds the environmental accounts in the use–make framework. Section 11.6 analyzes international spillovers.

11.2 Standards, taxes, or rights to pollute

Consider an economic activity that is harmful to the environment, such as the production of chemicals. Denote the activity level by $s = 0$, 1, 2, and 3. Let profit be 0, 3, 4, and 3, respectively. At the high level of activity, the firm would erode its own market. The price must be very low to sell all the output.[2] The utility of the local inhabitants is a declining function of activity with values 6, 5, 3, and 0, say. The profit maximizing level of activity is $s = 2$ (with profit 4). If the utility is also expressed in dollars, the socially optimal level of activity would be $s = 1$. At this level, the sum of profit and utility would be $3 + 5 = 8$. Table 11.1 shows that this is the maximum.

---

[1] At least in principle one may also think of "goods" which are added to and "bads" which are subtracted from the economy, but they would not constitute a problem of scarcity.

[2] Alternatively, one may think of decreasing returns to scale.

139

Table 11.1 *Profit and environmental impact of production*

Activity	Profit	Utility	Total
0	0	6	6
1	3	5	8
2	4	3	7
3	3	0	3

Taking into account the negative effect of the economic activity on the environment the market level of operation ($s = 2$) is too high. The three policies outlined above have the potential to correct this.

The first policy is to *set a standard* for pollution; the government may impose a limit on production, $s \leq s_0$. If the government sets the limit at 1, then a profit maximizing firm subject to the public control would operate at $s = 1$ (as $s = 0$ is less profitable) and hence serve the public interest. This solution is essentially the same as central planning. The government determines the optimal level of activity and imposes it as a constraint. There are at least two problems with this type of policy. First, any quantitative assessment of the optimal level of operation may well be beyond the power of the government. Second, even when optimal levels of extraction of pollution can be determined, it is difficult to allocate the quotas. Must incumbent producers all be limited by the same amount? Are the reductions relative or absolute? The policy has all the defects of central planning in general.

The second policy is to *tax* the activity. If we denote the tax by t, then after-tax profits would be 0, $3 - t$, $4 - 2t$, and $3 - 3t$, respectively. If the tax rate is sufficiently high, the firm is induced to limit its activity to level 1 rather than 2.[3] The tax is a mechanism to let the polluter pay for the disutility he or she causes; see Pigou (1920). The scheme does not require an allocation of activity by the government. Under the Pigovian tax, firms may act competitively as profit maximizers and the market mechanism regulates supply and demand. The determination of the tax is the subject of section 11.5. Pigovian taxes may become negative, in which case they are subsidies. This is appropriate when the effect on the environment is positive rather than negative. For example, the maintenance of landmarks does not only serve the proprietors, but has a positive external effect on passers by. Without the subsidy, the external effect does not enter the calculation of the decision-maker and the activity level would be set too low.

There is a formal relationship between standards and taxation policies. The relationship is precisely the same as between central planning and decentralized competition for the economies we investigated in preceding chapters, where we analyzed the maximization of the level of consumption subject to input constraints. The primal program determined the allocation of activity and could be used to set a central plan. The dual program determined the shadow prices under which the market would signal the activities to be undertaken.

---

[3] In fact, $t > 1$ is sufficient. The tax may not be excessive, as it would reduce the activity to the sub-optimal level of $s = 0$. We must therefore have $t < 3$.

We shall see below that Pigovian taxes are the shadow prices associated with environmental standards.

Although the taxation policy leaves more room for a competitive market, it still requires a cumbersome role for the government, as it is hard to calculate the tax. Once it is realized that the problem of the steel plant amid a population is the absence of a right to clean air, it is natural to assign that right. Property titles may be traded like commodities and a Coasian market is thus created. Let us analyze the two cases where the right to clean air is assigned to the proprietors of the plant and to the villagers, respectively. In the first case, the plant has the right to pollute. Yet table 11.1 can be used to conclude that the firm would scale down its activity. At the profit maximizing level, $s = 2$, the inhabitants are willing to pay up to $2 to have activity restrained by one unit. If the proprietor negotiates and cashes in on this willingness to pay, he more than offsets his reduction in operating surplus of $1. The inhabitants are not willing to compensate the entrepreneur for any further loss of profit (when he shuts down). Hence the level of activity will be $s = 1$, which is optimal. In the second case, the inhabitants have the right to clean air. The starting point of negotiations is now the top line of table 11.1. The inhabitants note that the entrepreneur is eager to set up production, as it would increase profit from zero to $3, far more than the disutility of one unit of activity. An increase from $s = 1$ to $s = 2$ would generate too little additional profit to be of interest to the consumer. So the outcome would again be the optimum.

The Coase Theorem states that any specification of property titles to natural resources and other ecotypes brings about an efficient and unique allocation of activity.[4] The first part of the Coase Theorem, claiming efficiency, is true. Once property rights are assigned, the natural resource or ecotype can be considered like labor or capital and competitive prices can be determined in the usual way. The second part of the Coase Theorem – that the specifics of the assignment is immaterial as regards the allocation – is also true in simple examples like the above one, but not in general, as has been noted by Hurwicz (1995) and will now be explained.

Clean air is a luxury: rich people are more keen to insist on it. Now the very assignment of such a title makes the recipients richer. If the assignment is egalitarian no one will become much richer, but if the right to clean air is given to a happy few, they become so powerful that they may tolerate only a very low level of activity. Whenever consumption coefficients, including one for clean air, vary with income, the allocation of activity between clean and dirty sectors will be affected by the distribution of income and, therefore, by the distribution of property rights, including the right to breathe clean air or to pollute.

The right to breathe clean air and to pollute are basically the same. In practice, the government auctions a certain amount of pollution. Whoever bids the most acquires the right to pollute by one unit. If you are an environmentalist, you can buy and not use but shelve the title and thus claim the right to clean air. The titles are exchanged in the market. In section 11.5 we show that the price equals the Pigovian tax.

---

[4] See Coase (1960).

11.3   Environmental accounting

A more detailed analysis of environmental policies requires a separate account for the natural resources and pollutants. Add it to the SNA (table 6.1).[5] The creation of the environmental account adds a row and a column to the system. The most important entry in the column is in the second position (production). Production yields not only goods and services, but also pollutants. The other feeder of the environmental column is account 6 (foreign flows). This cell accounts for the imports of pollutants. The environmental row has two similar entries, in the second and sixth positions, representing the use of natural resources and the exports of pollutants.

The environmental account is peculiar in two respects. First, the monetary values are typically zero. Hence the entries must be in physical units. Second, the account is not balanced. For balance one must add an environmental assets account, just like as foreign stocks account accommodates the balancing of the foreign flows account.

In addition to the environmental account, the production account may be refined to accommodate environmental activities such as the production of substitutes of natural resources and the abatement of pollutants. The first production unit is like a regular one. The second production unit has a negative output in the environmental cell of the production row; it eliminates pollutants.

Because of the non-monetary peculiarity of environmental accounts, they are not fully integrated in the SNA (United Nations 1993), but treated as so-called satellite accounts (United Nations *et al.* 2003). The most prominent extension of the SNA is the so-called Dutch National Accounting Matrix including Environmental Accounts (NAMEA), described by de Haan and Keuning (1996).

Some environmentalists argue that the national accounts should be "greened," so as to correct the standard GNP for the damage inflicted to the environment.[6] NAMEA does not do so. While in principle it is possible to price natural resources and pollution – we shall actually do so in the following sections – it is not advisable to apply this to the national accounts. There are three considerations. First and foremost, it is important to distinguish desirable *policies* – such as the polluter pays principle – from desirable *accounting*. The latter merely serves to picture the actual transactions in an economy, for right or for wrong. Just as accountants try to cover "black" transactions, such as services for which taxes are evaded, they also try to map industrial or household activity, be it dirty or clean, taxed or not. Second, intricate general equilibrium effects are involved with the pricing of damage to the environment. The income statements of clean activities would have to be changed as well, as sectors use each other's outputs as inputs. Third, if environmental damage were priced, producers and consumers would change their behavior, substituting cleaner techniques. It is messy to commingle actual transactions with the prices supporting desired transactions.

11.4   Energy policy

High on the environmental agenda stands the conservation of natural resources. To protect them, the subsidization of alternative sources is advocated. A prominent example is Brazil,

---

[5] The new account can be enlarged, like the other accounts, to detail the various natural resources and pollutants.

[6] A review of the issue is in Bartelmus with Vesper (2000).

where the production of gasoline from sugar instead of oil has been subsidized. In the case of energy, however, property rights are pretty well specified and interference in competitive markets through subsidies is suspicious.

Our model to analyze alternative energy policies is as an extension of the linear program of preceding chapters, where we maximized the level of consumption subject to commodity, factor, and international payment balances. Add a natural resource endowment. If there were no alternative energy sources, the energy resource could be modeled precisely like the capital and labor resources. In other words, we would measure the use of energy by sectoral activity and increases of activity levels would be feasible as long as the consequent demand for energy did not exceed the available supply. This is no different from capital and labor constraints. If, however, energy can also be produced, it becomes a commodity, and we have to reserve a commodity index – say, $i = 1$ – for energy, and a production unit index – say, $j = 1$ – for the alternative source. The material balance constraint becomes:

$$(V^\top - U)s + e_1 E \geq ac + z \tag{11.1}$$

On the left-hand side of inequality (11.1) we have the usual supply of commodities by the production units. In addition, there is the natural resource supply for commodity 1 through the first unit vector, (1.19), with $i = 1$; the level of this endowment is E. No further modifications are needed. The first row of use table U accounts for the intermediate consumption of energy and the first components of vectors a and z account for the final energy demand by the households and the foreign countries, respectively. The first column of the use table shows the input structure of the alternative energy source.

The alternative energy sector is typically unprofitable and proposals to subsidize it have been advanced and even implemented. Let us investigate non-profitability and its consequences. Denote the commodity price vector by p (the first component is the price of energy), the rental rate of capital by r, and the wage rate by w. Assuming for simplicity that the alternative energy sector has no secondary output, its unprofitability is expressed by the inequality:

$$p_1 v_{11} < p_1 u_{11} + p_2 u_{21} + \cdots + p_n u_{n1} + r K_1 + w L_1 \tag{11.2}$$

If the economy were a competitive market economy, this activity would not be undertaken according to the phenomenon of complementary slackness (corollary 4.5). Now this market test also proves appropriate from a narrow energy conservationist point of view. If the profitability test is negative, as in inequality (11.2), the energy balance of the alternative sector (sector 1) is also negative. The alternative source of energy is a net user of energy. Indeed, division by the price of energy yields the energy balance:

$$v_{11} < u_{11} + \frac{p_2}{p_1} u_{21} + \cdots + \frac{p_n}{p_1} u_{n1} + \frac{r}{p_1} K_1 + \frac{w}{p_1} L_1 \tag{11.3}$$

On the left-hand side of inequality (11.3) we have the supply of alternative energy. On the right-hand side we have the direct use of energy, u_{11}. The other inputs, u_{21}, etc., require energy in their production. Before explaining why this is an energy balance, note first that the dimensions are right. The first non-energy term in inequality (11.3) is:

$$\frac{p_2}{p_1} u_{21} \tag{11.4}$$

In expression (11.4) p_2 has the dimension of dollar per physical unit of commodity 2, p_1 of dollar per energy unit, and u_{21} of physical unit of commodity 2. The dollar and physical unit dimensions cancel and only the energy dimension in the denominator of p_1 remains. Since p_1 is in the denominator, expression (11.4) has the dimension of energy.

The possibility of reallocating activity between sectors offers a degree of substitutability and, therefore, scope for applying some neoclassical ideas. The main tool is theorem 4.5, by which competitive prices measure marginal productivities. The objective is consumption and, by theorem 4.5, the price of commodity i is the marginal productivity of an additional unit of y, the net commodity output:

$$p_i = \Delta c^* / \Delta y_i \tag{11.5}$$

In the case of energy, in view of the material balance constraint, (11.1), we have:

$$p_1 = \Delta c^* / \Delta E \tag{11.6}$$

For capital and labor, we have the marginal products:

$$r = \Delta c^* / \Delta M, w = \Delta c^* / \Delta N \tag{11.7}$$

Eliminating of c^* from (11.5), (11.6), and (11.7), we obtain the energy substitution values of the inputs:

$$\frac{p_i}{p_1} = \frac{\Delta E}{\Delta y_i}, \frac{r}{p_1} = \frac{\Delta E}{\Delta M}, \frac{w}{p_1} = \frac{\Delta E}{\Delta N} \tag{11.8}$$

Consequently, when prices are competitive and hence equal to marginal productivities, the right-hand side of inequality (11.3) measures the *energy value* of the inputs. The basic idea is that relative input prices measure the *marginal rate of substitution* (Baumol and Wolff 1981), a concept now explained.

The curve in figure 11.1 is an isoquant, representing input combinations that yield a common level of output. A cost minimizing firm would pick the point of tangency with the straight line, representing input combinations of equal value (cost C), given the input prices, p_1 (for energy) and p_2 (for another commodity). The slope at the point of tangency is pretty flat in figure 11.1, roughly one-half. This means that half a unit of commodity 2 is as good as one unit of energy. In other words, the marginal rate of substitution of commodity 2 for energy is 2. It is also called the *energy substitution value*. By the condition of tangency, the slope is equal to the slope of the straight line, p_1/p_2. Since we took the inverse slope to determine the marginal rate of substitution, we obtain that the latter is equal to p_2/p_1. The same logic applies to the last two inputs in inequality (11.3), capital and labor. Their prices relative to energy, given by expression (11.8), measure their energy substitution values.

On the right-hand side of inequality (11.3) we obtain the direct energy input plus the energy substitution value of the other inputs. The analysis requires only cost minimization given the input prices, and this condition holds not only for competitive markets but also for

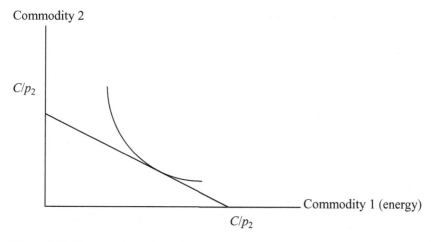

Commodity 2

C/p_2

Commodity 1 (energy)

C/p_2

Figure 11.1 Energy substitution value

other market forms, including even monopoly. A weakness of the analysis is the reliance on substitutability at the level of the firm, which is less plausible then at the macro level.

In input-output analysis the energy balance terms in (11.3) are confined to the commodities. For the relative prices, $p_2/p_1, \ldots, p_n/p_1$ in (11.8), one substitutes the energy contents of the commodities, listed by a vector $\overset{\circ}{p}$. This $(n-1)$-dimensional row vector of energy contents is computed as follows. The number of sectors is assumed to be equal to the number of commodities. The truncated use – make tables (without the energy rows and columns), are denoted by $\overset{\circ}{U}$ and $\overset{\circ}{V}$, respectively. The direct energy requirements of the sectors are given by row vector $u_{\bullet 1}$. The energy balance reads:

$$\overset{\circ}{p}\overset{\circ}{V}{}^{\top} = \overset{\circ}{p}\overset{\circ}{U} + u_{\bullet 1} \tag{11.9}$$

On the left-hand side of (11.9) we have the energy contents of the outputs of the respective sectors. On the right-hand side we have the energy contents of the commodity inputs as well as of the direct energy consumption. Equation (11.9) can be analyzed in precisely the same way as the financial balance (2.16) and the solution can be given a multiplier interpretation (section 3.2). More precisely, post-multiplying (11.9) with the inverse of the truncated make table, we obtain:

$$\overset{\circ}{p} = \overset{\circ}{p}\overset{\circ}{U}(\overset{\circ}{V}{}^{\top})^{-1} + u_{\bullet 1}(\overset{\circ}{V}{}^{\top})^{-1} \tag{11.10}$$

Equation (11.10) features the matrix of commodity input coefficients, $\overset{\circ}{U}(\overset{\circ}{V}{}^{\top})^{-1}$, and the row vector of *energy coefficients* $u_{\bullet 1}(\overset{\circ}{V}{}^{\top})^{-1}$ (see chapter 7). It is solved for *energy contents*, $\overset{\circ}{p}$, by application of the Leontief inverse to the energy coefficients; see (2.17) with the value-added coefficients v now replaced by $u_{\bullet 1}(\overset{\circ}{V}{}^{\top})^{-1}$. If the substitution of the energy contents in the relative prices of the energy balance (11.3) establishes the inequality by virtue of the first n terms on the right-hand side, then the new, alternative energy sector would be a net demander of energy.[7]

If the production of energy is unprofitable its contribution to the energy balance would be negative. Subsidization would cause the energy balance of the economy to deteriorate. The economics are straightforward. Energy does not enter an objective function directly; it is a productive input. If there is an alternative technique to make it, the market mechanism will render it profitable if it is to be activated in an efficient scenario. Conversely, if there is slack in the cost relationship of the new production unit, it would be inactive in an efficient scenario and a subsidy would thus activate a "wrong" sector.

Another interesting policy issue surrounds the unexpected discovery of an energy stock. If the value of the natural endowment rises suddenly, energy may draw the comparative advantage from other commodities. Some sectors will no longer be required to fulfill foreign demands. Reallocation of activity is warranted, with all the adjustment pain. The phenomenon that an expansion of resources may cause harm is called the *Dutch disease* after the case of the Netherlands where a discovery of natural gas shifted the comparative advantage towards energy and caused great adjustment problems such as unemployment (Dixit and Norman 1980, or Jones and Kenen 1985). The appropriate policy is to depreciate the currency. As energy becomes more abundant other factor inputs become scarcer. Their marginal products go up. As we saw in chapter 10, an increase of the shadow prices of foreign currency amounts to a depreciation of the national currency.

11.5   Pollution

Pollution is a more serious problem than energy conservation. The titles to energy are specified and the stuff can be priced in the market place. This is less possible with environmental resources like clean air. To limit pollution we cannot rely on the free market, but need a policy. In this section we analyze how pollution can be contained. We add an account for pollutants. These are "bads" rather than "goods." For goods, the material balance requires that supply is at least equal to demand. For the "bads," a constraint will require that supply is at most equal to an acceptable level of consumption. We also add a production account, for abatement. The output of this sector is a negative amount of pollutants (Leontief, 1970). The material balance reads:

$$\left(\begin{pmatrix} V^\mathsf{T} & 0 \\ v_{\bullet n+1}^\mathsf{T} & v_{m+1,n+1} \end{pmatrix} - \begin{pmatrix} U & u_{\bullet m+1} \\ 0^\mathsf{T} & 0 \end{pmatrix} \right) \begin{pmatrix} s \\ s_{m+1} \end{pmatrix} \begin{matrix} \geq \\ \leq \end{matrix} \begin{pmatrix} ac + z \\ a_{n+1}c \end{pmatrix} \tag{11.11}$$

The matrix on the left-hand side of inequality (11.11) is an $(n + 1) \times (m + 1)$-dimensional net output table. It acts on an $(m + 1)$-dimensional activity vector, yielding an $(n + 1)$-dimensional commodity vector. The first n components must be greater than or equal to $ac + z$, the final demand for goods. The last component, the net output of pollutants, must be less than or equal to ac. The consumption coefficients are given by vector a for the

---

[7] Traditional input-output analysis does not take into account the energy the opportunity cost of capital and labor terms on the right-hand side of (11.3).

goods and augmented with a for pollution. The consumption level is denoted by c. We have augmented the make table, V, with a column of pollutants, $v_{\bullet n+1}$. We have also augmented the use table, U, with a column of abatement inputs, $u_{\bullet m+1}$. This sector has a negative output of pollutants: $v_{m+1,n+1} < 0$.

The other constraints are as before:

$$Ks + K_{m+1}s_{m+1} \leq M, \, Ls + L_{m+1}s_{m+1} \leq N, \, \underline{p}z \geq -D, s \geq 0, s_{m+1} \geq 0 \quad (11.12)$$

In constraints (11.12) K_{m+1} and L_{m+1} are the capital and labor employed in the abatement sector, $\underline{p}$ is the row vector of world prices, z the vector of net exports, and D the deficit. Non-tradability constraints can be accommodated as in chapters 9 and 10. The vector of variables lists s, s_{m+1}, c, and z. Encompassing matrix notation for the pair of inequalities (11.11) and (11.12) is:

$$\begin{pmatrix} U - V^\top & u_{\bullet m+1} & a & I \\ v_{\bullet n+1}^\top & v_{m+1,n+1} & -a_{n+1} & 0 \\ K & K_{m+1} & 0 & 0 \\ L & L_{m+1} & 0 & 0 \\ 0 & 0 & 0 & -\pi \\ -I & 0 & 0 & 0 \\ 0 & -1 & 0 & 0 \end{pmatrix} \begin{pmatrix} s \\ s_{m+1} \\ c \\ z \end{pmatrix} \leq \begin{pmatrix} 0 \\ 0 \\ M \\ N \\ D \\ 0 \\ 0 \end{pmatrix} \quad (11.13)$$

Now denote the shadow prices associated with the constraints by p (for commodities), p_{n+1} (for pollutants), r (for capital), w (for labor), ε (for foreign currency), σ (for sectoral non-negativity), and σ_{m+1} (for abatement non-negativity). As in chapters 9 and 10, the objective is consumption:

$$e^\top ac = (0 \quad 0 \quad e^\top a \quad 0) \begin{pmatrix} s \\ s_{m+1} \\ c \\ z \end{pmatrix} \quad (11.14)$$

In expression (11.14) $e^\top a$ is observed consumption and c is the expansion vector. According to the dual equation (4.19), the product of the row vector of shadow prices and the matrix of constraint coefficients, see (11.13), equals the row vector of objective function coefficients, see (11.14):

$$(p \quad p_{n+1} \quad r \quad w \quad \varepsilon \quad \sigma \quad \sigma_{m+1}) \begin{pmatrix} U - V^\top & u_{\bullet m+1} & a & I \\ v_{\bullet n+1}^\top & v_{m+1,n+1} & -a_{n+1} & 0 \\ K & K_{m+1} & 0 & 0 \\ L & L_{m+1} & 0 & 0 \\ 0 & 0 & 0 & -\pi \\ -I & 0 & 0 & 0 \\ 0 & -1 & 0 & 0 \end{pmatrix}$$

$$= (0 \quad 0 \quad e^\top a \quad 0) \quad (11.15)$$

Writing out the dual equation (11.15) with a slight rearrangement of terms, we obtain:

$$p(V^{\top} - U) = p_{n+1}v^{\top}_{\bullet n+1} + rK + wL - \sigma$$
$$p_{n+1}(-v_{m+1,n+1}) = pu_{\bullet m+1} + rK_{m+1} + wL_{m+1} - \sigma_{m+1}$$
$$pa = e^{\top}a + p_{n+1}a_{n+1}$$
$$p = \varepsilon\pi$$

(11.16)

The first equation in (11.16) shows that prices must be such that value-added covers not only factor costs but also the price of pollution, $p_{n+1}v^{\top}_{\bullet n+1}$. Competitive analysis thus provides an economic foundation to the principle paraphrased by "the polluter pays." The second equation in (11.16) determines the price of pollution. Remember, $v_{m+1,n+1}$ is a negative figure, recording the removal of pollutants. The scalar p_{n+1} values the amount abated according to the costs of the abatement sector. Here we assume that the acceptable level of pollution, a_{n+1}, is sufficiently small, so that the constraint on pollutants is binding and, by the phenomenon of complementary slackness (theorem 4.2), slack variable σ_{m+1} is zero.[8] The prices include the cost of pollution, p_{n+1}, and, by the fourth equation in (11.16), the exchange rate, ε, will be higher. Using the analysis of chapter 10, this means that environmental controls weaken the currency of a national economy; devaluation is appropriate.

Apart from the macroeconomic effects, there are also microeconomic effects. When pollution is costly, the comparative advantage may shift from the sectors determined in chapter 10 to cleaner ones. In such a situation, politicians cater for the special interests of the threatened sectors. In the 1990s the Dutch government considered offering compensation for the trucking industry to continue their profitability in the face of an environmental tax. This is absurd. The point of departure of environmental policy is to protect the environment by containing damage. This requires a reallocation of activity which, indeed, can be brought about by a new set of market prices, given by the above equations and, therefore, reflecting the cost of pollution. If sectors are compensated, the reallocation will be frustrated. The market can respond to new conditions, such as environmental controls, provided prices are flexible. New activities, favorable to the new conditions, are stimulated by their achieved profitability. Resources are drawn from old activities, which are abandoned as they are no longer profitable. Compensation schemes frustrate the adjustment. With one hand the government taxes pollution and with the other it returns receipts to compensate and hamper reallocations. It would make more sense to accept current standards and not to introduce a new tax. Better still would be not to yield to special interests and drop the compensation schemes altogether.

The three policies introduced in section 11.2 are now related to each other. The policy of a standard is to set a limit on pollution, be it relative to the size of the economy (a_{n+1}) or an absolute limit ($a_{n+1}c$), and to interfere with the activity levels (s and s_{m+1}) so as to adhere to the pollution constraint. This requires detailed government interference, through

---

[8] If a_{n+1} is high, the pollution constraint is not binding and its shadow price p_{n+1} is zero by corollary 4.5. Then commodity prices are normalized in the usual way by $pa = e^{\top}a$, using the third equation in (11.16).

negotiations with the various production sectors. The second policy, taxation, is to set a tax, p_{n+1}, on pollution, as it is determined by the unit cost of abatement, by the second equation in (11.16). The third policy, the creation of a market for pollution rights, amounts to auctioning off the pollution shares of a_{n+1}. The market price will be equal to their marginal productivities, which is p_{n+1}. In other words, the cost of pollution would be the same and even accrue to the government (through the issuance of the shares) and ultimately to the abatement sector, but the market rather than the environmental or fiscal authorities would fix the price.

11.6   Globalization

Pollution can be ascribed to the producer or the consumer. For a closed national economy the distinction makes little difference, simply because the producers and the consumers are located in the same place. For an open economy, however, it makes quite a difference. One way to meet a national constraint on pollution is by importing the goods for which the production is dirty. In other words, pollution is exported by importing goods. From a global perspective such a policy merely shifts pollution and, to make things worse, the exported pollution may come back by a direct physical spillover, blown by the wind or floated on the rivers. Input-output analysis can account for these transfers.

What is needed, however, is a correspondence between pollution and products. Hence we will turn to the traditional input-output framework with as many sectors as goods and services, $m = n$, gross output $x = V^{\top}s$, commodity technology input-output coefficients (theorem 7.1), and abatement coefficients $a_{\bullet n+1} = u_{\bullet n+1}/(-v_{n+1,n+1})$. Then the material balance component of (11.11) reads[9]

$$x - Ax = ac + z + a_{\bullet n+1}(-v_{n+1,n+1}) \tag{11.17}$$

Introduce a row vector of pollution coefficients $b = v_{\bullet n+1}^{\top}(V^{\top})^{-1}$, then the pollution amounts to bx. Applying the Leontief inverse $B = (I - A)^{-1}$ to (11.17), pollution can be decomposed into three terms:

$$bx = bBac + bBz + bBa_{\bullet n+1}(-v_{n+1,n+1}) \tag{11.18}$$

On the left-hand side is the pollution of production. On the right-hand side are, respectively, the pollution due to domestic consumption, the pollution due to net exports, and the pollution due to abatement. For all substances contributing to acidification (NO_x, SO_2, and NH_3) or eutrophication (P and N), de Haan and Kee (2002) found that Dutch pollution responsibilities measured by domestic consumption, $bBac$, were lower than those measured by the activities, bx, because of a significant positive values of bBz.[10] The last term measures the pollution imported via the export of goods and services minus the pollution exported via the import of goods and services. Hence the Dutch *consumption* pattern is environmentally friendly,

---

[9] By the argument given in example 4.1, the material balance is binding.
[10] For acidification the emission is 338 m kg. Of this 221 is ascribed to domestic consumption, and the remainder (117) to the net exports of goods. Similarly, for eutrophication the emission is 1,701 m kg, of which only 1,260 is ascribed to domestic consumption.

but the rest of the world spills polluting activity into the country. From an environmentalist point of view it is fair to say that globalization harms the Netherlands. This drawback has to be weighed against the gain to free trade derived in section 10.4.

Similar imputations can be made further down the domestic level. Casler and Rose (1998) decompose the sources of change in CO_2 emissions in the United States over the 1972–82 timeframe using hybrid energy/value tables for the initial and terminal years. Their results show the significant effect of substitution within the energy sector and between energy and other inputs as the leading causes of the decline in carbon dioxide emissions.

Exercises

1. Show that the orderings of commodities by direct and total energy intensities may differ.
2. Provide a numerical example of an economy and trace the effects of a stiffer pollution constraint.
3. The government caps pollution to 1 percent of consumption and levies the appropriate tax, p_{n+1}. Determine the increase in the cost of living.

References

Bartelmus, P. with A. Vesper (2000). "Green Accounting and Material Flow Analysis: Alternatives or Complements," *Wuppertal Papers* 106

Baumol, W. J. and E. N. Wolff (1981). "Subsidies to New Energy Sources: Do They Add to Energy Stocks?" *Journal of Political Economy* 89 (5), 891–913

Casler, S. D. and A. Rose (1998). "Carbon Dioxide Emissions in the US Economy: A Structural Decomposition Analysis," *Environmental and Resource Economics* 11 (3–4), 349–63

Coase, R. H. (1960). "The Problem of Social Cost," *Journal of Law and Economics* 3, 1–44

Dixit, A. and V. Norman (1980). *Theory of International Trade: A Dual, General Equilibrium Approach*, Welwyn, Nisbet

de Haan, M. and P. Kee (2002). "Accounting for Sustainable Development: The NAMEA-Based Approach," Voorburg, Statistics Netherlands

de Haan, M. and S. J. Keuning (1996). "Taking the Environment into Account: The NAMEA Approach," *Review of Income and Wealth* 42 (2), 131–48

Hurwicz L. (1995). "What is the Coase Theorem?," *Japan and the World Economy* 7 (1), 49–74

Jones, R. W. and P. B. Kenen (eds.) (1985). *Handbook of International Economics*, Amsterdam, North-Holland

Leontief, W. (1970). "Environmental Repercussions and the Economic Structure – An Input-Output Approach," *Review of Economics and Statistics* 52 (3), 262–71

Pigou, A. C. (1920). *The Economics of Welfare*, London, Macmillan

United Nations (1993). *Revised System of National Accounts*, Studies in Methods, Series F, no. 2, rev. 4

United Nations, European Commission, International Monetary Fund, Organisation for Economic Co-operation and Development, and World Bank (2003). *Handbook of National Accounting: Integrated Environmental and Economic Accounting*, New York, United Nations

12 Productivity growth and spillovers

12.1 Introduction

An economy transforms factor inputs (capital, labor, or other services) into a bill of net outputs through a web of activities that reflects its technology. The level of final consumption may grow simply because more factor inputs are employed, or – perhaps more interestingly – because more output can be produced with the same input. The latter form of growth is called *productivity* growth and, in turn, can be decomposed into two further phenomena. The output/input ratio of an economy may improve because the PPF shifts (*technical change*) or because the economy moves closer to its frontier (*efficiency change*). In this chapter we show how to account for all these sources of growth.

One activity deserves special attention, namely international trade. Conceptually, international trade is like any production sector: a "black box" transforming one set of commodities (the "inputs") into another (the "outputs"). International trade requires commodity exports (which may be considered "inputs") and yields commodity imports (which may be considered "outputs"). As a production sector may improve its output/input ratio, or reduce its input-output coefficients, the trade sector may perform better by raising its import/exports ratio, which is an improvement in the terms of trade. The latter is equivalent to technical progress. If you think about it, it does not actually make a difference if Cuba becomes more efficient in producing sugar or the price of sugar goes up. In either case, the economy will be capable of raising the standard of living, by importing more commodities with the same resources.

Traditionally factor productivity growth is measured by the so-called Solow (1957) residual, which is the difference between the growth rates of the output and of the factor inputs of an economy. In other words, output growth that cannot be explained by sheer increase of inputs is deemed to measure technical change or efficiency change.

Growth accounting is introduced in section 12.2. Section 12.3 reinvokes the use–make framework to relate total factor productivity (TFP) growth to changes at the sectoral level in technical coefficients. Section 12.4 applies the analysis to the Canadian economy. A hot topic is spillovers. The benefits of technical change "leak" in the form of reduced prices to consuming industries and are eventually passed on to domestic and foreign consumers. This passive form of spillovers is analyzed in section 12.5. Innovations also have more direct spillovers, in the form of spin-offs in downstream industries. These are analyzed in section 12.6. Section 12.7 draws some conclusions.

12.2   Total factor productivity growth

We consider an open economy endowed with labor N, capital M (decomposed into various types), and an allowable trade deficit D. The economy is sub-divided into a number of sectors, each producing a vector of commodities. Part of the commodities is used as intermediate inputs and the rest flows to final demand (either domestic final demand or exports). The frontier of the economy is defined as the maximal expansion of its vector of final demand, while keeping the relative composition fixed. The composition reflects *preferences*. The frontier of the economy can be reached by an optimal allocation of inputs (primary and intermediate) and production across sectors and by an optimal trade of commodity with the rest of the world. Formally, the primal program (9.3) defines the *frontier* of the economy,

$$\max_{s,c,z} e^\top ac : (V^\top - U)s \geq ac + \begin{pmatrix} z \\ o \end{pmatrix} =: F,$$

$$Ks \leq M, Ls \leq N, \underline{p}z \geq \underline{p}d =: -D, s \geq 0 \qquad (12.1)$$

Program (12.1) features three variables (followed by their dimensions), namely activity vector s (# of sectors), level of domestic final demand c (scalar), and vector of net exports z (# of tradable commodities). The objective is the expansion of the level of domestic final demand, c. Domestic final demand comprises consumption and investment. Investment is merely a means to advance consumption, albeit in the future. We include it in the objective function to account for future consumption.[1]

All other symbols are given parameters. Preserving the proportions of domestic final demand a (# of commodities), we expand its level by letting the economy produce ac, where scalar c is the expansion factor. The level $c = 1$ is feasible (as it reflects the status quo) and $c > 1$ represents a movement towards the frontier of the economy. The model maximizes c, which, indeed, is equivalent to the maximization $e^\top ac$.[2] It is important to realize that vector a is not a variable, but an exogenous entity. The positive multiplicative factor in the objective, $e^\top a$, will control the nominal price level, since the value of the constraining entities such as labor equals the value of the objective function (including the multiplicative factor) according to theorem 4.1).

Let us explain the parameters in the constraints. As usual, V is the make table (# of sectors by # of commodities) and U the use table (# of commodities by # of sectors). F is potential final demand (# of commodities), K the capital stock matrix (# of capital types by # of sectors), M the capital endowment (# of capital types), L the labor employment row vector (# of sectors), and N the labor force. $\underline{p}$ is the world price row vector (# of tradables), d the vector of observed net exports (# of tradables), and D the observed trade deficit (scalar). We have listed the tradable commodities up front.

---

[1] As noted in chapter 9, Weitzman (1976) shows that for competitive economies domestic final demand measures the present discounted value of consumption.

[2] By (2.8), $e^\top a$ is the actual total domestic final demand.

The first constraint of the linear program (12.1) is the material balance: the net output of the production sectors must cover domestic final demand and net exports. The next constraints limit the use of capital and labor to what is available. The next to last constraint is the trade balance: net imports (at world prices) may not exceed the existing trade deficit. If this constraint were not present, importing whatever is needed could attain any standard of living. Finally, sector activity levels must be non-negative.

The linear program (12.1) basically reallocates activity so as to maximize the level of domestic final demand. Final demand also includes net exports, but they are considered not an end but a means to fulfill the objective of the economy.

The theory of linear programming (theorem 4.5) teaches us that the Lagrange multipliers corresponding to the constraints of the primal program measure the competitive values or marginal products of the constraining entities (the commodities and factors) at the optimum. We will use the Lagrange multipliers associated with the constraints of (12.1) in the definition of productivity growth. Now the multipliers are p (the shadow prices of the material balances, a row vector of commodity prices), r (the shadow prices of the capital constraints, a row vector of capital productivities), w (the shadow price of the labor constraint, a scalar for labor productivity), ε (the shadow price of the debt constraint, a scalar for the purchasing power parity (PPP) or exchange rate), and σ (the shadow prices of the non-negativity constraints, a row vector of slacks). The dual program (9.7), gives their interrelationship (eliminating $\sigma \geq 0$):

$$\min_{p,r,w,\varepsilon \geq 0} rM + wN + \varepsilon D : p(V^\top - U) \leq rK + wL, \, pa = e^\top a, \, p_T = \varepsilon \underline{p} \quad (12.2)$$

Dual program (12.2) minimizes the *factor costs* subject to the constraint that value-added is less than or equal to factor costs in each sector. Should value-added fall short of factor costs, the sector will remain inactive according to the phenomenon of complementary slackness (corollary 4.5). The second dual constraint normalizes the prices. Our commodities are measured in base-year prices and hence observed prices are one. The optimal competitive prices from the linear program will be slightly off, but we maintain the overall price level. The third and last dual constraint aligns the prices of the tradable commodities with their opportunity costs: the world prices.

Following Solow (1957), we define TFP growth as the residual between the final demand growth and aggregate-input growth, where each of them is a weighted average of component growth rates and the weights are competitive value shares. We need some notation for growth accounting. An ordinary *time derivative* is denoted by a prime, such as x'. Division by the level yields a *growth rate* and is denoted by a dot: $\dot{x} = x'/x$. The growth rate of domestic final demand for commodity i is $\dot{a}_i = a_i'/a_i$ and the (competitive) value shares are:

$$\frac{p_i a_i}{\sum_{i=1}^{n} p_i a_i} = \frac{p_i a_i}{pa} \quad (12.3)$$

Overall output growth sums to:

$$\sum_{i=1}^{n} \frac{p_i a_i}{pa} \dot{a}_i = \sum_{i=1}^{n} \frac{p_i a_i'}{pa} = \frac{pa'}{pa} \quad (12.4)$$

Inputs are aggregated in the same vein. The growth rate of labor is $\hat{N}$ and its competitive value share is $\beta = wN/(rM + \varepsilon D)$. Likewise, denote the competitive value shares of capital by α (a row vector) and of the trade deficit by γ (a scalar). Then overall input growth can be written as

$$\alpha \dot{M} + \beta \dot{N} + \gamma \dot{D} \tag{12.5}$$

Each term in (12.5) can be rewritten in time derivatives, as we have done for outputs. For example,

$$\beta \dot{N} = \frac{wN}{rM + wN + \varepsilon D} \dot{N} = \frac{wN'}{rM + wN + \varepsilon D} \tag{12.6}$$

TFP growth is the residual between overall output growth (12.4) and overall input growth (12.5), which we rewrite using (12.6) and similar expressions for capital and debt:

$$TFP = \frac{pa'}{pa} - \alpha \dot{M} + \beta \dot{N} + \gamma \dot{D} = \frac{pa'}{pa} - \frac{rM' + wN' + \varepsilon D'}{rM + wN + \varepsilon D} \tag{12.7}$$

In the growth accounting literature it is customary to assume that the economy is perfectly competitive. Unfortunately this assumption is seldom fulfilled. Observed prices are not perfectly competitive and the economy need not be on its frontier. For a related reason, vector p is not a device to convert values to real values, but the endogenous price vector that sustains the optimal allocation of resources in the linear program.

12.3   Measurement and decomposition

In the spirit of Nishimizu and Page (1982) and further frontier analysis, such as Data Envelopment Analysis (for example, Färe et al. 1994), we will decompose TFP growth (12.7) into a shift of the frontier and a movement towards the frontier:

$$TFP = FP + EC \tag{12.8}$$

In decomposition (12.8) *FP* is *frontier productivity* growth and *EC* is the rate of *efficiency change*. We will now define each of them.

Since real shadow prices measure the marginal products of the factors at the optimum (theorem 4.5), *FP growth* is the growth rates of the shadow prices of the factors (weighted by relative factor costs) minus the growth rate of the commodity prices:[3]

$$FP = \frac{r'M + w'N + \varepsilon'D}{rM + wN + \varepsilon D} - \frac{p'a}{pa} \tag{12.9}$$

FP growth defined by (12.9) corresponds to the dual expression of TFP growth for perfectly competitive economies elaborated by Jorgenson and Griliches (1967). It imputes

---

[3] Since prices are normalized at unity by the second dual constraint in (12.2), the price correction term is a sheer compositional effect. If the composition of domestic final demand, a, is constant (as a vector), then pa is also constant by the second dual constraint in (12.2), and it follows that $pa' = p'a = 0$. Otherwise the price correction term corrects marginal factor productivity growth rates for an inflationary effect, which does not reflect a change in the price level (since everything is already specified in real prices) but only a compositional effect.

productivity growth to factor inputs, which is beyond the scope of standard frontier analysis. The latter, however, is capable of accounting for efficiency change. Inefficiency is
measured by the degree to which the economy can be expanded towards its frontier, c. Conversely, recalling definition (9.4), efficiency is the inverse of expansion factor c. It follows
that the rate of efficiency change, denoted EC, is, using formula (1.2) (with $n = -1$) and
the chain rule (1.6):

$$EC = \frac{(c^{-1})'}{c^{-1}} = \frac{-c^{-2}c'}{c^{-1}} = \frac{-c'}{c} = -\overset{\bullet}{c} \tag{12.10}$$

In short, the efficiency change is simply measured by the negative growth rate or *contraction*
rate of the expansion factor. We must now demonstrate that FP growth and efficiency
change sum to total factor productivity growth. In other words, we must prove (12.8), given
definitions (12.7), (12.9), and (12.10). Now, by the main theorem of linear programming
(theorem 4.1), programs (12.1) and (12.2) have equal solution values – or, substituting the
price normalization constraint (12.2):

$$pac = rM + wN + \varepsilon D \tag{12.11}$$

This is the identity of national product and income, where national income consists of
factor costs. Notice that (12.11) is the identity at the frontier (with expansion factor c),
rather than the observed allocation. Differentiating (12.11) with respect to time, applying
the product rule (1.5), rearranging terms, and dividing through by (12.11) itself, we obtain
(12.8), completing our proof. It is interesting to notice that c cancels out everywhere, except
in the denominator under c', which yields the efficiency change.

FP growth can be broken down into technical change and the terms of trade effect. The
latter is not an add-on, but emerges naturally from our linear programming model of TFP
growth. It should not come as a surprise that terms of trade and sectoral technical changes
arise simultaneously. The trade sector is like a production sector, with multiple inputs
(namely exports) and outputs (namely imports). The technology is different, though. While
production sectors feature no substitutability, the trade sector features perfect substitutability
(with the marginal rate of substitution given by the terms of trade).

Our point of departure is TFP growth as defined in (12.7). Multiplying and dividing the
first term on the right-hand side of (12.7) by c, the two terms get a common denominator,
given by (12.11), and we obtain:

$$TFP = \frac{pa'c - rM' - wN' - \varepsilon D'}{pac} \tag{12.12}$$

We may substitute $M = Ks$, $N = Ls$,[4] and $D = -\underline{p}z$ in (12.12). The fourth term in the
numerator of (12.12) thus becomes:

$$\varepsilon(\underline{p}z)' = \varepsilon\underline{p}z' + \varepsilon\underline{p}'z = p_T z' + \varepsilon\underline{p}'z \tag{12.13}$$

---

[4] This is obvious if the labor constraint is binding at and near time t. If the labor constraint is non-binding at and
near time t, $w = 0$ by the phenomenon of complementary slackness (corollary 4.5), and one may substitute
anything. Strictly speaking t may also be a point of time where the constraint switches between binding and
non-binding, but we exclude this exceptional event. The argument for the other factor constraints is the same.

by the product rule (1.5) and the last equation in the dual program (12.2). Substitution of (12.13) reduces (12.12) to:

$$TFP = \frac{pa'c - r(Ks)' - w(Ls)' + p_T z' + \varepsilon \underline{p}'z}{pac}$$

$$= \frac{[p(ac + Jz)' - r(Ks)' - w(Ls)'] + \varepsilon \underline{p}'z - pac'}{pac} \quad (12.14)$$

Equation (12.14) yields the following important decomposition of TFP growth into technical change, the terms of trade effect, and efficiency change:

$$TFP = SR + TT + EC \quad (12.15)$$

The three terms are now defined. Recalling potential output $F = ac + \begin{pmatrix} z \\ o \end{pmatrix}$ from program (12.1), SR is the *Solow residual*:

$$SR = \frac{pF' - r(Ks)' - w(Ls)'}{pac} \quad (12.16)$$

The second term, TT, is the *terms of trade effect*:

$$TT = \frac{\varepsilon \underline{p}'z}{pac} \quad (12.17)$$

Finally, term EC is the efficiency change, derived earlier in (12.10). Comparison of TFP growth decompositions (12.15) and (12.8) reveals that we have effectively decomposed the structural change term, FP growth, into the technical change and terms of trade effects:

$$FP = SR + TT \quad (12.18)$$

The Solow residual, SR, can be broken down further, namely by sector. If the material balances are binding, then, by the first constraint in program (12.1), $F = (V^\top - U)s$, and, therefore, (12.16) becomes:

$$SR = \frac{p(V^\top s)' - p(Us)' - r(Ks)' - w(Ls)'}{pac}$$

$$= \frac{(pV^{\top\prime} - pU' - rK' - wL')s + (pV^\top - pU - rK - wL)s'}{pac} \quad (12.19)$$

$$= \frac{(pV^{\top\prime} - pU' - rK' - wL')s + \sigma s'}{pac}$$

Here we used the product rule (1.5) and the first constraint in the dual program (12.2) where the slack is σ. In fact, $\sigma s'$ vanishes by the analysis of chapter 4, (4.31): For small perturbations, inactive sectors ($s_j = 0$) remain inactive, so that $s_j' = 0$, while active sectors have $\sigma_j = 0$ by the phenomenon of complementary slackness (corollary 4.5). The consequent formula decomposes TFP growth into sectoral changes (Hulten 1978):

$$SR = \sum_{j=1}^m \frac{(pV_{\bullet j}^{\top\prime} - pU_{\bullet j}' - rK_{\bullet j}' - wL_{\bullet j}')s_j}{pac} = \sum_{j=1}^m D_j SR_j \quad (12.20)$$

In this so-called *Domar decomposition* the sectoral Solow residuals and the (Domar) weights are defined by:

$$SR_j = \frac{pV_{\bullet j}^{\top\prime} - pU_{\bullet j}' - rK_{\bullet j}' - wL_{\bullet j}'}{pV_{\bullet j}^{\top}}, \quad D_j = \frac{pV_{\bullet j}^{\top}s_j}{pac} \qquad (12.21)$$

In $pV_{\bullet j}^{\top\prime}$ the prime denotes time differentiation and the dot indicates that by taking all $pV_{kj}^{\top}$ elements over k, we obtain the jth column vector of $V^{\top}$, which is jth row vector of V. The pre-multiplication by the price vector p yields the value of output of sector j. The contribution of sector j per dollar of output is the change of value-added minus the change of factor costs.

The Domar weights do not sum to unity. The reason is that the sectoral productivity growth rates, SR_j, measure the gains per (dollar of) *gross* output, while the economy-wide Solow residual, SR of (12.16), measures the gain per unit of factor income or *net* output of the economy. The division by gross output in the sectoral productivity growth rates understates the contribution of the sector. This understatement is corrected by the Domar weight, which is the ratio of potential output to factor income. In fact, the Domar weights sum to

$$\frac{pV^{\top}s}{pac}$$

Here the denominator is, applying the phenomenon of complementary slackness (corollary 4.5) to linear program's (12.1) material balance and trade balance constraints, respectively, as well as the last constraint of the dual program (12.2):

$$pac = p(V^{\top} - U)s - p_T z = p(V^{\top} - U)s - \varepsilon pz = p(V^{\top} - U)s + \varepsilon D \quad (12.22)$$

In particular, when there is balance of payments, the Domar weights sum to the gross/net output ratio of the economy, $pV^{\top}s/p(V^{\top} - U)s$, which is also called the *Domar ratio*. Even in the general case Domar weights sum fairly accurately to the Domar ratio, because the trade deficit, εD, is small relative to potential output, $p(V^{\top} - U)s$. The Solow residual measures the shift of the PPF of the economy and this explains why the Domar weights feature activity scale corrections (s); the latter transform actual output to potential output. The corrections are merely allocative. The sum of the Domar weights – or, more precisely the Domar ratio, $pV^{\top}s/p(V^{\top} - U)s$ – is close to the observed gross/net output ratio, $pV^{\top}e/p(V^{\top} - U)e$, because the frontier corrections in the Domar ratio are made in the numerator as well as the denominator.

The subtlety that requires the taking of sectoral productivity growth rate weights which sum to *more* than unity is the other side of the coin we have encountered in national accounting. In chapter 6, we drew attention to the fact that the appropriate measure of the national product is based on the *net* output of the production sectors only. If one wrongly added the gross outputs of the production sectors, some products would be double counted as intermediate product and as final good, such as a car that is first sold to a dealer and then to a consumer. Just as the misuse of gross output would overstate the national product in national accounting, so it would understate productivity in growth accounting.

Still a further decomposition of productivity can be given if the data, (U, V, K, L), fulfill the commodity technology model (exactly or approximately, see chapter 7, and all sectors are active (for example by non-negativity constraints on net exports). Then, by theorem 7.1 and (7.31) and (7.32)

$$U = AV^\top, K = kV^\top, L = lV^\top \tag{12.23}$$

and, by the phenomenon of complementary slackness (corollary 4.5) applied to the first constraint of the dual program (12.2):

$$p(V^\top - U) = rK + wL \tag{12.24}$$

Substituting (12.23) into (12.20)

$$SR = \sum_{j=1}^{m} \frac{\left\{ p\left[(I - A)V_{\bullet j}^\top\right]' - r\left(kV_{\bullet j}^\top\right)' - w\left(lV_{\bullet j}^\top\right)' \right\} s_j}{pac}$$

$$= -\sum_{j=1}^{m} \frac{(pA' + rk' + wl')V_{\bullet j}^\top s_j}{pac} + \sum_{j=1}^{m} \frac{[p(I - A) - rk - wl]V_{\bullet j}^\top s_j}{pac} \tag{12.25}$$

Post-multiplication of (12.24) by the inverse of $V^\top$, using (12.23), renders the bracketed expression in the numerator of the last sum term of (12.25) zero. The first term can be simplified as well, defining Wolff's (1994) unit cost reductions π_i and (frontier) outputs x_i by the row and column vectors,

$$\pi = -pA' - rk' - wl', x = V^\top s \tag{12.26}$$

Substitution of (12.26) in (12.25), recalling that the second term vanishes, yields the Solow residual as a combination of reductions of input-output coefficients:

$$SR = \frac{\pi x}{pac} = \sum_{i=1}^{n} \frac{x_i}{pac} \pi_i \tag{12.27}$$

More precisely, (12.27) reveals the Solow residual as a Domar-weighted average of cost reductions per dollar of output.

The analysis has come to a close of the circle. TFP growth is the sum of the rate of EC and FP growth or technical change. The latter is the Solow residual (augmented with a similar cost reduction term for the trade sector). The final decomposition (12.27), confirms the intuition of Solow (1957), that his residual measures the shift of the PPF. In the process we have captured two components of TFP growth which are missed in Solow's idyllic perfectly competitive closed economy, namely efficiency change and the terms of trade effect. Our analysis makes the intuition very concrete by expressing technical change in reductions of input-output coefficients. The macroeconomic concept of TFP growth has been grounded in changes of microeconomic fundamentals.

Table 12.1 *Frontier productivity growth (FP) and the rate of efficiency change (EC) ((12.8), (12.9)), and (12.10), annualized percentages)*

	1962–74	1974–81	1981–91
FP	2.4	−0.8	3.6
EC	−0.6	0.9	−3.7
TFP	1.8	0.1	−0.1

12.4 Application to the Canadian economy

To illustrate our methodology, we present the productivity results obtained by ten Raa and Mohnen (2002), for the Canadian economy during the period from 1962 to 1991 at the medium level of disaggregation, which comprises fifty industries and ninety-four commodities. The linear program was solved for each year from 1962 to 1991 yielding the optimal activity levels and shadow prices for the TFP expressions.

Table 12.1 shows the decomposition of TFP growth into a shift of the frontier (FP growth) and a movement towards the frontier (EC). The healthy TFP growth rate of EC in the period 1962–74 reflects FP growth. The frontier slowed down – in fact, contracted – in the period 1974–81, but this was compensated by EC, yielding a tiny TFP growth rate. The period 1981–91 showed no recovery, but an interesting reversal of the components. The frontier moved out, but this effect was nullified by negative efficiency change. The economy became healthy, but there were severe adjustment problems. The shift of the frontier displays the well-known pattern of the golden 1960s, the slowdown in the 1970s, and the structural recovery of the 1980s.

Table 12.2 accounts for FP growth by factor input. The bulk of FP growth is attributed to labor, next to nothing to the trade deficit, and the remainder to capital. In the first period FP and labor productivity both grow by 2.4 percent. The 0.2 percent capital productivity growth is distributed very unevenly over the three types of capital, with infrastructure picking up 1.0 percent, equipment none, and buildings plummeting by 0.8 percent. The slowdown in the second period is ascribed to both labor (dropping to 0.4 percent a year) and capital (becoming −1.2 percent a year). As in the first period, infrastructure is decisive, now explaining all of the negative productivity growth in the second period. The successful FP growth in the last period is again a labor story. Labor productivity grew at a dramatic 4.8 percent a year, offsetting a reduction in capital productivity growth of 1.1 percent a year. Again, the latter is determined by the productivity of infrastructure. The price correction term, reflecting a change in final demand composition, played a minor role. (Demand has always tended to shift towards commodities requiring scarce resources, decreasing, but not by much, the positive effects of individual factor productivities on frontier productivity growth.)

Table 12.3 reveals the two sources of frontier shift, namely technical change and the terms of trade effect. In the first period the bulk of FP growth (2.4 percent) is caused by technical change (the Solow residual at shadow prices is 1.7 percent). The FP slowdown in the second

Table 12.2 *Frontier productivity growth (FP), by factor input ((12.9),
annualized percentages)*

	1962–74	1974–81	1981–91
Buildings	−0.9	0.4	−0.3
Equipment	0.0	0.1	0.3
Infrastructure	1.1	−1.5	−1.2
Capital, total	0.2	−1.0	−1.1
Labor	2.4	0.5	5.0
Deficit	−0.0	0.0	−0.1
Price	−0.2	−0.3	−0.2
FP	2.4	−0.8	3.6

Table 12.3 *Frontier productivity growth (FP), by Solow residual (SR) and
terms of trade effect ((12.16), (12.17), and (12.18), annualized
percentages)*

	1962–74	1974–81	1981–91
SR	1.7	−1.3	−0.3
TT	0.7	0.5	−3.8
FP	2.4	−0.8	3.6

period is also ascribed to a downturn in technology. The recovery in the last period, however, is due not only to a Solow residual (at shadow prices) increase of 1 percent, but above all to an improvement in the terms of trade effect from 0.5 to 3.8 percent annually. It may look strange to have some negative Solow residuals, albeit at shadow prices. How can technology regress? There are at least two serious explanations for this. First, technical progress does not show in the statistics right away. This is the argument raised by David (1990) to explain the productivity paradox. It takes time to absorb the new information technology and to use it to its maximal efficiency, just as it took time to adjust to using electricity at the beginning of the twentieth century. Second, the negative productivity growth is due to infrastructure, where the benefit may show up in the long run, and not in the short run because of adjustment costs.

12.5   International spillovers

So far, we have viewed an economy as a machine that transforms labor, capital, and foreign debt into a level of domestic final demand, subject to technological constraints and the terms of trade. TFP may grow because of efficiency change, technical change, or an improvement in the terms of trade. The latter component, however, is essentially a change in the relative prices of the tradable commodities. Like any price change, it should be the result of a change in the *structure* of the economic system, possibly in a foreign economy. For example, if an exports item becomes cheaper in the world market due to a process innovation in another major producing country, our economy will add less value in the sector producing it and, therefore, be less productive. This is an example of a *negative international spillover*. If, however, a foreign country enjoys an innovation in the production of a commodity that is *imported* by our economy, then the lower price of the imports is good news; the terms of trade improve and our economy gets more value for what it produces. The Solow residual in the foreign economy spills over to our economy, where it contributes to TFP growth. Taking a "helicopter" point of view of the world economic system, one might say that the sources of growth are changes in the structures of national economies, but that the beneficiaries may be in different economies and that the "benefits" may even be negative to other economies. It is as if a new water source somewhere in the world alters all the streams. Most will gain, but some may lose.

International productivity spillovers are analyzed by application of the productivity concepts developed in this chapter for a national economy to the system of national economies studied in chapter 10) (international trade). However, prices of the tradable commodities are not exogenous, but the solution to the linear program that determines the international equilibrium, (10.5). Notice that both in the general equilibrium model – see (10.8) – and the partial equilibrium model – see the last dual constraint in (12.2) – the relative prices of the tradable commodities in the economy at hand match those in the rest of the world. The only difference, really, is that in general equilibrium model changes in these relative prices are explained in terms of the fundamentals of the national economies. In general equilibrium, even the price levels match (the law of one price holds for tradable commodities); in terms of the partial equilibrium model this means that exchange rate ε is one and that the terms of trade effect (12.17) becomes $p'_T z / pac$.

Shestalova (2001) analyzes international spillovers in a general equilibrium model of the United States, Japan, and Europe[5]) for the years 1985 and 1990. She uses input-output tables and data on labor and capital stocks across sectors from two OECD databases: The Input-Output Data Base (IODB) and the Industrial Structure Data Base (ISDB). Sectors have been aggregated to a common number of 31. The input-output tables are converted to constant prices in 1990 US dollars. Data on capital stock by industry come from ISDB. For each industry, employed capital is defined as the capital stock of industry, corrected for capital utilization. Data on labor across sectors come from ISDB for all countries except for Japan, of which direct data are available. Data on labor force for the five countries are taken from the Labor Force Statistics (LFS) published by the OECD. Commodities produced by Construction and Non-market activities sectors are considered as non-tradable, since the input-output tables for all countries except for Germany reported zero values of export and import for these sectors.

The aggregate Solow residuals in the United States and Europe were found to be lower than those in Japan. Japan is identified as the TFP growth leader over the period 1985–90.

Table 12.4 shows that changes in efficiency were favorable to Europe, while relatively small in the United States and Japan. Japan was leading in technical changes over the period. The terms of trade effect was negative in both Japan and Europe, implying that free trade

---

[5] "Europe" is an aggregation of France, West Germany, and the United Kingdom.

Table 12.4 *Decomposition of annual TFP growth*

	Efficiency change	SR	Terms of trade effect	TFP growth
United States	0.25	−1.16	1.35	0.44
Japan	0.63	3.09	−1.15	2.56
Europe	3.03	0.03	−1.72	1.34

Source: Table 2 of Shestalova (2001). A slight correction has been made in the last two columns to be consistent with our trade term $\varepsilon D'$ in *TFP* expression (12.7).

transmits some of the welfare gains from changes in the fundamentals of the European and Japanese economies towards the United States. Although the observed level of the total net export from the system is preserved, the terms of trade effects for the three economies do not cancel, because different values of final demand are used in the denominators. The aggregate values of TFP growth evaluated at shadow prices are reported in the last column of table 12.4. In spite of the negative terms of trade effect, Japan appeared to be the leader in TFP growth.

12.6   Intersectoral spillovers

Technical progress causes a cost reduction. If an economy is competitive, the cost reduction leads to a price reduction and the productivity gain is thus passed on to other sectors and, eventually, to the consumers. This type of spillover, investigated in section 12.5, is *passive*. An improvement occurs somewhere and the benefits leak to all corners of the economy. Another form of spillover is more direct. An improvement in one sector may induce further improvements in other sectors. If computers become more powerful and cheaper, the service industries become more productive not only *simply* because they can produce the same output at a lower cost, adding more value, but also because new techniques of providing services or whole new services are developed. A productivity change in one industry yields more productivity change in other industries. To investigate such intersectoral productivity spillovers we must model the causes or sources of technical change.

The main cause of productivity growth is research and development (R&D). R&D expended in an industry creates technical change in the home industry and also in downstream industries. The latter is the intersectoral spillover. However, for R&D to spill over into TFP growth in other sectors, it must first be successful in the home sector, and this success is measured by TFP growth in the home sector. Thus, for any industry, TFP growth depends on R&D and on TFP growth in the supplying industries. The other side of the coin is that R&D in one industry can be associated with TFP growth in all industries. In other words, we may impute TFP growth to the sectors where the driving R&D takes place. This imputation amounts to a decomposition of TFP growth not by sector where it occurs (the Domar decomposition of section 12.3), but by sector that caused it – i.e. by source of growth.

In the United States, over the period 1958–87, the leading contributors to TFP growth were Trade & restaurants, Real estate, Agriculture, Transportation, and Food products. This is the result of a straightforward Domar decomposition (12.20) by ten Raa and Wolff (2000, table 3). Surprisingly, Computers are not in the list. As Bob Solow (1987) quipped, "You can see the Computer Age everywhere but in the productivity statistics." Now 1958–87 is quite an early period in the Computer Age and successful application of new techniques takes time. The productivity paradox of computers was thus considered an adjustment problem that would disappear eventually. However, ten Raa and Wolff (2000, table 3) discovered that if TFP growth is imputed to the *sources* of the spillovers, the leading sources of growth are Computers & office equipment, Electronic components, Plastics and synthetics, Scientific and control instruments, and Aircrafts and parts. In other words, Computers were successful not in the passive spillover sense (of their becoming cheaper) but in the *active* spillover sense of generating innovations elsewhere.

To understand all this, organize the R&D expenditures by sector in a row vector, RD. The ten Raa–Wolff (2000) model is

$$\pi = \alpha e^\top + \beta_1 RD(V^\top)^{-1} + \beta_2 \pi A \qquad (12.28)$$

In formula (12.28) α is autonomous growth, β_1 the return to R&D, β_2 the spillover coefficient, and A the matrix of input-output coefficients.[6]

That β_1 is the return to R&D requires some explanation. Substitution of (12.16) and (12.28) into the Domar decomposition (12.27) yields

$$pF' - r(Ks)' - w(Ls)' = [\alpha e^\top + \beta_1 RD(V^\top)^{-1} + \beta_2 \pi A]x \qquad (12.29)$$

Here we use the expression for (frontier) output given by (12.26). On the left-hand side of (12.29) is the additional net output. The second term on the right-hand side is $\beta_1 RD$ in view of (12.26). Hence β_1 measures the return to R&D. Only the direct return is captured by β_1: it ignores the spillovers. Since the cost reductions π are found on both sides of (12.28), there is a multiplier effect. The spillover term posts πA: Solow residuals in supplying sectors spill over in proportion to the input-output coefficients.[7]

The spillover analysis is a matter of solving (12.28). Denote the Leontief inverse of $\beta_2 A$ by $\tilde{B}$. Then the solution is:

$$\pi = [\alpha e^\top + \beta_1 RD(V^\top)^{-1}]\tilde{B} \qquad (12.30)$$

Substitution of (12.30) into the Domar decomposition (12.27) yields:

$$SR = [\alpha e^\top + \beta_1 RD(V^\top)^{-1}]\tilde{B}x/pac \qquad (12.31)$$

To develop some intuition, consider the case of no spillovers, then $\beta_2 = 0$, $\tilde{B} = I$, and $SR = [\alpha e^\top + \beta_1 RD(V^\top)^{-1}]x/pac$. Here the return to R&D is given by β_1, as we have argued before. Now, in (12.31) the spillovers multiply the direct rate of return β_1 by means

---

[6] Ten Raa and Wolff (2000) use $\hat{p}A\hat{p}^{-1}$, but we may normalize the commodity units, such that all prices are unity.
[7] Ten Raa and Wolff (2000) also include capital-embodied spillovers on top of the flow-embodied spillover πA, but we relegate the intersectoral modeling of capital to chapter 13.

of the Leontief inverse $\tilde{B}$. These *spillover multipliers* transform the direct rate of return into a total rate of return.

There are two ways to read (12.31), depending on how one groups the three factors in the numerator:

$$SR = [\alpha e^\top + \beta_1 RD(V^\top)^{-1}]\tilde{B} \bullet x/pac = [\alpha e^\top + \beta_1 RD(V^\top)^{-1}] \bullet \tilde{B}x/pac \quad (12.32)$$

The first reading, on the left-hand side of (12.32), is πx and amounts to the standard Domar decomposition, accounting for productivity growth by sectors where it is recorded. The second reading, on the right-hand side of (12.32), is the inner product of the vector of sectoral sources of growth, $\alpha e^\top + \beta_1 RD(V^\top)^{-1}$, and the vector of products of spillover multipliers and Domar weights, $\tilde{B}x/pac$. The alternative decompositions in (12.32) explain the difference in importance of sectors in productivity growth accounting and as sources of growth, respectively. Trade & restaurants record a lot of productivity growth (picking up a big term in the first decomposition), but Computers & office equipment are an important *source* of growth (picking up a big term in the second decomposition).

12.7   Conclusion

The output of an economy may grow because the inputs grow or because the output/input ratio or performance of the economy improves. The performance is measured by TFP. Its growth rate can be decomposed in a movement towards the frontier (efficiency change) and shift of the frontier (frontier productivity growth). The latter can be decomposed in sectoral productivity growth rates and a terms of trade effect. The terms of trade effects transmit technical and efficiency changes between economies. Innovations spill over passively by price reductions and actively by spin-offs in downstream industries. Perhaps surprisingly, all these effects can be calculated given input-output statistics of national economies.

Exercise

1. Consider exercise 4 of chapter 6 and exercise 2 of chapter 9. 1993 shows only two changes. Material costs in the service sector is reduced by 1 and domestic consumption of the good is increased by 1.
   (a) Determine TFP growth and explain why it can be ascribed to labor. Which technical coefficient change causes it? (Use the commodity technology model.)
   (b) Suppose the government wants to increase domestic consumption of the service by 1 as well. How much more capital and labor would be required?

References

David, P. (1990). "The Dynamo and the Computer," *American Economic Review, Papers and Proceedings* 80(2), 355–61.

Färe, R., S. GrossKopf, C. A. K. Lorell and Z. Zhang (1994). "Productivity Growth, Technical Progress and Efficiency Changes in Industrialised Countries," *American Economic Review* 84, 66–83.

Hulten, C. R. (1978). "Growth Accounting with Intermediate Inputs," *Review of Economic Studies* 45 (3), 511–18

Jorgenson, D. W. and Z. Griliches (1967). "The Explanation of Productivity Change," *Review of Economic Studies* 34 (3), 308–50

Nishimizu, M. and J. M. Page, Jr. (1982). "Total Factor Productivity Growth: Technological Progress and Technical Efficiency Change: Dimensions of Productivity Change in Yugoslavia, 1965–1978," *Economic Journal* 92, 920–36.

ten Raa, Th. and P. Mohnen (2002). "Neoclassical Growth Accounting and Frontier Analysis: A Synthesis," *Journal of Productivity Analysis* 18, 111–28; reprinted in Thijs ten Raa, *Structural Economics*, London and New York: Routledge (2004)

ten Raa, Th. and E. Wolff (2000). "Engines of Growth in the US Economy," *Structural Change & Economic Dynamics* 11, 473–89.

Shestalova, V. (2001). "General Equilibrium Analysis of International TFP Growth Rates," *Economic Systems Research* 13(4), 391–404

Solow, R. M. (1957). "Technical Change and the Aggregate Production Function," *Review of Economics and Statistics* 39 (3), 312–20

  (1987). "We'd Better Watch out," *New York Times Book Review* 36, July 12

Weitzman, W. (1976). "On the Welfare Significance of National Product in a Dynamic Economy," *Quarterly Journal of Economics* 20, 156–62.

Wolff, E. N. (1994). "Productivity Measurement within an Input-Output Framework," *Regional Science & Urban Economics* 24 (1), 75–92

13 The dynamic inverse

13.1 Introduction

Economies grow as more factor input becomes available or technology advances. The increased availability of labor is a matter of demography, but the increased availability of capital is a matter of economics. In this chapter we will model all the input requirements of future consumption, including the requirements of building the capital stock. In a static world, the total requirements were found through the Leontief inverse (2.18). Its extension to the capital requirements is the dynamic inverse (Leontief 1970).

An economy uses factor inputs capital and labor to produce the net outputs consumption, investment, and possibly net exports. The investment part of net output is a bill of commodities, which are added to the stock of capital. The stock of capital is expanded to increase the productive capacity of the economy, to further the level of consumption. When the investment in the stock of capital is accounted for period by period, the latter is no longer exogenous. The economy becomes a machine that transforms labor into consumption. Capital must be present, but is the product of past activity. It is preserved over the current cycle of production, except possibly a part that depreciates. The use–make framework is very suitable for the modeling of production with capital as a stock of produced commodities (von Neumann 1945). In this chapter we shall show how the material balance applies to stocks in a temporal setting. Basically, the input and output terms are no longer ordinary products between use and make matrices on the one hand and activity vectors on the other, but so-called "convolution products" (ten Raa 1986). We will also show how to go from stocks accounting to flows accounting, deriving the material balance for commodity flows. An example is the dynamic input-output model (Leontief 1970):

$$x = Ax + B\Delta x + y \tag{13.1}$$

In (13.1), matrices A and B display the flow and stock input coefficients, respectively, and Δ is the operator that takes an increment over time:

$$\Delta x(t) = x(t+1) - x(t) \tag{13.2}$$

The dynamic input-output model (13.1) will be shown to be valid only under a restrictive assumption on the lifetime of capital. The path of investment necessary to sustain capacities that may generate a certain consumption pattern is determined by a dynamic version of the Leontief inverse. The main ideas get across best by first considering a one-sector economy with a single commodity.

13.2   A one-sector economy

All we need to know about a one-sector economy with a single commodity is input u, output v, activity level s, and capital stock K. (We pay no attention to labor.) Some of the net output, $(v - u)s$, is added to the stock of capital and the remainder is consumed. Capital is a stock of the commodity that, unlike the material input u, is not absorbed in the process of production, but is carried over the cycle. One might say that input $u + K$ produces output $v + K$. The first term of the input represents the absorption of materials, including depreciation, and the second term the durable stock of commodities, such as housing and machinery. Marx (1974) refers to u as *circulating* capital and to K as *fixed* capital.

The classification of the means of production in circulating and fixed capital is a matter of degree. While electricity is circulating, buildings, machinery, and equipment are classified as fixed capital. But drills have to be replaced continuously and are therefore more like circulating capital. A unifying approach to circulating and fixed capital is through an account of the lifetime of process output.

A process centered at time 0 transfers inputs $u(t)$ at times $t \leq 0$ into outputs $v(t)$ at times $t > 0$. Time runs through the integers. The time profile of input u shows the lead times that must be observed in production. If production is instantaneous, then $u(t)$ is non-zero only for $t = 0$. The time profile of output v shows the lifetime of the product. By the time $v(t)$ reaches zero, the process is dead. If only $v(1)$ is non-zero, output is characterized by sudden death. If v is constant, we have the purely hypothetical case of a process with a completely durable product.

At age t, output depreciated by $-\Delta v(t)$. By definition (13.2), *depreciation at age t* amounts to $v(t) - v(t + 1)$, the amount of output at time t which is no longer available at the next period when the process is operated at the unit level. In case of sudden death, the entire output depreciates in the first period. In the case of geometric decay,

$$v(t) = (1 - \delta)^{t-1} \tag{13.3}$$

where δ is a number between zero and one. It is essentially the rate of deprecation, since depreciation, substituting formula (13.3) into the depreciation expression $-\Delta v(t)$ amounts to:

$$-\Delta v(t) = v(t) - v(t + 1) = (1 - \delta)^{t-1} - (1 - \delta)^t$$
$$= [1 - (1 - \delta)](1 - \delta)^{t-1} = \delta v(t) \tag{13.4}$$

The level of output is a sufficient statistic for the depreciation; age has no intrinsic role. This lifetime profile is crucial for the establishment of the dynamic input-output model below.

If the process were active only at time 0, then the amount of commodity present at time t would be $v(t)s(0)$, where $s(0)$ is the activity level of the process. The process centered in the next period (period 1), however, contributes $v(t - 1)s(1)$ to the stock of the commodity or *capital* at time t. Here $s(1)$ is the activity level of the process of time 1, and $v(t - 1)$ is its output at age $(t - 1)$, which it assumes at time t. And so on. The process centered at time $t - 1$ contributes $v(1)s(t - 1)$ to the stock at time t. By ascending age, the total stock of capital at time t amounts to:

$$K(t) = v(1)s(t - 1) + v(2)s(t - 2) + \cdots \tag{13.5}$$

The term structure is called the *vintage structure* of capital.

The *convolution product* of two functions of time, f and g, is defined by:

$$(f*g)(t) = \sum_{\tau=-\infty}^{\infty} f(\tau)g(t - \tau) \tag{13.6}$$

By definitions (13.5) and (13.6), capital is the convolution product of output and activity:

$$K = v*s \tag{13.7}$$

In (13.7) we put, without loss of generality, $v(\tau) = 0$ for $\tau \leq 0$.

A second application of the convolution product is the measurement of depreciation. Recalling that depreciation at age τ is defined as $-\Delta v(\tau)$, we obtain that at time t, depreciation of capital of vintage τ amounts to $-\Delta v(\tau)s(t - \tau)$, where $s(t - \tau)$ is the level of activity that prevailed when this capital was born. Summing over vintages $\tau > 0$, we obtain the *depreciation at time t*:

$$D(t) = - \sum_{\tau>0} \Delta v(\tau)s(t - \tau) \tag{13.8}$$

Except for one term, expression (13.8) is the convolution product of $-\Delta v$ and s. Since $v(\tau) = 0$ for $\tau \leq 0$, we have $\Delta v(\tau) = v(\tau + 1) - v(\tau) = 0$ for $\tau < 0$, but not for $\tau = 0$. Consequently:

$$-(\Delta v*s)(t) = - \sum_{\tau} \Delta v(\tau)s(t - \tau) = -\Delta v(0)s(t) - \sum_{\tau>0} \Delta v(\tau)s(t - \tau)$$
$$= -v(1)s(t) + D(t) \tag{13.9}$$

Equation (13.9) states that the convolution product of the depreciation profile and output equals current depreciation minus the product of the instantaneous output and the current activity levels.

13.3　The material balance

We are now prepared to set up the material balance, in terms of first stocks and then flows. The supply side of the stock balance is the amount of capital, (13.7). Some of the commodity stock is absorbed by the process centered at the time under consideration, t, namely $u(0)s(t)$. Since a process at unit activity level requires $u(-1)$ one period ahead of time, the process at time $t + 1$ requires $u(-1)s(t + 1)$ at time t. Total industry demand amounts $u(0)s(t) + u(-1)s(t + 1) + \cdots = (u*s)(t)$, where we put $u(t') = 0$ for $t' > 0$, without loss of generality. The stock of capital not claimed by industry goes to the households and is denoted $Y(t)$.

The stock balance thus reads:

$$v*s = u*s + Y \qquad (13.10)$$

Each term in (13.10) is a function of time. The transition from stocks to flows is by taking differences. A nice property of the convolution product is that the difference can be applied to just one factor, either the first or the second:

Lemma 13.1. $\Delta(f*g) = (\Delta f)*g = f*\Delta(g)$.

Proof. $\Delta(f*g)(t) = \Delta \sum_{\tau} f(\tau)g(t-\tau) = \sum_{\tau} f(\tau)\Delta g(t-\tau) = (f*\Delta g)(t)$ and

$$[(\Delta f)*g](t) = \sum_{\tau} (\Delta f)(\tau)g(t-\tau) = \sum_{\tau} [f(\tau+1) - f(\tau)]g(t-\tau)$$

$$= \sum_{\tau} \{f(\tau+1)g[t+1-(\tau+1)] - f(\tau)g(t-\tau)\}$$

$$= \sum_{\tau} f(\tau)g(t+1-\tau) - \sum_{\tau} f(\tau)g(t-\tau)$$

$$= \sum_{\tau} f(\tau)\Delta g(t-\tau)$$

$$= (f*\Delta g)(t) \qquad \qquad \square$$

Now let us apply lemma 13.1 to the differencing of the stocks balance, (13.10). Invoking (13.9), the left-hand side becomes $v(1)s(t) - D(t)$, of which we shift the second term to the right-hand side. The first term on the right-hand side of (13.10) becomes $(u*\Delta s)(t)$, which we spell out, using the fact that u is zero on the positives:

$$v(1)s(t) = D(t) + \sum_{\tau \leq 0} u(\tau)\Delta s(t-\tau) + \Delta Y(t) \qquad (13.11)$$

The supply side, on the left-hand side of balance (13.11), displays the instantaneous output of the current process. The demand side, on the right-hand side, comprises replacement investment, expansion investment, and an addition to the household stock. Material balance equation (13.11) bears out the dynamics of the stock equation, (13.10), and subsumes the dynamic input-output model.

13.4   Dynamic input-output analysis of a one-sector economy

For a one-sector economy, the dynamic input-output model, (13.1), reduces to:

$$x = ax + b\Delta x + y \qquad (13.12)$$

In (13.12) an output level x requires an input flow, ax, and a stock, bx. Here a is a flow input coefficient and b is a stock input coefficient. Residual y is the final demand flow. Since the stock is carried over to the next period, only the expansion, $\Delta bx = b\Delta x$, weighs on the demand side of the economy. The stock is proportional to the instantaneous rate of output. History does not matter; investment is independent of the vintage structure of capital.

We will justify the simplified model (13.12) for the case of geometric capital decay (13.3), whence depreciation is independent of the vintage structure of capital. The material balance of flows (13.11) reduces to, invoking (13.8), (13.4), (13.5), (13.7), and (13.10), and shifting $\delta Y(t)$ from the first to the last term on the right-hand side:

$$s(t) = \delta[u(0)s(t) + u(-1)s(t+1) + \cdots]$$
$$+ U(0)\Delta s(t) + U(-1)\Delta s(t+1) + \cdots + (\delta + \Delta)Y(t) \tag{13.13}$$

Equation (13.13) is future-driven, as current output fulfills current and future intermediate demand plus current final demand. The final demand flows replace and expand the household stock. Leontief (1970) assumed that production is instantaneous, ignoring production lead times. In this situation, only $u(0)$ is non-zero and (13.13) becomes the dynamic input-output equation, (13.12), with variable s playing the role of x and

$$a = \delta u(0), b = u(0) \tag{13.14}$$

Condition (13.14) validates the dynamic input-output model (13.12) for geometric capital decay and instantaneous production. It imposes quite a restriction on the stock and flow coefficients, namely $b = a/\delta$. If input-output coefficients fail to fulfill this restriction, one of the assumptions – geometric decay or instantaneity – is not fulfilled and one must be cautious, for the very derivation of Leontief's (13.12) is no longer valid and a return to material balance equation (13.13) is warranted.

As the Leontief inverse solves the static input-output model, the dynamic inverse solves the dynamic input-output model. The dynamic inverse is an extension of the Leontief inverse. To solve for the activity levels that sustain a desired bill of final goods, first consider an injection of final demand at time 0:

$$y(0) = 1, \ y(t) = 0 \ (t \neq 0) \tag{13.15}$$

Solutions are found backward. No future output is required:

$$x^*(1) = x^*(2) = \cdots = 0 \tag{13.16}$$

At time zero the flow balance, (13.12), equates output to the sum of input, investment and final demand:

$$x(0) = ax(0) - bx(0) + 1 \tag{13.17}$$

Since capital required in the next period is zero, the entire stock may be consumed. Hence investment is actually *dis*investment in the amount of $bx(0)$. The solution to (13.17) is:

$$x^*(0) = (1 - a + b)^{-1} \tag{13.18}$$

In the preceding period, the balance reads:

$$x(-1) = ax(-1) + b[x^*(0) - x(-1)] \tag{13.19}$$

Equation (13.19) is like (13.17), with time shifted and the unit of final demand replaced by

$bx^*(0)$, the capital stock to be left over. The solution, analogous to (13.18), is:

$$x^*(-1) = (1 - a + b)^{-1}bx^*(0) \qquad (13.20)$$

Repeating the argument and using (13.20),

$$x^*(-2) = (1 - a + b)^{-1}bx^*(-1) = [(1 - a + b)^{-1}b]^2x^*(0) \qquad (13.21)$$

And so on,

$$x^*(-t) = [(1 - a + b)^{-1}b]^t x^*(0) \qquad (13.22)$$

for $t > 0$ or $-t < 0$. For $t = 0$ the solution is given by (13.18) and for $t > 0$ it is zero.

Contrary to conventional wisdom, the capital coefficient need not be invertible. If $b = 0$, the solution (13.18) and (13.22) reduces to $x^*(0) = (1 - a)^{-1}$ and $x^*(t) = 0$ otherwise. The former exists and is non-negative if and only if $0 \le a < 1$ (theorem 2.2). This condition also ensures the existence of solution (13.22) if $b > 0$, and the output profile x^* is called the *dynamic inverse*. The dynamic inverse extends the Leontief inverse to the case $b > 0$. It fulfills the material balance at all times. Formally,

$$x^* = ax^* + b\Delta x^* + e_0 \qquad (13.23)$$

In (13.23) $e_0(t) = 1$ for $t = 0$ and zero otherwise. Now let us replace the simple final demand bill, e_0, by a general one, y. The sustaining activity levels are given by the convolution product of the dynamic inverse and final demand, $x*y$. This result is established by convolution of (13.23) with y:

$$x^**y = ax^**y + b(\Delta x^*)*y + e_0*y \qquad (13.24)$$

Substitute lemma 13.1 and the fact that $(e_0*y)(t) = \sum_\tau e_0(\tau)y(t - \tau) = y(t)$ in (13.24):

$$x^**y = ax**y + b\Delta(x**y) + y \qquad (13.25)$$

Equation (13.25) shows that the convolution product x^**y solves the dynamic input-output model, (13.12).

13.5   Multi-sector economies

The essence of capital is that production takes time or products have a lifetime. The extension of the preceding analysis of capital, depreciation, the material balance, and the dynamic inverse to multi-sectoral economies is trivial. Basically, final demand and activities become vectors and the use and make tables become matrix valued. The dynamic inverse continues to extend the Leontief inverse and the convolution product with final demand solves for the activity levels. The definition of the convolution product is easily extended from scalar valued functions to matrix valued function. If F and G are functions of time with $F(t)$ and $G(t)$ matrices of dimension $m \times k$ and $k \times n$, respectively, then their convolution product,

$F*G$, is the function of time with $(m \times n)$-dimensional matrices as values, defined by:

$$(F*G)(t) = \sum_{\tau=-\infty}^{\infty} F(\tau)G(t - \tau) \tag{13.26}$$

Taking a component of (13.26) reveals the relationship with the convolution product for scalar valued functions:

$$(F*G)_{ij}(t) = \sum_{\tau=-\infty}^{\infty} [F(\tau)G(t - \tau)]_{ij} = \sum_{\tau=-\infty}^{\infty} \sum_{l=1}^{k} f_{il}(\tau)g_{lj}(t - \tau)$$

$$= \sum_{l=1}^{k} \sum_{\tau=-\infty}^{\infty} f_{il}(\tau)g_{lj}(t - \tau) = \sum_{l=1}^{k} \left(f_{il}*g_{lj} \right)(t) \tag{13.27}$$

The technology of the economy is now represented by a pair of matrix valued functions of time, U and V. Inputs U are defined for times $t \leq 0$ and outputs V for times $t > 0$. The first process is given by the first column and row of U and V, respectively. Analogous to (13.7), *capital* is the convolution product of output and activity:

$$K = V^{\top}*s \tag{13.28}$$

The transposition in expression (13.28) is to get the dimensions right in the product required, just as in the static analysis. Analogous to definition (13.8), *depreciation at time t* is defined by

$$D(t) = -\sum_{\tau>0} \Delta V^{\top}(\tau)s(t - \tau) \tag{13.29}$$

Invoking the convolution product, (13.26), expression (13.29), analogous to (13.9) becomes:

$$D(t) = -(\Delta V^{\top}*s)(t) + V^{\top}(1)s(t) \tag{13.30}$$

Analogous to (13.10), the stock balance reads:

$$V^{\top}*s = U^{*}s + Y \tag{13.31}$$

In balance (13.31) Y is the household commodity stock, a function of time. Differencing the stock balance (13.31) and substituting (13.30), we obtain, analogous to the one-dimensional material balance (13.11):

$$V^{\top}(1)s(t) = D(t) + \sum_{\tau \leq 0} U(\tau)\Delta s(t - \tau) + \Delta Y(t) \tag{13.32}$$

The extension does not require that the number of processes be equal to the number of commodities.

The subsumption of the dynamic input-output model is analogous to the one-sector case. Leontief assumes that processes are pure (section 5.2), one for each commodity and, implicitly, that capital decays geometrically. Formally,

$$V(t) = (I - \hat{\delta})^{t-1} \tag{13.33}$$

The rate of depreciation of commodity i capital is δ_i. These rates are organized in vector δ and the cap creates a diagonal matrix. Analogous to (13.13), the material balance of flows reduces to:

$$s(t) = \hat{\delta}[U(0)s(t) + U(-1)s(t+1) + \cdots]$$
$$+ U(0)\Delta s(t) + U(-1)\Delta s(t+1) + \cdots + (\hat{\delta} + \Delta)Y(t) \tag{13.34}$$

Leontief assumes that production is instantaneous: Only $U(0)$ is non-zero. Equation (13.34) thus becomes the dynamic input-output model (13.1), where vector x replaces s and

$$A = \hat{\delta}U(0), \quad B = U(0), \quad (\hat{\delta} + \Delta)Y(t) \tag{13.35}$$

Condition (13.35) validates the dynamic input-output model (13.1) for geometric capital decay and instantaneous production. A restriction on the stock and flow coefficients must hold, namely the Bródy (1974, p. 153) condition:

$$B = \hat{\delta}^{-1}A \tag{13.36}$$

The dynamic inverse is determined the same way as for a one-sector economy; the B-matrix need *not* be invertible. First consider injections of final demand:

$$y(0) = e_i, \ y(t) = 0 \ (t \neq 0) \tag{13.37}$$

Denote the solution to balance equation (13.1) by $x_{\bullet i}^*$, a vector valued function of time. Organize the solutions in a matrix valued function of time, X^*; this is the *dynamic inverse*. Because future output $X^*(1) = X^*(2) = \cdots = 0$, the flow balances (13.1) at time zero (one column for each e_i-problem) read:

$$X(0) = AX(0) - BX(0) + I \tag{13.38}$$

The solution to (13.38) can be given explicitly by:

$$X^*(0) = (I - A + B)^{-1} \tag{13.39}$$

It exists if $U(0)$ fulfills the self-reliance condition that ensures the Leontief inverse (theorem 2.2). Completely analogous to the scalar case, (13.22), the other time components of the dynamic inverse are given by:

$$X^*(-t) = [(1 - A + B)^{-1}B]^t X^*(0) \tag{13.40}$$

For a general path of final demand, y, the convolution product with the dynamic inverse given by (13.39) and (13.40) yields the required gross outputs:

$$x = X^* * y \tag{13.41}$$

If the Bródy condition (13.36) is not met, the dynamic inverse may fail to exist, even when A has a Leontief inverse. For example:

$$A = 0, \quad B = \begin{pmatrix} 0 & 1 \\ 1 & 0 \end{pmatrix} \tag{13.42}$$

Under (13.42) balance (13.38) reads:

$$\begin{pmatrix} 1 & 1 \\ 1 & 1 \end{pmatrix} X(0) = \begin{pmatrix} 1 & 0 \\ 0 & 1 \end{pmatrix} \tag{13.43}$$

The first columns of (13.43) yield $(1\ 1)s(0) = 1$ and $(1\ 1)s(0) = 0$, a contradiction. This failure is a peculiar aspect of discrete time modeling. In continuous time, the productivity of matrix A ensures the existence of the dynamic inverse, whatever the value of matrix B.[1] It should be mentioned, however, that if the Bródy condition (13.36) is not met, the dynamic input-output model (13.1) should be replaced by the general stock equation, (13.31), or its flow derivative, (13.32).[2]

An illuminating example of dynamic input-output analysis is the case of a unitary production lag:

$$U(0) = A, \quad V(1) = I \tag{13.44}$$

and all other time components zero. This is the static input-output model, with one modification: outputs emerge only after one unit of (production) time. Under model (13.44) the balance equation, (13.31), reduces to:

$$x(t-1) = Ax(t) + Y(t) \tag{13.45}$$

By definition (13.2) of difference operator Δ, (13.45) is equivalent to

$$x(t) = Ax(t) + A\Delta x(t) + Y(t+1) \tag{13.46}$$

Now (13.46) happens to coincide with a special instance of the dynamic input-output model, (13.1), namely $B = A$. The specification is in agreement with the Bródy condition, (13.36). The dynamic inverse, (13.39) and (13.40), becomes:

$$X^*(-t) = A^t \tag{13.47}$$

Expression (13.47) is the representative term of the ordinary Leontief inverse (2.18). The terms of the Leontief inverse thus emerge explicitly when production takes a unit of time.

13.6   Conclusion

The dynamic material balance can be used as a constraint in the maximization of a function of the household stock, extending our linear programming approach to the dynamic model.[3]

---

[1] It involves a generalized inverse of B, not the Moore–Penrose inverse of statistics, but the one detailed in ten Raa (1986).

[2] Solving this equation requires an application of the theory of distributions; see ten Raa (1986, particularly the appendix).

[3] Since the household stock is a function of time, some discounting is implicit in the valuation function. The only factor input constraint is on labor. The growth rate of the economy is checked by the population growth rate. The wage rate at any point of time measures the marginal productivity of labor at that time. Since commodities are dated, prices will be functions of time. They determine the value of capital, since that is a stock of commodities. As commodity prices diminish through time, reflecting the discounting of the valuation function, so will the value of capitasl. This is the rate of interest. Note that interest rates may be specific to the type of capital (commodity).

Prescribing desired proportions on the household stock we could maximize its level, subject to material balances and a labor constraint. The imposition of desired proportions is troublesome in a dynamic context. Food may not be a substitute for a car, but a car now is certainly a substitute for a car tomorrow. The fixed proportions are therefore dropped in intertemporal settings. In fact, it is standard to go to the other extreme, to model current and future consumption as perfect substitutes by entering them into a linear function, where the coefficients are the discount factors. To avoid specialization in resource-extensive commodities, a non-linear contemporaneous utility function is used.

Commodities will not be wasted when reasonable utility functions are maximized. Consequently, the material balances will be binding and activity levels will depend on the final demand path of the economy as analyzed in this chapter. In particular, investment consists of replacement investment and investment in new capacity, where the latter is driven by future demand. Capacities are fully utilized. Inefficiencies may be decomposed as in chapter 9. It would be a waste of resources to invest in a sector with excess capacity. Full utilization of existing capacities is an easy way to raise the standard of living.

Exercise

1. Consider an economy with a unitary production lag, sudden death of output, and no secondary production. Write down the material balance in terms of stocks. Solve it to determine the activity levels that sustain a given household stock at time zero only.

References

Bródy A. (1974). *Proportions, Prices and Planning*, Budapest, Akadémiai Kiadó and Amsterdam, North-Holland

Leontief, W. (1970). "The Dynamic Inverse," in A. P. Carter and A. Bródy (eds.), *Contributions to Input-Output Analysis*, Amsterdam, North-Holland, 17–46

Marx, K. (1974). *Capital 2: The Process of Circulation of Capital*, New York, International Publishers

von Neumann, J. (1945). "A Model of General Economic Equilibrium," *Review of Economic Studies* 13, 1–9

ten Raa, Th. (1986). "Dynamic Input-Output Analysis with Distributed Activities," *Review of Economics and Statistics* 68 (2), 300–10; reprinted in Thijs ten Raa, *Structural Economics*, London and New York, Routledge (2004)

14   Stochastic input-output analysis

14.1   Introduction

Thus far, the economy has been given by a set of national accounts with unquestioned precision, but confidentiality, reporting, and measurement problems attach error components to economic data and render the derived constructs – multipliers, (potential) GNP, TFP, etc. – imprecise as well. There are two ways to analyze the transmission of errors. A pure error analysis, without imposition of any stochastic structure, involves the calculation of upper and lower bounds. For example, if GNP is to be determined on the basis of sectoral value-added data, the lower bound would be the sum of the lower bounds of the data and the upper bound of *GNP* would be the sum of the upper bounds of the sectoral value-added figures. A more interesting way to analyze the transmission of errors is by means of a *stochastic framework*; the errors are considered random variables, with given probability distributions. The worst-case and best-case scenarios may still occur, but with low probability, because it is unlikely that all (value-added) components assume their lower or upper values simultaneously. Errors tend to cancel out and hence sharper bounds can be derived for the economic variables of interest.

14.2   Stochastics

List data or underlying variables listed in vector a, estimated by random variable $\hat{a}$ with *mean* $E(\hat{a}) = a$ and *variance* $V(\hat{a})$. The former locates the levels of the data and the latter measures their precision. List the economic variables of interest in a vector b. They will be a function of the data: $b = \beta(a)$. The function summarizes the structure of the economic model. Application of the function to the data estimates yields an estimate of the economic variables, namely $\hat{b} = \beta(\hat{a})$.

It is critical if the function is linear or not. An example of a linear function is GNP. If a lists value-added by sector, then GNP is obtained by summation of the components: $b = \beta(a) = e^{\top}a$. The general formulation of a linear function is $b = \beta(a) = \beta_0 a$ where β_0 is a matrix. For linear functions our estimate is unbiased: if $\beta(a) = \beta_0 a$, then $E(\hat{b}) = b$. The proof of this statement is as follows:[1]

$$E(\hat{b}) = E[\beta(\hat{a})] = E(\beta_0 \hat{a}) = \beta_0 E(\hat{a}) = \beta_0 a = \beta(a) = b \qquad (14.1)$$

Linear constructs may therefore be estimated by plugging the estimates of the data or the underlying variables into the formula.

If the variable of interest is a non-linear function of the data, one must be more careful. Suppose we are interested in the square of a datum: $b = a^2$, where a is estimated by $\hat{a}$ with known mean and variance. Say $E(\hat{a}) = a = 0$ and $V(\hat{a}) = 1$. A simple example is $\hat{a} = \pm 1$ with probabilities one half each. Then $E(\hat{a}) = \frac{1}{2}(-1) + \frac{1}{2}1 = 0$ and $V(\hat{a}) = \frac{1}{2}(-1)^2 + \frac{1}{2}1^2 = 1$. In either case, $\hat{b} = \beta(\hat{a}) = \hat{a}^2 = (\pm 1)^2 = 1$ and, therefore, $E(\hat{b}) = 1$. However, $b = a^2 = 0^2 = 0$. Hence direct application of the functional relationship between the economic variables and the data yields an estimate with $E(\hat{b}) > b$. In other words, $\hat{b}$ is not an unbiased estimated of b; the bias is positive. It is instructive to express the inequality in terms of the data:

$$E(\hat{a}^2) > [E(\hat{a})]^2 \qquad (14.2)$$

On the right-hand side of inequality (14.2) we used $E(\hat{a}) = a$. For the quadratic function, the mean of the value exceeds the value of the mean.

The same logic applies to the Leontief inverse of scalar a ($b = 1 + a + a^2 + a^3 + \cdots$). Hence the mean of the Leontief inverse exceeds the Leontief inverse of the mean. This result extends to matrices A (Quandt 1958; Yershov 1969; Simonovits 1975). The first two terms in the Leontief inverse are linear and hence cause no bias, but the quadratic term and further terms produce a bias. Errors reinforce each other when squared or taken to even higher powers and this mechanism yields a relatively high mean of the Leontief inverse.

Kop Jansen (1994) reviews the distributional properties of the Leontief inverse (2.18). Generalizing the above observations, Simonovits (1975) proved that if all the elements of A are independent, random and symmetrically distributed, then the expected value of the Leontief inverse is underestimated by the Leontief inverse of the expected value of A:

$$E[(I - A)^{-1}] \geq [I - E(A)]^{-1} \qquad (14.3)$$

The main shortcoming of the analysis underlying inequality (14.3) is that the stochastics are imposed on the input-output coefficients. If possible, the errors are derived from the underlying data, such as the use–make tables.

For example, an employment multiplier measures the number of workers needed to satisfy a unit of a particular component of final demand. Formula (7.32) gives the commodity technology labor coefficients l and inflation by the Leontief inverse (2.18) yields the employment multipliers λ; see formula (7.35). We will demonstrate that theorem 7.1 reduces the estimation of employment multipliers to linear regression analysis. Substitute the commodity technology input coefficients (7.32) and (7.2) into employment multipliers

[1] The steps in derivation (14.1) are the definition of estimator $\hat{b}$, the linearity of function β, the linearity of expectation operator E, the assumed unbiasedness of estimate $\hat{a}$, the specification of function β, and the definition of function β, respectively.

expression (7.35):

$$\lambda = l(I - A)^{-1} = L(V^\top)^{-1}[I - U(V^\top)^{-1}]^{-1}$$
$$= L\{[I - U(V^\top)^{-1}]V^\top\}^{-1} = L(V^\top - U)^{-1} \tag{14.4}$$

Multiplication by the net output table further simplifies (14.4) to:

$$L = \lambda(V^\top - U) \tag{14.5}$$

For rectangular use–make matrices, with more activities than commodities, (14.5) is overdetermined and employment multipliers can be calculated as in the multiple linear regression analysis (7.29):

$$L = \lambda(V^\top - U) + \varepsilon \tag{14.6}$$

In (14.6) L is a row vector of order m with labor employment, λ is a row vector of order n with employment multipliers, V is a make matrix of order $m \times n$, U is a use matrix of order $n \times m$, and ε is a row vector of presumed independently normally random disturbance errors with zero mean and constant variance, with order m. Notice that m is the number of firms involved or the number of observed values.

The interpretation of regression equation (14.6) is straightforward. Since λ lists the amounts of labor required per unit of final demand or *net* output, multiplication by the net output table yields employment. The first column of $V^\top - U$ is the net output commodity vector of the first sector, firm, establishment, or, in general, observation. Multiplication by λ yields the labor requirement.

14.3   Application

Ten Raa and Rueda Cantuche's (2004) analyze regression (14.6) for the Andalusian economy in the year 1995. The number of firms considered is 18,084 and the employment multiplier estimates are presented in table 14.1.[2] For comparison, the second column displays the employment multipliers based on published use–make matrices. The model has been estimated for eighty-seven commodities by means of ordinary least squares. Seventy-six estimated multipliers are significant at the 95 percent confidence level.[3]

Remarkably, fifty-seven out of eighty-seven commodities have lower employment multipliers than those calculated with published use and make matrices.[4] In other words, most employment multipliers obtained by using published data *over*estimate our values (which are unbiased and consistent), contrary to Simonovits' (1975) result (14.3), but confirming the intuition of Dietzenbacher (1995) and Roland-Holst (1989).

600,000 euros generate large employment (numbers of workers in parentheses) if spent on the final demand categories household employers (115.2), private social services industry (40.2), cleaning services industry (32.7), personal services industry (31.9), or private

---

[2] The Institute of Statistics of Andalusia provided all the available data.   [3] R^2 is 0.9948.

[4] Only nineteen commodities have higher employment multipliers.

Table 14.1 *Employment multipliers (number of workers per 600,000 euros)*

	Description	Estimated multiplier	Multiplier (MIOAN95)	p-value	Lower bound	Upper bound
89	Household employers services	116.2	116.2	0.0000	116.2	116.2
83	Private social services	40.2	40.6	0.0000	39.2	41.2
88	Personal services	31.9	32.6	0.0000	31.6	32.3
75	Cleaning services	32.7	32.1	0.0000	31.6	33.7
74	Security services	23.5	31.6	0.0004	10.5	36.4
5	Forestry and related services	30.0	30.3	0.0000	29.5	30.5
79	Private education services	31.8	28.1	0.0000	29.8	33.8
82	Public social services	25.6	25.7	0.0000	25.4	25.9
1	Fruits and vegetables	23.9	24.1	0.0000	23.3	24.6
44	Furniture	9.7	23.1	0.0017	3.7	15.8
24	Cork and wood products	8.0	22.6	0.0413	0.3	15.7
55	Retail trade and repair domestic and personal effects	42.9	22.1	0.1186	−11.0	96.8
73	Marketing services	1.5	21.5	0.3509	−1.7	4.7
4	Livestock and hunting	21.1	21.3	0.0000	20.7	21.5
2	Olive and vine	21.0	21.2	0.0000	20.5	21.5
70	Research and development	20.1	19.9	0.0000	19.5	20.6
76	Other business services	4.3	19.7	0.7309	−20.3	29.0
85	Social services	22.2	18.8	0.0000	14.2	30.2
57	Bars and restaurants services	31.1	18.8	0.0000	23.2	39.1
77	Public administration	19.0	18.6	0.0000	18.2	19.8
23	Leather tanning, leather products, and footwear	7.2	18.5	0.0013	2.8	11.5
22	Clothing products	4.4	18.4	0.0186	0.7	8.0
51	Preparing, installation, and finishing construction services	18.3	18.4	0.0000	17.7	18.8
6	Fish and fishing products	11.0	18.3	0.0000	9.7	12.4
71	Accounting and law activity services	72.0	18.1	0.1060	−15.3	159.3
32	Ceramics, clay, bricks, and other products for building	11.7	17.7	0.0000	8.6	14.7
52	Petrol and motor vehicles trade services	18.1	17.6	0.1137	−4.3	40.4
13	Canned and preserved fish, fruit, and vegetables	15.0	17.5	0.0000	12.1	17.9
78	Public education services	18.3	17.5	0.0000	17.4	19.2
59	Other earthbound transportation services	17.0	17.1	0.0000	16.1	17.8
80	Public medical and hospitals services	16.6	16.8	0.0000	16.4	16.8
72	Engineering and architecture technical services	23.2	16.5	0.0203	3.6	42.8
84	Public drainage and sewerage services	23.8	16.5	0.0000	20.5	27.1

(cont.)

Table 14.1 (cont.)

	Description	Estimated multiplier	Multiplier (MIOAN95)	p-value	Lower bound	Upper bound
53	Repair motor vehicles services	15.9	16.3	0.0000	15.5	16.3
65	Insurance	12.1	15.9	0.0000	10.3	13.9
35	Fabricated metal products	6.6	15.6	0.0001	3.3	9.9
16	Grain mills, bakery, sugar mills, . . .	4.6	15.6	0.0000	2.7	6.5
33	Stone and glass products	7.1	15.5	0.0000	5.2	9.1
66	Allied financial services	6.4	15.4	0.0021	2.3	10.5
42	Naval transportation and repairing services	2.3	15.4	0.1319	−0.7	5.4
3	Other agriculture and related services	14.6	14.8	0.0000	14.2	15.1
45	Miscellaneous manufactured products	14.6	14.6	0.0000	13.9	15.3
14	Fats and oils	3.4	14.5	0.0000	2.2	4.7
56	Hotels services	19.4	14.1	0.0000	12.8	26.0
36	Machinery and mechanic equipment	14.1	14.0	0.0000	13.4	14.8
60	Sea and river transportation services	7.2	13.7	0.0000	5.0	9.4
7	Coal mining	7.2	13.7	0.0000	5.0	9.3
62	Allied transportation services	8.1	13.6	0.0007	3.4	12.8
69	Computer services	15.1	12.7	0.3185	−14.6	44.9
54	Wholesale trade	3.4	12.4	0.3184	−3.3	10.2
87	Other amusement, cultural, sport, and recreation services	9.6	12.4	0.0000	8.4	10.9
50	Constructions	7.0	12.2	0.0000	5.2	8.7
49	Water and sewerage services	10.8	11.8	0.0000	8.1	13.5
18	Wines and alcoholic beverages	7.7	11.7	0.0000	6.2	9.3
15	Milk and dairy products	11.5	11.6	0.0000	6.5	16.4
46	Recycling products	9.8	11.1	0.0000	8.0	11.5
58	Railway transportation services	10.6	11.1	0.0000	9.9	11.2
68	Machinery and equipment rental	8.8	11.0	0.0001	4.5	13.2
11	Non-metallic and non-energetic minerals	11.0	10.9	0.0000	10.1	12.0
26	Printing, publishing, and editing services	33.9	10.7	0.0868	−4.9	72.7
43	Miscellaneous transportation equipment	1.5	10.5	0.2899	−1.2	4.2
21	Textile mill products	10.6	10.5	0.0000	10.2	11.0
63	Post and communications services	5.2	10.4	0.0000	4.7	5.8
31	Cement, lime, and allied products	4.3	10.2	0.0018	1.6	7.0
12	Meat and meat products	6.4	9.8	0.0001	3.2	9.7
40	Professional and scientific instruments	3.6	9.2	0.0664	−0.2	7.4
64	Finances	8.7	9.1	0.0000	7.9	9.5
30	Rubber and plastic products	3.3	9.1	0.0001	1.6	4.9
10	Metallic minerals	7.0	8.8	0.0000	4.2	9.8

(cont.)

Table 14.1 *(end)*

	Description	Estimated multiplier	Multiplier (MIOAN95)	*p*-value	Lower bound	Upper bound
29	Other chemical products	5.0	8.7	0.0185	0.8	9.2
41	Motor vehicles transportation equipment	11.3	8.6	0.0000	6.4	16.2
38	Electrical and electronic machinery	3.6	8.6	0.0166	0.7	6.6
81	Private medical and hospitals services	4.9	7.6	0.0008	2.0	7.8
61	Air transportation services	8.4	7.6	0.0000	4.7	12.1
39	Electronic materials, radio, and television equipments	7.7	7.5	0.0000	6.9	8.5
19	Beer and soft drinks	5.5	7.2	0.0000	4.7	6.3
25	Paper and allied products	3.6	7.1	0.0000	2.0	5.1
20	Tobacco products	5.4	7.0	0.0478	0.1	10.7
17	Miscellaneous food products	6.0	6.8	0.0010	2.4	9.5
37	Computers and office equipments	5.5	5.9	0.0000	4.7	6.3
86	Cinema, video, radio, and television services	29.1	5.9	0.0000	25.2	33.0
28	Basic chemical products	2.2	5.1	0.0079	0.6	3.7
48	Gas and water steam, and irrigation services	3.5	3.8	0.0000	2.1	5.0
47	Electricity and irrigations services	2.8	3.4	0.0000	2.6	2.9
34	Primary metal products	0.8	2.3	0.0050	0.2	1.3
67	Real estate	2.1	2.0	0.0000	1.6	2.6
27	Petroleum refining products	2.0	1.6	0.0000	1.5	2.6

education (31.8), while little employment is generated in metallurgy (0.8), petroleum refining (2.0), real estate (2.1), or basic chemicals (2.2).

Household employers, electricity and irrigation services industry, and public medical and hospitals services industry have very precise confidence intervals. On the contrary, architecture and engineering technical services industry, security services industry, and social activities have less precise confidence intervals.

14.4   Conclusion

Statistical offices combine use–make flow data (including inversion of the make matrix) to construct input-output coefficients and economists invert the Leontief matrix to determine the output and cost multipliers of the economy. The construction and the inversion are non-linear operations with complicated errors transmission and have been studied in relative isolation. This chapter shows, however, that a shortcut from the use–make data to the multipliers provides simple, unbiased estimates.

References

Dietzenbacher, E. (1995). "On the Basis of Multiplier Estimates." *Journal of Regional Science* 35, 377–90

Kop Jansen, P. S. M. (1994). "Analysis of Multipliers in Stochastic Input-Output Models," *Regional Science & Urban Economics*, 24 (1), 55–74

Quandt, R. E. (1958). "Probabilistic Errors in the Leontief System," *Naval Research Logistics Quarterly* 5, 155–70

ten Raa, Th. and J. M. Rueda Cantuche (2004). "How to Estimate Unbiased and Consistent Input-Output Multipliers on the Basis of Use and Make Matrices," Economic Working Papers E2004/14, centrA

Roland-Holst, D. W. (1989). "Bias and Stability of Multiplier Estimates," *Review of Economics and Statistics* 71, 718–21

Simonovits, A. (1975). "A Note on the Underestimation and Overestimation of the Leontief Inverse," *Econometrica* 43 (3), 493–8

Yershov, E. B. (1969). "Uncertainty of Information and Stability of Solutions to the Static Planned Input-Output Models," *Problems of Macroeconomic Optimum*, Moscow, Ekonomika (in Russian)

Solutions to exercises

Chapter 1

1. n, m, m, No, Yes
2. $2n$, $2n + 2$, Yes, Some, Some
3. Distinguish two cases.

    If $M > 0$, then $M/N < k_i/l_i$ (all i) implies $l_i < Nk_i/M$ (all i) and, therefore, $lx = \Sigma l_i x_i < \Sigma Nk_i x_i / M = Nkx/M \le N$ by the capital constraint.

    If $M = 0$, then $k_i > 0$ (all i) by the assumed intensity inequality and, by the capital constraint, $x = 0$, hence $lx = 0 < N$ (as M/N is finite).

    In either case, the labor constraint is not binding. The wage rate will be zero by (1.15).

Chapter 2

1. Sufficient, Both
2. Gross output (2.37) x is non-negative, for matrices fulfilling theorem 2.2. Net output $x - Ax$ is positive; denote it by y. Then $x = Ax + y \ge 0 + y > 0$.
3. By (2.20), the columns of the Leontief inverse are the solutions to $x - Ax = e_1$ and $x - Ax = e_2$, respectively.

    Take the first equation,

    $$x_1 - a_{11}x_1 - a_{12}x_2 = 1$$
    $$x_2 - a_{21}x_1 - a_{22}x_2 = 0.$$

    It is easy to find the solution: Substitution of $x_2 = \frac{a_{21}x_1}{1-a_{22}}$ into the first component yields $x_1 = \frac{1-a_{22}}{(1-a_{11})(1-a_{22})-a_{12}a_{21}}$ and, therefore, $x_2 = \frac{a_{21}}{(1-a_{11})(1-a_{22})-a_{12}a_{21}}$. These are non-negative if and only if $a_{12}a_{21} < (1 - a_{11})(1 - a_{22})$ and $a_{22} < 1$.

    Similarly, the second column of the Leontief inverse is non-negative if and only if $a_{12}a_{21} < (1 - a_{11})(1 - a_{22})$ and $a_{11} < 1$.

    Summarizing, we have the class of all 2×2-dimensional productive matrices is the set of non-negative matrices $\begin{pmatrix} a_{11} & a_{12} \\ a_{21} & a_{22} \end{pmatrix}$ with $a_{11} < 1$, $a_{22} < 1$ and $a_{12}a_{21} < (1 - a_{11})(1 - a_{22})$.

Chapter 3

1. If the total income multipliers exist and are non-negative, then so does the Leontief inverse of $A + av$ by theorem 2.1 (or 2.2). Hence the Leontief inverse of A exists and is non-negative, ensuring the existence and non-negativity of the production income multipliers.
2. Since A fulfills theorem 2.2, by (2.35)–(2.37) $x \geq Ax + 2e$ for some $x \geq 0$. Pick $v > 0$ such that $avx \leq e$. Then $x \geq (A + av)x + e$. Hence $A + av$ fulfills theorem 2.1. Its Leontief inverse exists and is non-negative by theorem 2.2. Hence the total income multipliers exist for this $v > 0$.
3. Consider a unit increase in the ith component of v. Then p goes up by $e_i^\top \sum_{k=0}^\infty A^k \geq e_i^\top$.
4. When input-output coefficients are nominal and all value-added is income, then $v = p - pA = e^\top (I - A)$ and, therefore, $vB = e^\top$, so that all production income multipliers are one and government expenditure can be targeted on any commodity. If some value-added, $p - pA$, is not income, but non-competitive imports, for example, then v may be different. For example if $A = 0$, $v = (1\ \frac{1}{2})$, and $l = (\frac{1}{2}\ 1)$, then income and employment policies are best targeted on sectors 1 and 2, respectively.

Chapter 4

1. F F T F T F T T F F T.
2. $\min f(x)$ s.t. $g(x) \leq b$ can be written as $\max -f(x)$ s.t. $g(x) \leq b$.
3. $\max f(y)$ s.t. $g(y) \leq b^\top$ can be written as $\max f'(y^\top)$ s.t. $g'(y^\top) \leq b$ where f' is defined on column vectors x by $f'(x) = f(x^\top)$ and the same for g'.
4. $\begin{pmatrix} g \\ -g \end{pmatrix}(x) \leq \begin{pmatrix} b \\ -b \end{pmatrix}$ stands for $g(x) \leq b$.
5. $\min \lambda b$ s.t. $\lambda C = a$ can be written as $\max -\lambda b$ s.t. $\lambda C = a$ and $\lambda \geq 0$ (by 2) or

$$\text{max-}b^\top \lambda^\top \text{ s.t. } \begin{pmatrix} C^\top \\ -C^\top \\ -I \end{pmatrix} \lambda^\top \leq \begin{pmatrix} a^\top \\ -a^\top \\ 0 \end{pmatrix}.$$

6. $\min_{\mu,\nu,\rho \geq 0} (\mu \quad \nu \quad \rho) \begin{pmatrix} a^\top \\ -a^\top \\ 0 \end{pmatrix} : (\mu \quad \nu \quad \rho) \begin{pmatrix} C^\top \\ -C^\top \\ -I \end{pmatrix} = -b^\top.$

7. $\max_{\mu,\nu,\rho \geq 0} a(\nu - \mu)^\top : C(\nu - \mu)^\top = b - \rho^\top$. Because the set of points $(\nu - \mu)^\top$ with $\mu, \nu \geq 0$ equals the set of column vectors x with x free, this can be rewritten further as $\max_{\rho \geq 0} ax : Cx = b - \rho^\top$ or $\max ax$ s.t. $Cx \leq b$, the primal.
8. $\max_{x \geq 0} ax : Cx \leq b$ can be written as $\max ax : \begin{pmatrix} C \\ -I \end{pmatrix} x \leq \begin{pmatrix} b \\ 0 \end{pmatrix}$ which has dual
$\min_{y,z \geq 0} (y^\top \quad z^\top) \begin{pmatrix} b \\ 0 \end{pmatrix} : (y^\top \quad z^\top) \begin{pmatrix} C \\ -I \end{pmatrix} = a$, $\min_{y,z \geq 0} b^\top y : C^\top y = a^\top + z$, or $\min_{y \geq 0} b^\top y : C^\top y \geq a^\top$.
9. Denote the technical coefficients by matrix A and row vector l and the final demand proportions by column vector a. Then $\max_{x,c} c$ s.t. $x \geq Ax + ac$, $lx \leq N$, $x \geq 0$. If A fulfills theorem 2.2, then $x = Ax + a$ has the solution $\bar{x} = \left(\sum_{k=0}^\infty A^k\right) a$. Hence $x = \frac{N}{l\bar{x}}\bar{x}$, $c = \frac{N}{l\bar{x}}$

is feasible. Hence the level of final demand is positive. $x \geq Ax + ac \geq ac > 0$: all sectors are active. The dual constraints are $(p \quad w \quad 0) \begin{pmatrix} A - I & a \\ l & 0 \\ -I & 0 \end{pmatrix} = (0 \quad 1)$ or $p = pA + wl$

with $p = wl \sum_{k=0}^{\infty} A^k$ and $pa = 1$. Hence $p = wl \sum_{k=0}^{\infty} A^k$ with $w = \left(l \sum_{k=0}^{\infty} A^k a \right)^{-1}$. Because a is defined up to an arbitrary scaling factor, it may be compressed or expanded so as to put $l \sum_{k=0}^{\infty} A^k a = 1$. Then $p = l \sum_{k=0}^{\infty} A^k$. Under free trade the economy would specialize in the commodity with the most value-added (at world prices) per worker: the answer is no.

Chapter 5

1. If $U = 0$ and $V = \begin{pmatrix} 1 & 1 \\ 0 & 1 \end{pmatrix}$, then net output is positive whenever the first sector is active.
2. Rescale the use – make data of the sectors so as to render the labor inputs equal to unity. Order the sectors by decreasing net output ratio of commodity 1 over commodity 2. Then sector 1 produces commodity 1 and sector 3 produces commodity 2. If sector 2 produces commodity 1, we must choose between sectors 1 and 2. (If it produces commodity 2, an analogous analysis applies to sectors 2 and 3.) The net output of sector 2 is $\begin{pmatrix} v_{21} & -u_{12} \\ v_{22} & -u_{22} \end{pmatrix}$. The same proportions may be achieved by operating sectors 1 and 3 at levels $0 < \theta < 1$ and $1 - \theta$, preserving the unit labor input.
$$\theta \begin{pmatrix} v_{11} & -u_{11} \\ v_{12} & -u_{22} \end{pmatrix} + (1 - \theta) \begin{pmatrix} v_{31} & -u_{13} \\ v_{32} & -u_{23} \end{pmatrix} = \lambda \begin{pmatrix} v_{21} & -u_{12} \\ v_{22} & -u_{22} \end{pmatrix}.$$
This is a system of two equations for two unknowns, θ and λ. If $\lambda < 1$, this arrangement yields less net output, so that sectors 1 and 2 constitute the non-substitution table. Otherwise sectors 1 and 3 constitute the non-substitution table.
3. Consider $V = \begin{pmatrix} 1 \\ 1 \end{pmatrix}$, $U = 0$, $K = (1 \ 0)$, $L = (0 \ 1)$, $M = N = 1$. Then two units of output is feasible, but not by means of one technique.

Chapter 6

1. F T F T T F T F F.
2. $b = V - U^{\top} - N)t$ yields $t = (V - U^{\top} - N)^{-1} b$ (or $t^{\top} = b^{\top}(V^{\top} - U - N^{\top})^{-1} = b^{\top}\{[I - U(V^{\top})^{-1} - N^{\top}(V^{\top})^{-1}]V^{\top}\}^{-1} = b^{\top}(V^{\top})^{-1}\sum_{k=0}^{\infty}[U(V^{\top})^{-1} + N^{\top}(V^{\top})^{-1}]^k)$. With more commodities than sectors, there will be multiple ts fulfilling $b = (V - U^{\top} - N)t$. With more sectors then commodities, this equation will be overdetermined and must replaced by $(V - U^{\top} - N)t \geq b$. In either case, one may pinpoint a t by minimizing linear form at with weights given by row vector a.
3. (a) Balancing the factors account, savings are 8. Investments of the goods are 1, 1 + 6, respectively, by the accounts of goods 1 and 2 and of capital. Factor income from or to abroad would drive a wedge between savings and investment.
   (b) Balancing the account of good 3, its imports must be 2, matching exports. Once more, factor income from or to abroad would drive a wedge.

(c) GNP in goods 1, 2 and 3 are $(9 + 1 + 1 - 1)$, $(9 + 1 + 1 - 1)$ and $(9 + 6 - 2 - 3)$, respectively. GNI in sectors 1, 2, and 3 are given in the factors row: 10, 10, and 10, respectively. The equality holds no longer sector by sector if the use table contains off-diagonal elements.

(d) $1/(9 + 1 - 1) = 11\%$, $1/(9 + 1 - 1) = 11\%$ and $3/(9 + 6 - 3) = 25\%$ for goods 1, 2, and 3, respectively.

4. The national accounts are balanced as follows.

	Goods	Services	Manufacturing	Service sector	Factors	Foreign
Goods			0	3	5	0
Services			0	0	5	1
Manufacturing	6	0				
Service sector	1	6				
Factors			$3 + 2 + 1$	$1 + 2 + 1$		
Foreign	1	0				

Profits (1 in manufacturing and 1 in the service sector) are the residuals between revenues and costs. GNI amounts 6 in manufacturing plus 4 in the service sector. The shares of capital, labor, and entrepeneurs are 4, 4, and 2, respectively. GNP must also be 10 and consists of 0 investment, 0 net exports, and hence 10 consumption. The latter is split between goods and services, both 5. Demand for goods is $3 + 5$ and production is only $6 + 1$, so that 1 must be imported. Similarly, services exports are 1. The product composition of GNP is 4 goods and 6 services.

5. All VAT contributions come from sectors. By reducing one sectoral contribution without increasing the others, the total VAT collected must be less. In other words, the tax base would be eroded. The Minister of Finance is right. The logic of the Minister of Economic Affairs is flawed. From the answer to question 1 we see that if the number of sectors equals the number of commodities, a reduction of a component of b reduces all components of t.

Chapter 7

1. The direct capital coefficients are $6/10$, $3/20$, and $2/30$, respectively. The direct labor coefficients are $3/10$, $5/20$, and $8/30$, respectively. Post-multiplication by the Leontief inverse (2.18), $\begin{pmatrix} 1 & 0 & 0 \\ 0 & 2 & 0 \\ 0 & 0 & 3 \end{pmatrix}$, yields total capital coefficients $6/10$, $6/20$, and $6/30$, respectively, and total labor coefficients $3/10$, $10/20$, and $24/30$, respectively.

2. $a_{ij}(U, V) = u_{ij} / \sum_k v_{jk}$.

Scale invariance: $a_{ij}(U\hat{s}, \hat{s}V) = u_{ij}s_j / \sum_k s_j v_{jk} = u_{ij} / \sum_k v_{jk} = a_{ij}(U, V)$.

Consider $U = \begin{pmatrix} 1/2 & 0 \\ 1 & 1/2 \end{pmatrix}$, $V = \begin{pmatrix} 1 & 1 \\ 0 & 1 \end{pmatrix}$, $s = \begin{pmatrix} 2 \\ 1 \end{pmatrix}$, and $p = (2.1)$. Then $A(U, V) =$

$\begin{pmatrix} 1/4 & 0 \\ 1/2 & 1/2 \end{pmatrix}$ and, therefore $A(U, V)V^\top = \begin{pmatrix} 1/4 & 0 \\ 1 & 1/2 \end{pmatrix}$. The material balance is violated because $A(U, V)V^\top e \neq Ue = \begin{pmatrix} 1/2 \\ 3/2 \end{pmatrix}$. The financial balance is violated because $e^\top A(U, V)V^\top \neq e^\top U = (3/2 \ \ 1/2)$. Price invariance is violated because $a_{11}(\hat{p}U, V\hat{p}) = 1/3 \neq p_1 a_{11}(U, V)/p_1 = 1/4$.

3. $A(U, V) = (U - \check{V}^\top)\hat{V}^{-1}$. Scale invariance:
$$A(U\hat{s}, \hat{s}V) = [U\hat{s} - (\hat{s}\check{V})^\top](\hat{s}\hat{V})^{-1} = (U\hat{s} - \check{V}^\top\hat{s})\hat{s}^{-1}\hat{V}^{-1} = (U - \check{V}^\top)\check{V}^{-1} = A(U, V).$$
Price invariance:
$$A(\hat{p}U, V\hat{p}) = [\hat{p}U - (\check{V}\hat{p})^\top](\hat{V}\hat{p})^{-1} = (\hat{p}U - \hat{p}\check{V}^\top)\hat{V}^{-1}\hat{p}^{-1}.$$
Consider $U = \begin{pmatrix} 1/2 & 0 \\ 1 & 1/2 \end{pmatrix}$ and $V = \begin{pmatrix} 1 & 1 \\ 0 & 1 \end{pmatrix}$ Then $A(U, V) = \begin{pmatrix} 1/2 & 0 \\ 0 & 1/2 \end{pmatrix}$ and, therefore, $A(U, V)V^\top = \frac{1}{2}\begin{pmatrix} 1 & 0 \\ 1 & 1 \end{pmatrix}$ creating the same inequalities as in excercise 2.

Chapter 8

1. Scale each production unit, i, such that factor inputs (K_j, L_j) yield one unit of value-added each. Plot these points in the labor–capital plane. Connect them by the unit isoquant. The slope of this isoquant goes monotonically from minus infinity to zero. The absolute value of this slope is the marginal rate of substitution of capital for labor. The marginal rate of substitution of capital for labor is not affected by proportional input changes, that is a straight move to the origin in the labor–capital plane. As the labor force increases, the marginal rate of substitution is therefore given by the slope of the unit isoquant at a point more to the right. Hence it goes monotonically from infinity to zero.

For $F(M, N) = M^\alpha N^\beta$ the marginal rate of substitution, ΔM, is determined by $(M + \Delta M)^\alpha (N - 1)^\beta = M^\alpha N^\beta$ or $\left(1 + \frac{\Delta M}{M}\right)^\alpha = \left(\frac{N-1+1}{N-1}\right)^\beta = \left(1 + \frac{1}{N-1}\right)^\beta$, or $\Delta M = \left[\left(1 + \frac{1}{N-1}\right)^{\beta/\alpha} - 1\right]M$ which is decreasing in N, from infinity to zero.

2. The marginal rate of substitution of a smooth production function is the absolute value of the slope of an isoquant in the labor–capital plane. Iso-cost lines have slopes with absolute value $\frac{1/r}{1/w} = w/r$. The point of an isoquant residing on the lowest iso-cost line is a point of tangency, where the slopes are equal.

3. No finite amount of capital is sufficient to compensate individual production units for a reduction of labor input. Hence individual marginal rates of substitution are infinite and not w/r.

Chapter 9

1. (a) The unit cost line connecting $(1/r, 0)$ and $(0, 1/w)$ must be below the sectoral points, as close as possible to the endowment point, $(M, N) = (6 + 3 + 2, 3 + 5 + 8) = (11, 16)$. The direction of the latter is between sectors 1 and 2. It follows that the unit cost line passes through the points of sectors 1 and 2. Here factor costs per unit of value-added are now unity. Sectors 1 and 2 break even and sector 3

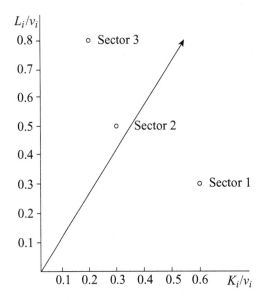

is unprofitable. Note that the unit cost line has well defined intercepts; r and w are positive. By complimentary slackness, all activity is in sectors 1 and 2 and employment of capital and labor is full. Hence $6s_1 + 3s_2 = 11$ and $3s_1 + 5s_2 = 16$ Hence the activity levels are $s_1 = 1/3$ and $s_2 = 3$.

(b) Sectors 1 and 2 break even: $0.6r + 0.3w = 1$ and $0.3r + 0.5w = 1$. Hence $r = 20/21$ and $w = 10/7$. Optimum GDP amounts $10s_1 + 10s_2 = rM + wN = \frac{20}{21}11 + \frac{10}{7}16 = 33\frac{1}{3}$. Only 30 is realized. Inefficiency is 3 out of 33, or 10 percent.

(c) The endowment goes up and its direction is now between sectors 2 and 3. Activity relocates from sector 1 to sector 3. The slope of the iso-cost curve, r/w, becomes bigger. (In fact, $r = 15/7$ and $w = 5/7$ by a cost calculation for sectors 2 and 3.)

2. By the dual constraints, $6 = r \cdot 3 + w \cdot 2$ and $7 - 3 = r \cdot 1 + w \cdot 2$. Hence $r = 1$ and $w = 3/2$. The objective function value is, by the main theorem of linear programming (theorem 4.1), $1 \cdot (3 + 1) + (2 + 2)$ or 10. This is realized. The efficiency is one.

Chapter 10

1. Given terms of trade p, value-added per unit output is given by $p(I - A)$ while labor per unit output is given by l. The economy would specialize in sector i with the greatest ratio of $\underline{p}_i - \sum_j \underline{p}_j a_{ji}$ to l_j.

2. There are two possible answers. If debt is zero or indexed, then $\underline{p}$ and D turn $\lambda \underline{p}$ and λD where $\lambda > 1$ represents inflation. The new trade constraint is equivalent to the old one and all primal variables, sectoral activity, consumption, and net exports, remain the same. Prices of commodities and factor inputs still solve the dual constraint, provided ε becomes ε/λ, which is smaller. The total currency is appreciated.

Another answer applies when debt is not indexed and only p becomes λp. This is equivalent to a replacement of D by D/λ, a smaller debt. A tighter debt constraint will increase its shadow price, ε, and hence depreciate the local currency. The other factor input constraints will be less stringent. Their shadow prices, r and w, will be lower.

Chapter 11

1. Consider $\overset{\circ}{V} = \overset{\circ}{I}$ and $A = U = \begin{pmatrix} 1 & a \\ 0 & 1 \end{pmatrix}$. Then the Leontief inverse is $\begin{pmatrix} 1 & a \\ 0 & 1 \end{pmatrix}$. Denote the direct energy intensities by $(u_{11} \; u_{12})$. Then the total energy intensities are given by $(u_{11} \; au_{11} + u_{12})$. If commodity 1 has a greater direct energy intensity, its total energy intensity is smaller, for a sufficiently close to one.

2. Consider an economy that makes two goods in respective sectors. The world prices are unity and the consumption pattern is one to one. For example, $U = 0$, $u_{\bullet 3} = 0$, $V = I$, $K = 0$, $K_3 = 0$, $a = e$, and $\underline{p} = e^{\top}$. Then the dual constraints become

$$p = p_3 v_{\cdot 3}^{\top} + wL - \sigma$$
$$-v_{33} p_3 = wL_3$$
$$pe = 2 + p_3 a_3$$
$$p = \varepsilon e$$

when the pollution constraint is binding ($\sigma_3 = 0$). First we show that only one product will be made. Otherwise, by complimentary slackness (corollary 4.5), $\sigma = 0$ and, therefore, $\varepsilon = p_3 v_{13} + wL_1$, $\varepsilon = p_3 v_{23} + wL_2$, $-v_{33} p_3 = wL_3$, $2\varepsilon = 2 + p_3 a_3$. Expressing all prices in p_3, the first equation reads $p_3 = 1 + \frac{1}{2} p_3 a_3 = p_3 v_{13} - \frac{v_{33} p_3}{L_3} L_1$ and the second $1 + \frac{1}{2} p_3 a_3 = p_3 v_{23} - \frac{v_{33} p_3}{L_3} L_2$. The solutions are, respectively, $p_3 = 1/(v_{13} - v_{33} L_1/L_3 - \frac{1}{2} a_3)$ and $p_3 = 1/(v_{23} - v_{33} L_2/L_3 - \frac{1}{2} a_3)$ which is consistent only if $v_{13} - v_{33} L_1/L_3 = v_{23} - v_{33} L_2/L_3$. In general, this will be false. (If the equality happens to be valid by chance, it can be shown that the economy is indifferent between the two activities.) So, the economy will specialize. Either $\sigma_1 = 0$ or $\sigma_2 = 0$. The dual constraints become, respectively,

$$(\sigma_1 = 0) \qquad \varepsilon = p_3 v_{13} + wL_1$$
$$\varepsilon = p_3 v_{23} + wL_2 - \sigma_2$$
$$-v_{33} p_3 = wL_3$$
$$2\varepsilon = 2 + p_3 a_3$$

and

$$(\sigma_2 = 0) \qquad \varepsilon = p_3 v_{13} + wL_1 - \sigma_1$$
$$\varepsilon = p_3 v_{23} + wL_2$$
$$-v_{33} p_3 = wL_3$$
$$2\varepsilon = 2 + p_3 a_3$$

The solutions are, respectively,

$$(\sigma_1 = 0) \quad p_3 = 1/\left(v_{13} - v_{33}L_1/L_3 - \tfrac{1}{2}a_3\right)$$

$$w = -\frac{v_{33}}{L_3}/\left(v_{13} - v_{33}L_1/L_3 - \tfrac{1}{2}a_3\right)$$

$$\varepsilon = 1 + \frac{1}{2}a_3/\left(v_{13} - v_{33}L_1/L_3 - \tfrac{1}{2}a_3\right)$$

$$\sigma_2 = p_3(v_{23} - v_{33}L_2/L_3 - v_{13} + v_{33}L_1/L_3)$$

and

$$(\sigma_2 = 0) \quad p_3 = 1/\left(v_{23} - v_{33}L_2/L_3 - \tfrac{1}{2}a_3\right)$$

$$w = -\frac{v_{33}}{L_3}/\left(v_{23} - v_{33}L_2/L_3 - \tfrac{1}{2}a_3\right)$$

$$\varepsilon = 1 + \tfrac{1}{2}a_3/\left(v_{23} - v_{33}L_2/L_3 - \tfrac{1}{2}a_3\right)$$

$$\sigma_2 = p_3(v_{13} - v_{33}L_1/L_3 - v_{23} + v_{33}L_2/L_3)$$

Note that the sign pattern (zero or positive) of the expressions for σ_2 and σ_1 are not influenced by a_3. A stiffer pollution constraint does not reverse the pattern of specialization. A lower a_3 does reduce the expression for w ($-v_{33}$ is positive!) and, by the main theorem of linear programming (theorem 4.1), the level of consumption. The reduction of labor costs also reduces the price of abatement, p_3, and of the products, ε. (Note, however, that ε remains higher than in the situation where a_3 is so large that the pollution constraint is not binding: $\varepsilon = 1$ by the last dual constraint.)

3. The cost of living, pa, increases from $e^\top a$ to $e^\top a + p_{n+1}a_{n+1}$, hence by $p_{n+1}a_{n+1} = p_{n+1}/100$.

Chapter 12

1. (a) By (12.7) *TFP* is 10 percent of GNP (exclusively due to the leading term). The change is caused by Δa_{12}. Since this is in the relatively labor-intensive sector, labor becomes more short, and hence productive.

(b) As regards the analysis of the government program, there are two possible answers, one in terms of activities and one in terms of multipliers:

Activities $(V^\top - U)\Delta s = \begin{pmatrix} 6 & -1 \\ 0 & 6 \end{pmatrix}\begin{pmatrix} \Delta s_1 \\ \Delta s_2 \end{pmatrix} = \begin{pmatrix} 0 \\ 1 \end{pmatrix}$ hence $\Delta s_1 = 1/36$ and $\Delta s_2 = 1/6$.

Capital requirement $K\Delta s = (3 \quad 1)\begin{pmatrix} 1/36 \\ 1/6 \end{pmatrix} = 1/4$ and labor requirement $L\Delta s = (2 \quad 2)\begin{pmatrix} 1/36 \\ 1/6 \end{pmatrix} = 7/18$.

Multipliers   By the commodity technology model, manufacturing determines the input coefficients of the good: $a_{\bullet 1} = 0$, $k_1 = 1/2$ and $l_1 = 1/3$. It follows that in the service sector the inputs designated for the service output are 2 (materials), 1/2 (capital), and 5/3 (labor). Hence $a_{\bullet 2} = \begin{pmatrix} 1/3 \\ 0 \end{pmatrix}$, $k_2 = 1/12$ and $l_2 = 5/18$.

Capital requirement $k(I + A + A^2 + \cdots)\begin{pmatrix} 0 \\ 1 \end{pmatrix} = (1/2 \quad 1/12)\left(\begin{pmatrix} 1 & 0 \\ 0 & 1 \end{pmatrix} + \begin{pmatrix} 0 & 1/3 \\ 0 & 0 \end{pmatrix} + \begin{pmatrix} 0 & 0 \\ 0 & 0 \end{pmatrix}\right)\begin{pmatrix} 0 \\ 1 \end{pmatrix} = (1/2 \quad 1/12)\left(\begin{pmatrix} 1/3 \\ 0 \end{pmatrix}\right) = 1/4,$ and labor requirement $l(I + A + A^2 + \cdots)\begin{pmatrix} 0 \\ 1 \end{pmatrix} = (1/3 \quad 5/18)\begin{pmatrix} 1/3 \\ 0 \end{pmatrix} = 7/18.$

Chapter 13

1. Stock balance (13.31) reads $V^\top * s = U * s + Y$. Because of the unitary production lag, only $U(0)$ is non-zero – say, A. Because of the sudden death, only $V(1)$ is non-zero – say, I. This reflects the absence of secondary production and a scaling of production processes. By definition of the convolution product, the balance at time t becomes $s(t - 1) = As(t) + Y(t)$. Since $Y(t) = 0$ for $t > 0$, no production is required at time zero. At preceding times, $s(-1) = Y(0)$, $s(-2) = As(-1) + 0 = AY(0)$, $s(-3) = As(-2) + 0 = A^2Y(0)$, $s(-4) = A^3Y(0)$, $s(-5) = A^4Y(0)$, etc. The activity levels are given by the terms of the Leontief inverse, each times $Y(0)$. The unitary time lag dates the terms of the Leontief inverse in consecutive points of time. This exercise reviews (13.44)–(13.47).

Index

Page numbers in **bold type** are where a key concept is defined.

Printed in the United States
By Bookmasters